SHAKESPEARE'S LONDON

AMS PRESS

NEW YORK

LONDON BRIDGE
(From an engraving by Visscher, 1616)

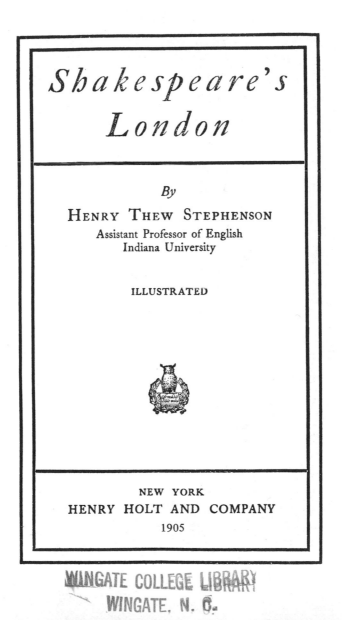

Shakespeare's London

By

HENRY THEW STEPHENSON

Assistant Professor of English
Indiana University

ILLUSTRATED

NEW YORK
HENRY HOLT AND COMPANY
1905

Library of Congress Cataloging in Publication Data

Stephenson, Henry Thew, 1870-1957.
    Shakespeare's London.

    1. London--Description--To 1800. 2. Shakespeare,
William, 1564-1616. I. Title.
DA680.S84 1973   914.21'04'55   74-176435
ISBN 0-404-06258-X

Reprinted from the edition of 1905, New York
First AMS edition published in 1973
Manufactured in the United States of America

AMS PRESS INC.
NEW YORK, N. Y.   10003

To

William A. Procter

THIS BOOK IS
AFFECTIONATELY
DEDICATED

PREFACE

So much time and study have been given of late to the surroundings of Shakespeare and his fellow-dramatists, that everything in connection with Elizabethan times is of considerable interest to a large class of people. Though it is true that many, if not most, of the following facts are to be found in modern works or reprints, it is also true that they are so scattered as to be available only after the most prolonged search, and so inaccessible as to be out of reach of one who has not access to a large library.

Furthermore, no work of the present kind has yet appeared, if we except the contemporary *Survey of London* by John Stow. Some recent attempts to accompany prints of old London with letter-press have resulted in inaccuracies that render the works wholly useless to the person who wishes to be well informed. The present writer has attempted with great care to verify his facts and to draw as largely as possible upon contemporary sources.

While the book is primarily a topographical

description of the city as it was seen by Shakespeare, the task could not be performed satisfactorily without frequent references to the manners and customs of the people. The introductory chapter, however, and the description of a theatrical performance do not, it is hoped, encroach materially upon the field of a companion volume with which it is expected to follow this one, a volume devoted wholly to manners and customs.

In addition to the printed sources mentioned in the text, the writer wishes to acknowledge his indebtedness to the libraries of the British Museum and of the London Guildhall, where every possible courtesy and consideration is extended to the foreign student.

H. T. S.

INDIANA UNIVERSITY,
February 14, 1905.

CONTENTS

ILLUSTRATIONS

SHAKESPEARE'S LONDON

CHAPTER I

THE ELIZABETHANS

SHAKESPEARE'S record is essentially a record of Elizabethan life and times. His plays teem with local colour. Not the history plays alone refer to London. It appears elsewhere, often disguised by a different name, but evident to the familiar eye. One may be sure that the London 'prentice of the time recognised his brother 'prentices, armed with good English oak, rallying to the well-known cry of " Clubs, Clubs!" notwithstanding the fact that the title above the stage reads in plain letters, " Verona— A public Place."

One can best understand the temper of the Elizabethans by drawing an analogy between the defeat of Spain, in 1588, and our own brief war with that venerable nation. If, a few years ago, we had found ourselves at war with all of Europe; if, in addition, we had been on the eve of civil strife at home; if thirty miles of water instead of three thousand had separated us from our enemy, we should then have been in much the same condi-

tion as England at the sailing of the Armada.
Imagine all the odds against us, imagine the country rising like one man in brotherhood, stilling
a deep-rooted civil conflict in order to repel the
foe; imagine a victory, overwhelming and complete, at a time when victory was faithfully believed
to be the direct judgment of God upon the
favoured nation—imagine all this, and it is more
possible to come near the exuberant spirit that
characterised the Elizabethans at the close of
1588.

Is it any wonder that the whole nation burst
forth in one peal of joyous song and action! It
found vent in many ways. Some travelled for
profit, others for culture; some set out to colonise
the forbidden territories, others remained to reap
at home; one and all, high and low, realised that
the danger was over, that England in one bound
had sprung into the forefront of civilisation and
power.

By the defeat of Spain travel upon the continent became not only possible and safe, but the **fad**.
Every youth must make the grand tour, and in
the course of such travels were gathered and
brought home the manuscripts and texts that, upon
translation, blossomed into the Elizabethan drama.

This people, in a sense, was an ignorant people.
Those of the highest rank were well and labori-

ously educated according to the contemporary standard; but the rank and file paid no attention to learning. They neither read, wrote, nor thought. One to-day is astonished at the ignorance of the then common people concerning public affairs. Compare a history like Holinshed's with a history like Froude's or Gardiner's. You find in the former no exposition of principles, no attempt to sift tradition from fact, no sense whatever of the dignity of a thousand page folio in black letter. On the other hand, we read in Holinshed of a terrible storm that killed a dog in Essex, or of a cow that gave birth to a five-legged calf in Kent. Street parades, tiltings, trivial and momentous events alternately, mere gossip, above all, inspired utterances in the form of public proclamations from the crown—this is the sum and substance of Holinshed and Stow—and the people were well satisfied.

The matter-of-fact critic of to-day is too apt to condemn the Elizabethan dramatists for the credulity evinced by their characters. But such criticism is often misplaced. The Elizabethans were credulous people. The opening chapter of Kingsley's *Westward Ho!* relates a number of foolish inducements held out by Salvation Yeo and John Oxenham, two prospective sailors of the South Seas. But the inducements were not con-

sidered foolish then. Kingsley, in his charming
way, points a little pleasantly at the inconsistency
of English inscriptions upon the wondrous horn
of ivory that had been picked up in the land of
the Incas. Even here, the amusing sarcasm is
slightly misplaced. The Elizabethans would not
allow themselves to be troubled by such trifles.
The golden city of Monoa was as real to them
as Paradise or Hell. The chapter, in fact, is
almost a literal transcript of a contemporary
pamphlet, doubtless produced in perfect faith.
Even Shakespeare, judged by our modern stand-
ards, may not have been a really sophisticated man ;
the ring of truth in Othello's tales to Desdemona
may be due to a believing heart.

There was going on all the time a rapid change
in the social scale. The middle class was rising
into prominence. It was no longer necessary to be
born a peer in order to become a man of wealth
and position. The story of Whittington was
repeating itself every day ; and, what is more to
the point, the people were daily growing more and
more proud of the fact.

As the age of Elizabeth was the golden time of
literature, so it was the golden time of superstition. There was one Banks, a hanger-on of the
Earl of Essex, who lived in the Old Bailey and

who possessed a wonderful horse named Morocco, shod with shoes of silver. This horse could dance to music, count, make answer to questions; do a thousand and one other tricks, among which was his reputed ascent of St. Paul's steeple. London looked upon Banks and his horse as little short of the supernatural; and in later years all street-London wept at the news from Italy, where both master and horse were burned to death on the charge of sorcery.

With this execution the Londoners could heartily sympathise, for they were superstitious to a degree incomprehensible at the present day. None was so ready as Sir Walter Scott himself to acknowledge that the fatal flaw in *The Monastery* was the demand put upon the credulity of an incredulous people by the introduction of the White Lady of Avenal. Nothing so well illustrates this difference between the time of Shakespeare and our own as a comparison of the failure of *The Monastery* and of the success of *Hamlet*. A serious tragedy based upon a trivial motive is likely to degenerate into out and out farce. Had the audience of Shakespeare believed as we do in regard to superstition, both *Hamlet* and *Macbeth* would have probably missed the public approbation. We should certainly think a logic-loving philosopher

or an iron-nerved general tainted in his wits, if he
allowed his reason to be swayed by a shadowy ap-
parition, or his intrigues to be governed by a trio
of vanishing witches; yet Shakespeare was making
use of the most powerful motive at his command.
Doubtless every person in The Globe play-house
shuddered at the appearance of Hamlet's ghost, for
it was true, actually true to them, that this might
be either Denmark's spirit or the very devil in a
pleasing shape.

John Stow, the annalist of E-gland and author
of the *Survey of London*, was, next to Camden,
the most famous antiquarian student of the age;
yet this man, whose *Survey* is the great store-
house of knowledge about Elizabethan London—
learned, careful, and methodical—thus interprets
the effect of a church struck by lightning:

"And here a note of this steeple: as I have oft
heard my father report, upon St. James's night,
certain men in the loft next under the bells, ringing
of a peel, a tempest of lightning and thunder did
arise, an ugly shapen sight appeared to them, coming in at the south window, and lighted on the
north, for fear whereof they all fell down, and lay
as dead for the time, letting the bells ring and cease
of their own accord; when the ringers came to themselves, they found certain stones of the north win-

dow to be razed and scratched, as if they had been so much butter, printed with a lion's claw; the same stones were fastened there again and so remain until this day. I have seen them oft, and have put a feather or small stick into the holes where the claws had entered three or four inches deep. At the same time certain main timber posts at Queen-hithe were scratched and cleft from the top to the bottom; and the pulpit cross in Paul's churchyard was likewise scratched, cleft, and overturned. One of the ringers lived in my youth, whom I have often heard to verify the same to be true."

The people not only believed in ghosts and witches, but in magic of every sort. Alchemy was a common hobby, and many a man of brain wasted his time and ruined his fortune in the vain search for the philosopher's stone long after the practice had been held up to ridicule upon the stage by Ben Jonson.

Astrology, or astronomical fortune-telling, was so thoroughly a factor of the age that every one desired the casting of his horoscope. Leicester consulted Doctor Dee, the astrologer, to discover a propitious date for the Queen's coronation. The great Queen herself consulted him upon an occasion, instead of her family physician, in order to charm away the tooth-ache. Again, a waxen image of Elizabeth was picked up in one of the fields near London. Doctor Dee was immediately sent for to counteract by his charms the evil effect of this familiar kind of sorcery.

People, one and all, believed in fairies. The usual critical opinion, that the opening scenes of *A Midsummer Night's Dream* owe their arrangement to a desire to lead gradually from the real to the unreal, would have caused an Elizabethan to laugh, if not outwardly, in his sleeve. There is nothing unreal about the fairies of that delightful comedy except their size. Any one might not only have seen the pleasant fairies, but also the wicked, and might have become blind by the sight, if he did not take care to protect himself by charms. A grown man did not feel foolish in those days if when in the neighbourhood of a lonely and ghost-haunted wood at night he wore his coat inside out. There were innumerable superstitious rites performed at births, christenings, weddings, on certain days of the year, and in certain places; as, the churchyard, the cross-roads, etc. Every hour in the day, every article in the world—stone, plant, or animal—had its cluster of superstitions.

The time was further characterised by a general freedom of manners. We often find personal ridicule and abuse, as well as praise, levelled at individuals from the stage. Different companies and rival play-wrights fought out their private battles on the public boards. A play of ancient setting, such as *Hamlet*, does not scruple to allude to current events of interest to Londoners. The mob in *Romeo and Juliet* rallies to the cry of the London 'prentice lads. The actors talked to people in the pit, who in turn pelted an unpopular player from the stage. There existed, likewise, a coarseness of speech in every-day talk that would be quite intolerable to-day. Queen Elizabeth swore like a trooper, spat at her favourites, or threw her slipper at the head of an obdurate councillor. The artificial refinement of our age requires the lines of many of Shakespeare's heroines to be curtailed; yet Beatrice and the like talk no more broadly than did that paragon of female excellence, " Sidney's sister, Pembroke's mother."

The great popularity of the stage at once suggests the chief characteristic of the age: artificiality. About the middle of the century appeared Lyly's *Euphues*. This book, a kind of tale, owed its great vogue to its quaintness of phrase, its antitheses, and its elaborate conceits. The book sold by wholesale. No one was considered fit to appear in public unless he could talk the fustian fashion of the *Euphues*. The book is intolerably

dull to most of us, but the perusal of a few pages
will repay the curious, as an object-lesson in the
rubbish spoken by the cultivated Elizabethan
courtier.

Part of the Euphuistic training was the art of
compliment. This habit was fostered by the vanity
of the Queen. Elizabeth, so some of the foreigners who saw her tell us, possessed several undesirable
characteristics, among others a hooked nose and
black teeth, and there is no doubt that her skin
wrinkled as she grew near seventy. Yet, to the
very end of the great Queen's life, the obsequious
courtier was welcome who would assure her that he
is like to die if he is debarred the sight of that ala-
baster brow, of those cheeks of rose covered with
the bloom of peaches, of those teeth of pearl. Besides the elaborate compliments to the Queen that
were frequently introduced into plays and masques,
a common custom was to set up a tablet to her honour in the parish church. Here is an example of
their inscriptions:

" Spain's rod, Rome's ruin, Netherland's relief,
  Heaven's gem, Earth's joy, World's wonder, Nature's chief.
  Britain's blessing, England's splendour,
  Religion's nurse and Faith's Defender."

Gossipping was one of the favourite pastimes of
the Elizabethans, and London was not yet too large

for the practice to be thoroughly effective. Gossip
started from the barber-shop and the tavern-table—
the Elizabethan equivalent of the afternoon tea—
and spread thence in every direction. Space pre-
vents the enumeration of many of the indications
of freedom of manner that are to be discovered in
every direction. Gossip led to frequent quarrels,
that were more hot and bitter because side arms
were worn upon all occasions. The fine woman of
the time would jostle with the rudest peasants in
the pit of the bull-ring and the theatre. Wakes
and fairs were of daily occurrence, in which every
one joined, irrespective of previous acquaintance.
During the yule-tide festivities all distinctions of
class were considered as temporarily non-existent.
Elizabeth showed herself so often and so intimately
to the common people that they considered the
acquaintance almost personal. So much for the
happy-go-lucky spirit that characterised the
time.

The extent of gaming is lamented by all the
contemporary writers who have a leaning towards
reform. Dicing, card playing, and racing, though
to a less extent than the others, were practised
upon every hand; while cheating was but too common. In former times it was considered almost a
crime to take interest for money loaned, but by

the reign of Elizabeth this prejudice was so completely overborne that usury was practised by all the money lenders, who did not scruple to turn the screws upon the least occasion.

The people were greatly addicted to showy dress, but show in dress was a mere bagatelle. Pageants of all sorts were planned upon the least occasion. Coronations, funerals, and progresses were always got up upon the most spectacular basis. The riding watches, the parades of civic officials in their gaudy robes of state, the Livery Companies upon the river in their brilliant barges, manned by oarsmen in full livery, the Queen coming to St. Paul's in 1588, to render thanks for the victory over Spain —all such spectacles were provided with gorgeous pageants, triumphal arches, side-shows, and so forth, that would be weeks preparing.

Though the plays of Shakespeare were produced upon a stage practically devoid of scenery, and wholly without costume as we understand the word, the private masques at court were accompanied by elaborate stage machinery and gorgeous dresses that quite overshadowed the lines of the poet, and that often cost a fortune for a single presentation. Heraldry, likewise, received due attention; private households swarmed with servants; Gervase Markham, a contemporary cook-book writer, suggests

DOMESTIC ARCHITECTURE
(Winchester Street.   From an etching by J. T. Smith, drawn 1804)

sixteen dishes of meat and sixteen other dishes for an ordinary family dinner. To be sure, the splendid monasteries had been shorn of their magnificence, but the Papal plate went to enrich still further the decoration of the tables belonging to the Tudor sovereigns and their favourites. So much for the general spirit of excess that pervaded English life three hundred years ago.

The people were extremely fond of out of door life. Of a summer evening they would set the tables by the sidewalks, or by the door in unimproved streets, for supper. Whenever possible, the last course of dinner, called the banquet, was served in the garden. Open air sermons were thoroughly popular. The theatres were open to the sky. Hawking, hunting, and field sports were the favourite amusements.

When one attempts to describe the architecture of any age he usually selects that which in later time is known to have then originated, but which was at the time itself so new as to appear novel rather than characteristic. Though there is a style of building that we associate with Elizabethan times, the people for the most part lived in houses that had long been built, and were usually of the hollow-square pattern. The fact that capability of defence was no longer an important consideration had caused the moat and wall gradually to disappear, and the isolation of the lodge or gate-house into a separate structure. In the later part of the Elizabethan era great changes were introduced in the ground plan and the façade; but once within, whether the house were old or new, a fairly uniform set of conditions confronted the observer.

In the domestic architecture of the time there was a great deal of elaborate ornamentation, such as delicately carved wood-work, plaster, moulding, wrought fire-places, etc. A great deal of colour was used throughout the house, both in the way of pictures and heraldic designs, and in the tapestry. There was much regularity about all the ornamental patterns, and many straight lines, as in the panelling. Brackets, hinges, knockers, etc., were usually of the most elaborate wrought iron or brass.

The plan familiar to us, from Bacon's essay *Of Building*, was followed by many of the Elizabethan builders, though lack of means to build, and room for the double court, in the London houses, often led to a considerable alteration. One need but walk along Holborn to-day and glance at the Staple Inn, that still serves its purpose as well as it did three centuries ago, to realise how substantially they were wont to build in those days. Oak and chestnut entered largely into the construction, and

the ceilings were omitted in the great halls in order
to show the timber framework of the roof, which
was often beautifully and elaborately carved. This
framework was sometimes painted and gilded, but
more frequently depended for its ornament upon
the deep, grotesque carvings or decorated heraldic
designs. Crosby Hall, however, is an exception to
this rule; for the hall is provided with an arched
ceiling divided into panels. In any case, the hall
was usually the only room left unceiled. These
ceilings were often of the finest execution. The
walls were variously adorned. Sometimes they were
gilded. The use of pictures came into vogue largely
during the reign of Elizabeth. At first they were
let into the walls or painted upon wooden panels
over the fire-place, the rest of the room being pan-
elled. It was a common custom to keep pictures
covered with a cloth. Oftentimes the walls of a
room were covered with arras or tapestry, which,
because of the damp climate, was not attached
directly to the wall, but stretched upon light wooden
frames distant a foot from it; hence, "behind the
arras" was a convenient place of hiding. In
meaner houses the place of tapestry was taken by
painted cloths, which served the same purpose of
decoration, and had the double advantage of being
inexpensive and a fair imitation of the more desir-

able display of wealth. The tapestry was frequently adorned with mottoes, and mottoes were
often hung up alone, especially in the sleeping
rooms of the domestics, to remind them of their
duty.

It was the common custom to cover the floors of
rooms with a layer of rushes—a great source of
uncleanliness. Often new rushes were placed over
the old, and the whole mass removed as seldom as
twice a year. This habit husbanded all sorts of
filth, and vermin was a common ailment of the home
apartments; bad odours rising therefrom gave rise
to a whole profession, that of perfumer. It was a
perfumer's business to sweeten the atmosphere of a
room without removing the cause of the stench.
The timber of the house front was also often elaborately carved, and sometimes painted in bright colours. In some of the old houses, beneath the second story on the outside, were rows of iron hooks.
These were used to hold up the hangings that were
put out as street decorations in time of public festivity.

The main room in a mansion that was built in the
form of a square was the hall. It served often as
dining-room, drawing-room, and place of festivities. About the walls were hung all sorts of weapons, relics of the chase, etc. Even in London

DOMESTIC ARCHITECTURE
(Part of Duke Street, West Smithfield. From an etching by J. T. Smith, drawn 1807)

houses this was the custom; for it must be remembered that hunting and hawking were carried on where is now the centre of the city, and that Crosby Hall, in the days of Elizabeth, was not ten minutes' walk from the open country. There were chairs and stools in the hall, and chests, handsomely carved or delicately inlaid with ivory and pearl. When meals were served tables were brought in or taken down from their place against the walls. These tables consisted of leaves hinged together and laid temporarily on trestles. In *Romeo and Juliet* Capulet refers to such tables being removed preparatory to clearing the hall for a dance, when he cries:

> " A hall, a hall! give room! and foot it, girls.
> More light, you knaves; and turn the tables up."

In the bedroom were usually two beds: one a standing bed in which slept the occupant of the room; the other, a truckle bed, on which slept the attending page or lady's maid. The truckle bed was pushed under the standing bed during the daytime. The bed was frequently covered with a costly counterpane, highly wrought and brilliantly coloured. Ivory coffers and cypress chests elevated upon carved legs were highly esteemed as bedroom furniture, and were often of extreme value

and fine workmanship, which consisted of ornamental scrolls and inlaid heraldic devices. Here,
as elsewhere, the floor was covered with rushes, and
the best mansions could boast nothing better.
"Rushes that grow upon dry ground," observes
Dr. Bulleyne, "be good to strew in halls, chambers,
and galleries, to walk upon, defending apparal, as
trains of gowns and kirtles from dust."

A necessary adjunct to the bedroom was the
wardrobe for keeping clothes. Drawers were not
then in use, chests taking their place; most of the
garments, however, were hung upon pegs about the
room, and in great houses a special apartment,
called the wardrobe, was reserved for this purpose.
Rooms were lighted by candles or torches thrust
into sconces. A favourite form of candlestick was
an image with the hands clasping the candle-socket.
On state occasions the candles were held in sockets
carried by human beings. The office of candle-
bearer at court was a desirable one and always
performed by the members of the Gentlemen Pen-
sioners. Watch lights, as they were called, were
candles so divided by rings as to indicate how long
they had been burning. They were common only
in the houses of the wealthy.

Every house of any pretension possessed a
library, though reading was not a common habit

among the lower classes. "Trulie," says Harrison, "it is a rare thing with us now, to heare of a courtier which hath but his owne language. And to saie how manie gentlewomen and ladies there are, that beside the sound knowledge of the Greek and Latine toongs, are thereto no lesse skillful in the Spanish, Italian, and French, or in some of them, it resteth not in me: sith I am persuaded, that as the noblemen and gentlemen do surmount in this behalf, so these come verie little or nothing at all behind them for their parts, which industrie God continue, and accomplish that which otherwise is wanting!" It would be impossible to say what books these libraries contained, for the simple reason that at a time when books were so scarce, one picked up whatever he could find. The Chronicles, of course, were in everybody's library. As for the rest, a large proportion was in the form of unique manuscripts, many of which had been brought home for translation, soon to become easily accessible in English. The famous astrologer, Dr. Dee, at his death left a library of four thousand volumes, which was considered large. Much attention was paid to binding. The covers were often held shut with clasps of gold heavily studded with jewels. Such books were placed on the shelves with the edges of the leaves facing out for the purpose of

exhibiting the clasps. Brief manuscripts and documents were rolled and laid upon the shelf. They
were furnished with a label attached to a string
that hung out of the end, thus enabling one to
search for what he wanted when the rolls were piled
one upon another.

As has been said, dinner and supper were usually
served upon movable tables, which were covered
with tablecloths of linen, often called carpets. The
hour for dinner was twelve o'clock; supper was
served at six. Wooden trenchers were still seen
upon the tables of the rich. Pewter in its best form
was a costly material, and wealthy persons often
rented their stock of pewter by the year. It was,
however, in plainer forms, slowly working its way
into the houses of the common people, hardly any
of whom did not boast, at least, a few pewter dishes.
Silver, gilt plate, cut glass, and china, the latter
sparingly, were in use. Before 1563 people ate
with their fingers; hence the frequent circulation at
table of a bowl of water and a towel. Knives were
introduced in 1563, but forks came some time later.

Dinner was usually served in three courses: the
first, meat; the second, game; and the third, sweets.
The last, called the banquet, was, when possible,
served in the summer-house in the garden, from
which, after sufficient time spent in conversation,

the family adjourned to evening prayer and then prepared for supper. The people were extremely lavish in the matter of provision, and extravagant in their tastes. The consumption of wine was then far greater than now. Harrison mentions fifty-six French wines, thirty-six Spanish, and several made at home. Englishmen were very fond of sugar, which it was customary to mix with every kind of wine.

Servants were then far more numerous than now, and a more essential mark of gentility than at any other age. They wore their master's arms upon the left sleeve; their distinctive dress was a blue coat. The feeling that dignity depended largely upon the size of the train of servants pervaded all ranks of society. The domestics, at least while they were within doors, were kept under the strictest discipline. John Harington, in 1566, drew up a set of rules by which the servants of his house were governed. Such documents were common; the following selection illustrates the character of the supervision:

1. A servant shall not be absent from morning or evening prayer without excuse, upon fine of 2d each time.

3. No man shall leave any door open that he findeth shut, without cause—fine 1d.

5. No bed shall be left unmade, nor fire or candle box unclean, after 8 A. M.

8. No man shall wait at table without a trencher in his hand except for good cause—fine 1d.

14. No one shall provoke another to strike, or strike another on pain of dismissal.

15. No man shall come to the kitchen without reasonable cause—he shall be fined 1d and the cook 1d.

20. The court gate must be shut during each meal.

The fines are to be bestowed upon the poor.

The lady's maid and the page were important personages in the household. The duty of the former was to assist her mistress at her toilet, to talk to her, to play games with her, and to be general companion. The page performed all sorts of small duties. If his mistress went to church the page walked before her with prayer book. If his master went into the street the page walked behind with his sword. The page ran errands, kept secrets, tidied up the room, and did a number of other services that did not fall to the lot of any particular servant. It was a common custom to lend a page to some other master for a time, an act that was considered the highest compliment one could pay.

Before leaving the subject of servants, let us see what was required of their mistresses. Gervase Markham, a contemporary writer upon domestic affairs, has a good deal to say in *The English Housewife* concerning the duties of the mistress of the house. She should be skilled in many things that have passed out of fashion.   To begin with, she ought to understand medicine and nursing. Markham assists her to a sufficient knowledge of such things by descriptions of the various diseases and by prescriptions for their cure.   Here is a fair example, the manner of treatment of quotidian fever: " You shall take a new laid egg, and opening the crown, you shall put out the white, then fill up the shell with very good aquavitae, and stir it and the yoke very well together, & then as soon as you feel your cold fit begin to come upon you, sup up the egg, and either labour till you sweat, or else, laying great store of clothes upon you, put yourself in a sweat in your bed, and thus do while your fits continue, and for your drink, let it be only cool posset ale."

The housewife should also have a knowledge of cookery, " else she can perform but half her vow in marriage."   She should have a knowledge of all kinds of herbs, their uses, when to sow them, and when to gather them.   " At any time sow Asparagus & colworts . . . . in the February new moon Spike and Garlick . . . . . full   moon Parsley . . . . . March new moon Marigolds and violets . . . . etc."   She must also know when and what herbs are to be transplanted.   Concerning her ability to cook, Markham says, " she must have a quick

eye, a curious nose, a perfect taste, and a ready
eare; (she must not be butter-fingered, sweet-
toothed, nor faint-hearted;) for, the first will let
everything fall, the second will consume what it
should increase, and the last will lose time with too
much niceness. She must know how to prepare
salids, simple and compound; salids for show only;
how to adorn the table," etc., etc. Moreover, the
housewife should understand the art of cutting up
meat, the making of cheese and butter, and the care
of poultry.

Markham lays great stress upon the proper serving of a meal. He offers the following suggestion: "Thus you shall order them in your closet;
but when they go to the table you shall first send
forth a dish made for show only, as Beaste, Bird,
Fish, or Fowle, according to invention: then your
marchpane, then your preserved fruit, then a paste,
then a wet sucket, then a dry sucket, marmelaide,
cumfits, apples, pears, wardens, oranges, and lem-
ons sliced; then wafers and another dish of preserved fruits, and so consequently all the rest before: no two dishes of one kind going or standing
together, and this will not only appear delicate to
the eye, but invite the appetite with the much variety thereof." The foregoing description refers to
the lighter part of the repast, known usually as the

banquet, the dishes being often set upon the table first and the meat and game courses then served. For a family not too large, Markham says that sixteen dishes of meat and sixteen dishes of salads and vegetables will, if properly distributed, be sufficient.

Another duty of the housewife was distilling. She ought to furnish herself with stills, and learn their use in the preparation of medicines, perfumes, sauces, etc. She should know all about the ordering of wines, she should be a competent brewer, and know how to gauge wine and ale casks. Then, a knowledge of wool was necessary. "The housewife should know when to send it to the dyer, yet, in case of emergency, she should understand dyeing, the action whereof must be got by practice, not by relation." All about flax was a part of her knowledge, and skill in dairy work. Markham, after enumerating all these various duties with descriptions and receipts, belittles the value of his own volume by saying the housewife must not only find time to read and study about these things, but also to practise them all, else the study will prove of no avail. The modern reader should bear in mind that the English housewife in the time of Elizabeth was actually skilled in all these various duties, and that it often fell to her lot to train ser-

vants in them, even though she did not usually perform them herself.

Traders, except those who put up temporary
booths in Cheapside and the market fairs, lived in
the house where they carried on their business. To
their aid was called the service of several apprentices, who were bound to their master for a term of
years, each party to the agreement assuming certain responsibilities, the neglect of which was pun-
ishable by law. The apprentice lived in his master's house, learned his trade or business, and when
discharged was considered sufficiently skilful to
set up in business on his own account. The feeling of brotherhood among the 'prentice lads was
very strong. If one was insulted, all were insulted,
and many a sudden row assumed serious proportions. Though allowed to carry no weapon except
the " club," the apprentice often became a formidable foe, as was the case at the time of the great
uprising known to history as Evil Mayday. The
position of apprentice was not considered one of
degradation, and the frequent practice of a master's daughter or widow marrying with his apprentice was not frowned upon by public opinion.

One who would comprehend the style of Elizabethan dress must, for the time-being, set aside all
notion of simplicity or fit. In fact, the people of

DOMESTIC ARCHITECTURE
(Old Houses at Chancery Lane and Fleet Street. From an etching
by J. T. Smith, drawn in 1789)

that time carried their idea of what was proper in wearing apparel to such a ridiculous extreme that they were made the subject of innumerable satires; and dress was the most popular point of attack by all the abusive writers on reform. Bright colours, elaborate trimming, and padding were the most notable characteristics of Elizabethan dress; padding was so full that all semblance of the human body was lost, both to men and women.

"There is not any people under the zodiac of heaven," says Philip Stubbs, "how clownish, rural, or brutish soever, that is not so poisoned with this arsenic of Pride, or hath drunk so deep of this cup as Aelga [England] hath." Harrison, a contributor to *Holinshed's History*, wrote, "The phantastical folly of our nation (even from the courtier to the carter) is such that no form of apparel liketh us longer than the first garment is in the wearing, if it continue so long, and be not laid aside to receive some other trinket newly devised by the fickle-headed tailors, who covet to have several tricks in cutting, thereby to draw fond customers to more expense of money . . . . And as these fashions are diverse, so likewise it is a world to see the costliness and the curiosity, the excess and the vanity, the pomp and the bravery, and finally the fickleness and folly, that is in all degrees, insomuch that nothing is more constant in England than inconstancy of attire."

This magnificent extreme obtained in all ranks of life, as Harrison says, "from the courtier to the carter." The only difference was that the rich man dressed in more expensive stuffs; he wore diamonds and rubies where the poor man wore beads of coloured glass. He bought clothes oftener than the poor man; yet they were all alike in this: they dressed as fine and finer than their pockets would allow.

The kind of dress worn upon any occasion was not dependent upon the time of day. A man would appear at court in his gaudiest clothes, whether the time was day or night, morning or afternoon. The garments were stiffened and stuffed till the wearer could not move with any comfort. A man in full dress was laced from head to foot. His doublet was laced or buttoned in front; the sleeves were often laced to the armholes; the doublet was laced to the hose; the hose was laced; sometimes even the shoes were laced. A man could not dress himself without assistance. Dressing, or "making-ready," was such an undertaking that, once accomplished, a man was glad to keep the same clothes on all day. Women carried dress to an even greater extreme than men. They put on a complete frame-work of whalebone and wire before they began to assemble the outer garments. When the process was completed resemblance to a figure was obliterated. Women were wide and round and stiff, and as rigid as if made of metal; and their dress abounded in straight lines and sharp angles.

What women achieved by means of wire and bone men accomplished by means of wadding. Wool, hair, rags, and often bran, were used to pad out the doublet and hose. A writer in 1653 [Bulwer, *Artificial Changeling*] tells a story of a young gallant "in whose immense hose a small hole was torn by a nail of the chair he sat upon, so that as he turned and bowed to pay his court to the ladies, the bran poured forth as from a mill that was grinding, without his perceiving it, till half his cargo was unladen on the floor."

Holme, in his *Notes on Dress* (Harl. 4375), relates the following: "About the middle of Queen Elizabeth's reign, the slops, or trunk hose, with peascod-bellied doublets, were much esteemed, which young men used to stuff with rags and other like things, to extend them in compass, with as great eagerness as women did take pleasure to wear great and stately verdingales; for this was the same in effect, being a sort of verdingale breeches. And so excessive were they herein, that a law was made

against them as did stuff their breeches to make
them stand out; whereas, when a certain prisoner
(in these times) was accused for wearing such
breeches, contrary to law, he began to excuse himself of the offence, and endeavoured by little and
little to discharge himself of that which he did wear
within them; he drew out of his breeches a pair of
sheets, two table-cloths, ten napkins, four shirts, a
brush, a glasse, a comb, and night-caps, with other
things in use, saying: 'Your lordships may understand that because I have no safer a store-house,
these pockets do serve me for a room to lay my
goods in; and though it be a straight prison, yet it
is a store-house big enough for them, for I have
many things yet of value within them.' And so
his discharge was accepted and well laughed at;
and they commanded him that he should not alter
the furniture of his store-house, but that he should
rid the halle of his stuffe, and keep them as it
pleased him."

"The women," says Stubbs, "when they have
all these goodly robes upon them, seem to be the
smallest part of themselves, not natural women, but
artificial women; not women of flesh and blood, but
rather puppets or mawmuts, consisting of rags and
clouts compact together."

People of high rank sometimes built the hair into

towering masses on the crown of the head; as a rule, however, the hair was dressed plain, though frequently covered with jewels. The Elizabethan women, as well as the men, dyed their hair, not to conceal the fact that it was turning gray, but to please a passing fancy. There was no attempt to disavow this practice, nor was the same colour always used. In fact, the colour of the hair was made to harmonise with the garments worn upon any particular occasion. Those who did not care to dye their hair wore wigs. The Elizabethans revelled in wigs. The Records of the Wardrobe show that Elizabeth possessed eighty at one time. Mary Stuart, during a part of her captivity in England, changed her hair every day. So usual was this habit, and so great the demand for hair, that children with handsome locks were never allowed to walk alone in London streets, for fear they would be kidnapped, and their tresses cut off.

Men wore hats of all shapes, sizes, and colours. The most popular material was velvet. All sorts of feathers were used by. men to decorate the hats; black feathers eighteen inches or two feet in length were in great demand; a common decoration was a twisted girdle next the brim, called a " cable hat-band." Some hats, however, were perfectly plain, of soft felt; others were velvet caps with a jewelled clasp. Occasionally small mirrors were worn in the hat. The place for the hat was frequently upon the head; but quite as often dangling down the back by a ribbon. It was worn in either place, either within or without doors. The hair was usually cut short, with, however, a long lock behind one or both ears. This was called the love-lock, and was adorned with bows of ribbon. Men painted the face quite as much as women. The moustache was sometimes left very long. Hair, moustache, and beard were coloured as fancy prompted. The following from *The Midsummer Night's Dream* is to be understood quite literally: " Either your straw-coloured beard, your orange-tawny beard, your purple ingrain beard, or your French crown-coloured beard, your perfect yellow." (I. ii. 96.) "Forsooth, they say the King is budded Another of a pure carnation colour, Speckled with green and russet." (Ford: *The Broken Heart*, II. i.) Harrison writes: " Neither will I meddle with our variety of beards, of which some are shaven from the chin like those of the Turks, not a few cut short like the beard of the Marquis Otto, some made round like a rubbing brush . . . therefore if a man have a lean, straight face, a Marquis Otto's cut will make it broad and large; if it be platter like, a long slender beard will make it seem narrower. . . .

Some lusty courtiers also, and gentlemen of courage do wear either rings of gold, stone or pearl, in their ears, whereby they imagine the workmanship of God not to be a little amended."

Stubbs writes in 1583: "They, the barbers, have invented such strange fashions of monstrous manners of cutting, trimming, shaving, and washing, that you would wonder to see." He mentions the French cut; the Spanish, Dutch, and Italian; the new, the old, the gentleman's, the common, the court, and the country cuts. He concludes with: "They have also other kinds of cuts innumerable; and therefore when you come to be trimmed they will ask you whether you will be cut to look terrible to your enemy, or amiable to your friends; grim and stern in countenance, or pleasant and demure, for they have divers kinds of cuts for all these purposes, or else they lie." Is it any wonder that such words as fool, wretch, ape, and monkey were used as terms of endearment!

When one thinks of costume in the age of Elizabeth, one naturally thinks of three things as most characteristic: the ruff, the huge padded hose, and the farthingale. Of these three, the first is the unique feature of the dress of that age. Ruffs of our own time convey no idea of what ruffs were in 1600. During the time of the early Tudors par-

telets, or narrow collars, of divers colours, generally made of velvet, were much worn by the nobility. These began to grow in size and use during
the reign of Elizabeth. As was usual in those
days, the new fashion was introduced by the men;
but the women were quick to follow in the adoption
of the ruff. Ruffs were made of linen, often decorated with gold and silver thread, and adorned with
jewels. They were expensive garments and could
be worn but a few times. In 1564, however, a
woman became the great benefactor of English
society. This woman was Mrs. Dingham, wife of
a Dutch coachman in the service of the Queen. Mrs.
Dingham brought to England the art of starching.
The use of starch gave the ruff a new birth. It
could now be worn more than once; and, in a trice,
ruffs were within the reach of all. Elizabeth wore
her ruffs closed in front, close under her chin; most
women, however, who had fairer skin and shapelier
necks, preferred to wear the ruff open in front.

The ruff was made of linen, much plaited, and
starched stiff, usually with white starch. For a
while yellow starch was popular, but the fad was
of short duration. Starch was also used in other
colours. Stubbs tells us that the women used "a
certain kind of liquid matter which they called
starch, wherein the devil hath willed them to wash

and die their ruffs well; and this starch they made of divers colours and hues—white, red, blue, purple, and the like; which, being drye, will then stand stiff and inflexible about their neckes."

What made the ruff so conspicuous was the size. When first introduced it was modest and unpretentious; but nothing on which fashion then took a fair hold could remain " confined within the modest limits of order." We hear of ruffs that contained eighteen or nineteen yards of linen. The fashionable depth was one-fourth of a yard. Sometimes they were as much as one-third of a yard deep. Imagine the head of a man or woman, like the hub of a cartwheel, firmly gripped in the midst of a mass of starched linen extending a foot on all sides! So cumbersome were these articles of dress that it became necessary to underprop them with a framework of wire to keep them from tumbling over of their own weight, and to prevent them from dragging their wearers' heads down with them. What a stiff, unnatural carriage the habit of wearing ruffs gave to the upper part of the body is fully illustrated by the following: " He carries his face in 's ruff, as I have seen a serving man carry glasses in a cypress hat band, monstrous steady for fear of breaking." (Webster: *White Devil*, II. iv.) One's head in the midst of such a ruff was free to move, of course, only within limits. In fact, people found it most difficult to eat and drink. In France—for this fashion was imported from Paris, where it was carried to a greater extreme than in England—we read of a loyal lady who found it necessary to take soup out of a spoon two feet long.

The upper part of a woman's body was cased in a neat, tightly laced bodice, that followed the contour of the body closely. This was the only part of the figure that retained its natural shape. The bodice frequently projected downwards in a long, sharp point below the stomach; and was often open towards the top to show the breast, or the stomacher of brightly coloured silk beneath the crossed laces.

The corresponding garment for men was the doublet. It was, however, usually padded and stuffed till nearly twice the natural size of the body. The doublet was cut and slashed in front and sides so as to show the gay-coloured lining of costly material. It sometimes laced, but more frequently buttoned up the front. Two or three buttons at the top were left open and the shirt of delicate white lawn pulled out a little way. The doublet sometimes projected downward in front, when it was called a peascod-bellied doublet; sometimes it surrounded the hips like a short skirt. The sleeves were usually removable and laced to the doublet about the arm-holes. Working people who, of course, wore doublets or jerkins that were only slightly padded, often wore no sleeves at all, the arms covered by the sleeves of the shirt. A pair of draw-strings working opposite the small of the back enabled one to tighten or loosen his doublet at will.

There used to be a punishment in vogue in the colony of New York, by which a man was compelled to walk about encased in a barrel; his head projected from one end, and his feet from the other. The Elizabethan women did not carry a barrel about their hips, but they carried a corresponding bulk. What would correspond to a skirt in our time was then called a farthingale. This name, however, was properly applied to the framework of whalebone and wire which a woman buckled on before she began to dress. It clamped her tightly about the waist and was absolutely rigid. One style gave a curve from the waist line downward; the other extended level from the waist, and met the vertical line of drapery at right angles. In either case the nether garments were supported by this framework, much as we support the week's wash on a rotary drier. The appearance of a fashionable woman when completely dressed was not unlike the colonial culprit in his humiliation barrel, save that the farthingale reached to the floor and was richly begirt with jet beads, strings of pearls, jewels, and gold thread. The women of that day thoroughly understood the art of tight lacing. Some of the old pictures of a woman with a wasp-like waist and huge farthingale look very much like a tin soldier soldered to his base. In 1563 a law was passed in France to limit farthingales to an ell, or about four feet in diameter; and the satirists tell us that in this respect England outdid France.

The nether garment for men was called the hose. Its size was likewise carried to a ridiculous extent. The man, however, laboured under an additional dis-advantage. Instead of spreading himself out with whalebone, he gained his volume by padding. It was from this garment that the poor fellow already described took out his tablecloth, napkins, sheets, and other household goods.

The shoes of this period were of various shapes and of many colours. They were frequently slashed below the instep in order to show the colour of the stocking. At parting, Ralf, in the *Shoe-maker's Holiday* (I. i.), gives Jane a pair of shoes "made up and pinked with letters for thy name." Hamlet speaks of "provincial roses in my razed shoes." Razed were slashed shoes. "Provincial roses" refers to the habit of wearing roses or rosettes upon the instep. They were generally made of lace, and often decorated with gold thread, spangles or even jewels. At times the roses were worn very large, four or five inches in diameter. " Why, 'tis the devil, I know him by a great rose he wears on 's shoe to hide his cloven foot." (*White Devil*, V. iii.) Corks, so often referred to in the old plays, were shoes with cork soles that increased in thickness toward the heel, where they might be two or three inches thick. Their purpose was the same as high heels, and when more fully developed became known by another name. The chopine was a device used by women principally, for the purpose of increasing their height, and to keep their embroidered shoes and farthingales out of the mud when they walked abroad. The chopine was an extension of the high heel; though, in its extreme fashion, it is better described as a short stilt. The shoe was fastened to the top, and the chopine was frequently a foot high. The fashion came from Venice, where the height of the chopine corresponded roughly to the rank of the wearer. Persons of very high rank have been known to wear chopines eighteen inches high. The Venetian woman so dressed could not walk alone, but required the assistance of a staff, or to be led about upon the arm constable-fashion. There is a line in one of the old plays to the effect: when a woman walks on chopines she cannot help but caper.

CHAPTER II

THE EARLY GROWTH OF THE CITY

A LITTLE less than a century ago Sir Walter Scott lamented the new service of quick steam-packets that had been introduced between London and Edinburgh, on the score of the danger of individuality being blotted from the various parts of the city. This facility of communication, he thought, would give to London an undue share in fashioning the thought and habits of the whole kingdom. If the fear of the Wizard of the North has been realised, the present state of affairs is but a harking back to old conditions. In the time of Queen Elizabeth London possessed, to an extent unknown even to-day, an influence and domination over the rest of England. It is not so much to point this relation as to describe the city which exerted it that the following pages are written. London, through the fire of 1666, has lost more of its ancient landmarks, and through the Puritan domination more of its habits and customs, than almost any other city of equal antiquity. Hence description and illustration must combine to re-present the city of our great dramatist before our eyes. Street names in the City recall the ancient places, but the places themselves are gone forever.

In early times, before the coming of the Romans, much of the site of London was low, marshy ground. The position and direction of some of the old roads hint that it was a place of much importance, but there is no positive record to substantiate the fact. The earliest known event in connection with the rising city is the building of the bridge; and, though the exact date is unknown, the bridge was probably built during the Roman occupation.

London was still a small unwalled town when next met with on the page of history, when, in A. D. 286, Carusius issued money coined at London. The wall that converted the cluster of houses from an insignificant village to a town of strength was built some time late in the fourth century; and nothing more definite can be said of its origin. It occupied very nearly the site of the wall described in the next chapter, and must have, therefore, included much territory that was then open fields. There is no evidence at present either in the form of remains or of records that imply the existence of Christian worship in the Roman city; and it is fairly certain that the London of that day was not a city of any particular magnificence.

Difficult as it is to write a history of Roman
London, it is even more difficult to write a history
of Saxon London. What happened after the flight
of the Romans is altogether unknown. Concerning
the fate of the unhappy Britons left in the city
the page of history is blank. When we next hear
of London it has already become the chief town of
a flourishing Saxon kingdom. " In short," says
Mr. Loftie, "there are evidences, rather negative
than positive, it is true, to show that the East
Saxons found London desolate, with broken walls
and scanty population, if any; that they entered
upon possession with no great feeling of exulta-
tion, after no great military feat deserving mention
in their chronicle; and that they retained it only
just so long as the more powerful neighbouring
kings allowed them." It is probable that the wall
was destroyed in the Saxon conquest, inasmuch as
no defence was made against the Danes, and it had
to be rebuilt by Alfred. The new Saxon occupants
renamed everything, and, with the possible exception of Dowgate, no Celtic name remains. London
at this time was a source of weakness rather than
of strength to its possessor.

It was probably as a renewal of the dilapidated
wall that Erkenwald built the gate that has been
called after him to this day: Bishopsgate. In the

meantime London had become Christianised and had received its first bishop, Mellitus, in 604. From this time dates the foundation of Saint Paul's and perhaps of Westminster. Shortly afterward London drove out its religious representatives and relapsed again into paganism. The church of Saint Ethelberga probably dates from this period, as does the church of Saint Osith, and doubtless the four churches dedicated to the patron saint of East Anglia: Saint Botolph. After 800 London may be said "to be no longer the capital of one Saxon kingdom, but to be the special property of whatever kingdom was then paramount in all England." (Loftie.) Again and again London was ravished by the Danes, and whatever vestige of the Roman occupation survived the Saxon conquest must have then disappeared.

In 878, by the treaty of Wedmore between King Alfred and the Danes, the kingdom was divided and the part containing London was given to the foe. The Danes, however, put little faith in walls, preferring to meet their enemies in the open fields. They therefore paid little attention to fortifying their new possession. But Alfred was a wiser monarch. He used the period of peace that followed the treaty merely to recuperate his strength, then recaptured the city and drove away the invaders.

He at once repaired or rebuilt, as alluded to above, the ruined wall.

Four times during the reign of Ethelred the Unready the citizens drove away King Sweyn; then, when the Danes had mastered all else, the Londoners saw that further opposition would be useless. They abandoned Ethelred to his fate and compounded with the enemy. They rebelled, however, against Cnut, son of Sweyn, and summoned Ethelred back. He came, accompanied by King Olaf of Norway. The bridge turned out to be the great strategic point. Olaf roofed his boats to protect his crews, rowed boldly up to the bridge, and fastened ropes about the piers. Then he gave orders to row away, and literally tore the bridge down. By this means the Danes in London and those in Southwark were separated and became easy prey.

The coronation of Edmond Ironside, son of Ethelred, took place in London, 1016. This is the first recorded instance of Londoners taking part in the election of a king. When Edward, later in the year, was compelled to make terms with Cnut, he was able to retain possession of London. At his death in 1017, however, Cnut was acknowledged king over all England. Thus the city once more passed into other hands. From this period have survived the names of St. Olave, St. Magnus, and possibly St. Clement Danes. It is during the reign of Cnut that civil government begins to be mentioned in contemporary documents.

This is a meagre list of facts for a thousand years of history, but it is all. It sounds strange to say so, but it is the fact, that the history of London has remained unwritten till our own time. Historian after historian, and there have been many, have written what was called the history of London, copying each other's errors and asserting as facts the hazy traditions that fill those delightful old story books, the Chronicles. It was not till Mr. Loftie's history appeared that we possessed anything like a narrative of the early time which stood upon a basis of fact rather than upon tradition. To be sure, he was compelled to write lines where others had written pages; but this cannot be helped, and there is hope that research and investigation will multiply details. Until that time, however, we possess a history that, though meagre in detail, is thoroughly trustworthy. Since the appearance of Mr. Loftie's book another by Mr. Sharpe, that indefatigable searcher among the Guildhall archives, has come before the public. It is far more continuous and complete than the former, to which it is a complement rather than a rival: for Mr. Loftie deals mainly with topographical devel-

opment, Mr. Sharpe with the development of political institutions. It is needless to say how far the
present writer is indebted to these volumes for the
substance of this chapter.

After the Norman conquest London ceased to be
the residence of the sovereign. When successive
kings had occasion to reside in the neighbourhood
they made their residence at Westminster or at the
Tower—for the Tower, strictly speaking, was not
a part of the city. This change in residence of the
kings was far from ill for London. The city became far more independent and manly in its temper and grew to depend more and more upon its
own internal resources. William the Conqueror
granted to London the first of that long series of
charters that eventually secured the rights of the
citizens and their numerous fondly cherished customs and privileges. He had, however, no idea of
rendering the newly chartered corporation too independent of himself, a condition of affairs he began
to prepare for by commencing the construction of
the White Tower, which was intended both to overawe and to protect the city.

It should be remembered that the old Roman
wall ran directly south towards the river, which it
joined. Part of this wall was removed—perhaps
the very foundation was in part used in the con-

struction of the Tower raised upon its site.   Thus
doubtless arose the tradition, which found believers
in Shakespeare's time, that the Tower was originally
built by Julius Cæsar.   The enclosure that contained the walls and moat surrounding the White
Tower was half within and half without the old
city boundary; but the whole was thenceforth considered to be without the city.   This question gave
rise to many subsequent quarrels over the proper
jurisdiction to be exercised by the Lord Mayor and
the Constable of the Tower, and was not fully settled even in the time of Elizabeth.

The Tower was begun about ten years after
Hastings and was carried on by Rufus, but it was
long before it assumed the splendid proportions
described in a later chapter.   In 1087, the year of
the accession of William Rufus, a great fire occurred in the city, by which the cathedral of Saint
Paul was destroyed.   The rebuilding on a more
magnificent scale was the beginning of the structure familiar to the eyes of Shakespeare.

A new charter granted by Henry I. still further
guaranteed the citizens in their rights.   They were
absolved from the payment of any feudal services,
and, what was of even greater value to them, they
were granted the farm of the revenues of Middlesex, and were given leave to appoint their own jus-

ticier, and were relieved from resorting to any court outside the city. The importance and power of London was shown when Stephen in his contest with Maud threw himself for support upon the good will of the citizens. They claimed their ancient privilege of being heard in the election of a king, and proceeded to elect Stephen, who had thus politically flattered their vanity. Each swore fidelity to the other, an oath firmly kept by the city, but soon broken by the faithless king. Within a few years he robbed them of their right to elect their chief officer, and only restored the privilege after the payment of a heavy fine.

In 1136 occurred the first great fire of London. It broke out in the neighbourhood of London Stone, and burned eastward as far as the gate over the Essex Road, westward to the cathedral, and southward till it destroyed the approaches to London Bridge.

With the accession of Henry II. a period of comparative prosperity set in. The city received confirmation of all the privileges granted by his grandfather, many of which had been rescinded by Stephen and Maud. It was during this reign that Fitzstephen wrote the earliest descriptive account of London, so frequently quoted in the pages of Stow. The city was then young and hardy, having been almost entirely rebuilt since the Conquest. The aggressive citizens felt secure of their rights. Fitzstephen paints it all in glowing colours, with great pride and prophetic hope of the future greatness of the corporation.

Times, however, were soon to change. With the accession of Richard I. the chief magistrate assumed the title of mayor, which he has borne ever since. But from this time till the accession of Edward I. the history of London is one long and bitter struggle on the part of the citizens for their rights against the encroaching kings. Now one side gained a victory, now another. Towards the end of the reign of Henry III. fate set steadily against the city, till it was reduced to a state of abject servitude. Yet the haughty spirit of the sturdy Londoners would not for long brook this state of affairs. Nearly all that had been lost was won back during the next reign. The rule of Edward I. was stern but just. Before his rule was well under way order was restored; and for some time there was no further serious infringement of civic liberties. In 1290 the list and limits of the wards became substantially what they are to-day.

"The twenty-five councillors who advised the king in the reign of King John had gradually become identified with the aldermen; and this title, which was at first applied to the heads of trade guilds and other functionaries, was thenceforth confined to the rulers of the wards. The city was parcelled out into twenty-four divisions. Each division was to elect its alderman except Portsoken, of which the Prior of Aldgate was *ex officio* alderman. There were many signs in other wards that the old hereditary system was long in dying out, and the aldermanry of Farrington, which then comprised both the modern wards of that name, continued to be vested in William Farrington, who had bought it, and his son Nicholas, for no less than eighty years." (Loftie.)

In the reign of Edward I. we have the first distinct mention of the Livery Companies, which leads to a short digression. From very early times there were guilds, mainly religious, but also connected with the crafts, in London. Out of these may have grown the Livery Companies, but there is no positive evidence to connect the two sets of organisations. The trading companies come into notice in 1272, when Walter Hervey was elected Lord Mayor of London. There was strife between the oligarchic party in the city and the commons or tradesmen. Whatever system existed under the old order of guilds was insufficient to bond the commonalty together. Hervey solved the difficulty.

" No longer striving for one great union against
the city guild, he organised all the city trades sep-
arately, and, assuming as chief to the city execu-
tive the right to grant charters of incorporation to
the craftsmen, he called a new force into existence.
Bringing order out of disorder, he faced the aldermen with a hydra-headed combination, against
which the struggle was found to be useless. The
charters he granted were not called into question
while he remained mayor." (Loftie.)   Early in
January, 1274, all these charters were annulled.
This fact, however, did not vanquish the new power
that had been called into existence. The craftsmen
were becoming still more powerful, and before long
began to seek charters of incorporation from the
King himself; and they soon became so influential
as to be, so to speak, the very city itself.   The
earliest royal charters date from 1327, when the
incorporation took place of the goldsmiths, the
tailors and armourers, and the skinners.   Edward
III. also gave charters to the grocers, fishmongers,
drapers, and vintners.   " The work of incorporation went on merrily during this and several succeeding reigns.   Eight of the twelve Great Companies were chartered before the end of Edward's
life.   Exclusiveness and monopoly were, of course,
the object of each society thus formed.   They de-

sired to regulate trade and also to regulate traders.
They fixed the prices. They fixed the method of
manufacture. They made rules as to the conduct
and even the dress of the members. It is apparent
that to do this effectually they required to have
power to forbid all interference from without. No
one must carry on their trade who was not of their
mystery. It will be remembered how the charters
of William Hervey were superseded for the want
of this power. The royal charters conferred it,
though it may be doubted if the mayor's charters
may not have been legally quite efficient—and every
new company as it was formed sought for the distinction of a grant from the king himself."
(Loftie.)

The companies had now become all powerful
governors of the city's trade. One step more
made them the rulers of the city government. The
old method of electing the mayor did not work satisfactorily. "In 1375, accordingly, it was superseded, and the Great Companies were recognised in
an ordinance by which the power of nomination
was taken from the wards and given to the companies, and by which the persons so nominated were
to be summoned to the council and to the elections."
(Loftie.)

This is the period of greatest civic importance,

though not of mercantile prosperity, of the Livery Companies. "Not only was the common council to be elected in future by the guilds, but the guilds were also to elect the mayor and the sheriffs. The aldermen and commons were to meet together at least once a quarter, and no member of the common council was to serve on inquests, nor to be appointed collector, or assessor of taillage." (Sharpe.)

This new power of the Livery Companies was not to be enjoyed long. This pre-eminence in civic affairs ended in 1384, when it was said that the new system had been forced upon the citizens. It was therefore resolved to revert to the old system of election by wards. At that time the municipal government became substantially what it is to-day.

The history of London during the Wars of the Roses is mainly of events rather than of civic development. The legend of Richard Whittington is known in every nursery. King Edward was still alive when the lad of thirteen came up to London to be apprenticed to a wealthy mercer and to begin his wonderful career. In due time he was made free of the Mercers' Company; and in 1397 King Richard, who had been attracted by the energetic shrewdness of the young man, undertook to make him mayor in an underhand way. At the death of a mayor during his term of office the King arbitrarily appointed Whittington in his place. This infringement of their liberties, however, did not seriously offend the citizens, a sterling tribute to the popularity of the new mayor. He was not mayor the year Henry IV. came to the throne, but was re-elected in 1406.

About this time a new force enters the history of England and becomes closely related to the history of London. The city by this time had become so large and so wealthy and so stable that every movement of importance in the realm was concerned to know how it would be received by the citizens. The day of popularity of the great mediæval religious institutions was verging towards its close. Though a century and a half was to elapse before their final spoliation under Henry VIII., their doom was virtually sealed by the conditions that required the passage in 1401 of an act for burning heretics. From the beginning of Lollardry, the forerunner of the Reformation, London was intimately connected with the fate of the religious orders. The first victim of the law was William Sawtree, a mass priest of Saint Osyth, who was "brent in Smythfelde . . . for erysse." In 1414 came the Lollard insurrection under the leadership of Sir John Oldcastle, which resulted in the death of this good man. During these years London was sorely distracted; but we can easily imagine the turn towards joy and pride that took place when news of their beloved King's victory came from Agincourt.

In 1419 Whittington was mayor for the last time. The exact date of his death is not known, though his will was proved in 1423. His name is worth remembering by all who have a homely pride in London. His gifts to the city of his prosperity continued after his death. In addition to the college for priests in St. Michael, Paternoster Royal, he gave books and a building to Greyfriars, and has the credit for founding the first city library. He rebuilt Newgate, set fountains in various parts of the city, and left a multitude of other small bequests.

In 1418, during the mayoralty of Sir Henry Barton, the lighting of the streets with lamps was made compulsory. In 1423 the infant Henry VI. entered London. The streets of the city at once became the battleground of the factions at war with each other during the King's minority. He was crowned at Paris in 1429, but matters were not bettered at home. For years London was now in the hands of York, now in those of Lancaster. In general, the records of this time are very meagre, but they are full and authentic concerning that strange rebellion of the Kentish men under the leadership of Jack Cade. For a few days he fully possessed the panic-stricken city. He sat himself down in the Guildhall, whence he pompously issued orders to the assembled mayor and aldermen. But he overshot himself, and in a few days Cade was a fallen star, with his head alone still high, elevated upon a staff to ornament London Bridge.

Up to 1452 the city was thoroughly loyal to King Henry. The triumphant entry of York, who conducted the King a prisoner to London after the battle of St. Albans in 1455, left no doubt that the temper of the citizens had changed from its former loyalty. There was a momentary hesitation on the part of London when the tide of battle turned in favour of that "tiger's heart wrapped in a woman's hide," but their spirit returned with the appearance of the warlike son of the Duke of York. London hastened to exercise its ancient privilege and proclaimed Edward IV. King of England.

"From the accession of Edward IV. a change comes over our city annals. The civic constitution was now settled. The outermost ring of suburbs had been enclosed. The last touches had been put to the fabric over which rival aldermen and common councillors had contended for centuries. The city had become venerable. Her citizens had begun to 'think upon her stones.' The repair of the Roman wall, carried out in 1476, is one of the first examples of modern ' restoration,' namely, the falsification of the history of a building. The first of the long series of London antiquaries, the first dramatist who was to illustrate her history, her people, her streets, for readers of all generations, were not yet born, but their time was drawing very nigh, and the printing press was already at work. Fortunately for us the old associations had begun to be studied before Cromwell and the fire came to obliterate them. Stow has made the stage and painted the scenery, and Shakespeare has put in the figures. . . . In writing the plays that relate to London in those times he could speak of what was actually before his eyes. The Wars of the Roses were not more remote from him than the Scots' Rebellion is from us. He stood with respect to the sad story of Henry VI. nearly as we stand to that of George III." (Loftie.)

Edward retained the good will of London till his death. The city was proud of his victories, and the people loved his extravagant expenditure. Trade revived and all went merrily for a few years. The city gave a cold welcome to Richard III., as all may read in Shakespeare's play, and, though they allowed him to act as if he had been honestly proclaimed king by the city itself, it was a half-hearted tolerance they gave him, and they joyfully welcomed the conqueror who found the crown of England upon a bush on Bosworth Field.

With the accession of the Tudors this brief note on the development of the city may suitably close. It had become in appearance and extent practically what is described in the following pages. Henry VII. began what was the policy of the Tudors throughout: high-handed tyranny executed by force. What in earlier times would have been encroachments on the city rights, were under the Tudors merely violations, not denials of those rights. The moment the strong hand was removed the city sprang upright with its personality unimpaired. Henry VIII. during his long reign, in which occurred the Dissolution of the Monasteries, was always popular in London. The city was dumb with horror during the Marian persecution, but were loyal to the Maiden Queen for nearly half a century.

CHAPTER III

A GENERAL VIEW OF LONDON

ROUGHLY speaking mediæval London began with the building of the White Tower by William the Conqueror, and ended with the great fire of 1666. Throughout this long period changes were made from year to year; but, after the great religious establishments were once built, the face of London changed so slowly that the picture of one generation is the picture of the next. The most sudden sweeping change was made at the Dissolution of the Monasteries, and the period of most rapid expansion was the reign of Elizabeth. It is the London of the latter half of the sixteenth century and the beginning of the seventeenth, the most brilliant period in its history between Hastings and the Fire, that the following pages essay to present.

Three hundred years ago the relative importance of London to the rest of England was even greater than it is to-day. All the theatres and all the publishers of note were in London or in the immediate vicinity. The court was held for most of the time at Westminster. There was but one Royal Exchange in the kingdom. All persons of any pretence to wealth or influence possessed their town house or inn. The city set the manners and furnished the news for the whole island; it was, indeed, the heart of the kingdom.

In order to draw a fancy picture of the Elizabethan city as Shakespeare knew it, one who is familiar with the modern metropolis must blot from his mind all present associations—not only in regard to size, but also in regard to outward aspect, and in the manners and customs of the people; for in these respects the city of that day was wholly different from the city of this. It should be remembered that the fire of 1666 practically swept away all but the suburbs of Elizabethan London. Hardly a town in the world of ancient origin preserves so few of its original structures as does the capital of England. One can go about the city to-day and encounter practically nothing besides the street names that reminds him of times before the Fire. Roughly speaking, a line connecting the Tower, Crosby Hall, Christ Church, Ludgate Circus, and the approach to Blackfriar's Bridge includes the part of the city destroyed by the great conflagration. And this area, though it is but a small part of the city we know, constituted the major part of the city in 1600.*

* The part of the modern metropolis known as The City approximates in area the Elizabethan city.

LONDON

(From an engraving by Hollar, about 1620)

1. St. Paul's
2. Whitehall
3. Suffolk House
4. York House
5. Savoy
6. Somerset House
7. Arundel House
8. St. Clemen's
9. St. Dunstan's
10. The Temple
11. St. Bride's
12. St. Andrew's

13. Baynard's Castle
14. Queenhithe
15. St. Sepulchre's
16. Three Cranes
17. The Waterhouse
18. The Steelyard
19. Bow Church
20. Guildhall
21. St. Michael's
22. St. Laurence
23. Fishmongers' Hall
24. The Old Swan

25. The Bridge
26. Gray Church
27. St. Dunstan in the East
28. Billingsgate
29. Custom-house
30. The Tower
31. Tower Wharf
32. St. Catharine's
33. St. Olave's
34. St. Mary Overy
35. Winchester House

36. The Globe
37. Bear Garden
38. The Swan
39. Harrow on the Hill
40. Hamsted
41. Highgate
42. Hackney
43. Pontney
44. Ell Ships
45. Galley Fuste
46. Cold Harbour

In the latter part of the sixteenth century a Dutch traveller by the name of Hentzner visited England, and afterward wrote a very interesting account of his foreign travels. He visited London, and his quaint account of the sights is full of the local colour of which we are so desirous. Let us for a moment station ourselves where he must have been when he first caught a glimpse of what was then, as it is to-day, one of the chief cities of the world.

We are on the Surrey side, approaching London along the old Roman road which leads to the bridge. Perhaps before Hentzner crossed the river he visited St. Mary Overies. If he had ascended the Tower he would have seen a splendid sight. Across a river that was as unlike the modern Thames as imagination can picture lay the bustling city. The river was clear and shining, sparkling with swans that swam gracefully in miniature fleets of snowy whiteness. Behind, on either side, and beyond the busy capital were green fields spotted with flowers or covered with golden grain and emerald turf. The city itself was nestled upon three hills. On an eminence to the right rose the many-towered walls of the citadel surrounding the lofty White Tower of William the Norman. Two small valleys rendered visible by the dip in the red-tiled roof line separate it from the great cathedral pile of St. Paul's. This church was the glory of all England. No other cathedral in the kingdom was so beautiful, the source of so much pride; and one who looks at the modern structure that occupies its site sighs with deep-felt regret over the ignominious contrast.

What perhaps impressed the Dutch traveller most was the innumerable collection of spires that rose from the densely populated city. The Dissolution of the Monasteries had not fallen lightly upon London; in fact, it had left it, as Mr. Besant says, a city of ruins. For all that, the parish churches had been spared. Hardly one had fallen in the national game of snatch-grab that followed the Dissolution. Stow tells us that there were no less than a hundred and twenty, and all of these were provided with towers or steeples. Yet, high above the clustered mass of slender spires rose the great bulk of the cathedral. Its lofty, graceful spire, however, had been burned some years before, and only a mutilated stump replaced it.

If we pause for a moment to listen we can hear the mingled peals of bells and the roar of the city, for it was even more noisy then than now. People lived in the streets and used them constantly as a daily convenience that is suggested to one by modern Paris, not by London.

Immediately beneath us lies the only bridge

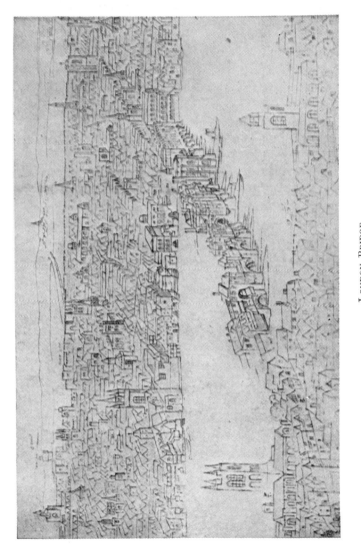

LONDON BRIDGE
(From the drawing by Wyngaerde)

across the Thames. London Bridge of those days was a little east of the present structure; in fact, it crossed the river just where St. Magnus' Church now stands. It was an arched bridge of nearly a score of arches, no two of them exactly the same in width. About the piers were timber frameworks of wood that so encroached upon the waterway that the flow while the tide was rising and falling was greatly impeded. Such obstacles were these lozenge-shaped " starlings," that the backing up of the water at mid-tide produced a fall beneath the bridge of several feet. Pennant alludes to the sound of the falling waters in the following words: " Nothing but use could preserve the rest of the inmates who soon grew deaf to the sound of falling water, the clamours of watermen, or the frequent shrieks of drowning wretches." The old plays sometimes refer to the sound of the bridge being heard over the whole city. This natural water-fall was pressed into use to operate a set of force pumps that supplied water to a large part of the city. Much of the local travel that is now carried on in cabs was then performed upon the river in small boats. The cry with which one hailed a waterman was Westward ho! or Eastward ho! according to the direction. If, in the journey, it was necessary to cross the bridge at mid-tide the passenger had to land and wait. Sometimes they "shot" the bridge, that is, took their chances of mishap and went over the fall. The danger that attended this kind of rapid transit gave rise to the proverb: London Bridge was made for wise men to walk over and fools to go under. When the Princess Elizabeth, afterwards the Queen, was conveyed a prisoner to the Tower, it was necessary for the boatmen to row about in the neighbourhood of the bridge for an hour before it was deemed safe to "shoot."

What to us appears the most peculiar feature of this old bridge was not the starlings or the noisy river, but the covered way or arcade that capped the arches throughout the entire length. From end to end, with the exception of two small openings, London Bridge was covered with houses that enclosed and roofed a narrow street: dwellings above and shops below. There were many kinds of shops, but in the time of Elizabeth the bridge was especially noted for the manufacture of pins, and the fair dames of London often bargained among the narrow stalls above the water for this indispensable article of dress.

At the southern end of the bridge was a huge towered gate-house whose principal use in the days of Queen Bess was to afford a resting place for traitors' heads. Imagine the trait of character that prompted the people to flock to an execution by the hundred, in holiday attire, and afterward gaze unshocked upon a score of bloody heads on pikes, grinning ghastly from the battlemented tower. About midway on the bridge was a handsome chapel. Beneath the last three arches of the northern end were the pumps for forcing water to which allusion has already been made. At the London approach was another tower, almost in ruins by the third quarter of the century, and taken down by the end.

Unless Hentzner hailed a boat at the stairs of the Bear tavern by the bridge foot with the cry of Northward ho! he must have entered the city along the gloomy bridge. The roadway through this structure was scarcely wider than a single cart, and in the press one had to exercise considerable ingenuity to escape collision, the bridge being always a busy thoroughfare. At two places only were open spaces where people could stand for safety.

Instead of following the Dutch traveller to his tavern, let us take a general view of the outward appearance of the city in methodical order. The city, as has been said, was then comparatively small; it was also comparatively open in the manner of building. For, though the streets presented solid and continuous lines of house fronts, there were gardens behind most of them. In fact, many of the city blocks resembled open courtyards occupied on the four sides with buildings. There were numerous churches, and about most of them burying grounds of considerable size. Furthermore, it was but a short walk to the country in any direction. Ten minutes was sufficient for a person to reach the open fields from any part of London afoot. Hunting and hawking were still common sports of the neighbourhood and were carried on as near the centre of the city as the British Museum or the Liverpool Street Station.

Elizabethan London, which in area corresponded closely with the modern City was surrounded by a wall that remained almost intact on three sides till a time long subsequent to that under description. Even so early as the days of Fitzstephen the river side of the wall had disappeared, leaving no trace of its existence except in such names as Dowgate and Billingsgate. The course of the Elizabethan wall was from the north side of the Tower ditch, along the Minories in a northwesterly direction to Aldgate; then, curving west and north, followed Camomile and Wormwood Streets and London Wall. The angle of the wall at the northwest corner is still marked by the existing base of the tower which stands in the churchyard of St. Giles, Cripplegate. From this point the wall turned directly south along the present Noble

LONDON WALL
(A portion in churchyard of St. Giles's, Cripplegate. From an etching
by J. T. Smith, drawn in 1793)

Street, west, crossing Aldersgate Street, and south-west between St. Bartholomew's the Great and Christ's Hospital to a point west of Newgate prison. Thence it ran south to Ludgate Hall, west to Ludgate Circus, and south again to the river.

The wall was built, except for a small portion, upon the foundation of an earlier Roman wall. The more recent structure was partly of rough stone and partly of tile, and was capped by a battlemented wall of brick and stone. At short and irregular intervals were small towers in addition to the fortified gate-house. None of these smaller towers has survived, nor is there any accurate description of them. The base of one in St. Giles churchyard has been mentioned and another was discovered after a fire about a century ago. It was two and twenty feet in height, but not complete.

There were several gates: the Tower postern, Aldgate, Bishopsgate, Moorgate postern, Aldersgate, Greyfriar's postern, Newgate, and Ludgate. These, with the exceptions of the posterns, were huge towered structures, with, usually, a triple passage: one for vehicles, the others for pedestrians. The latter were closed at night by heavy doors, the former by ponderous portcullises. Newgate and Ludgate were used as prisons, the others often as private dwellings for those who guarded the gates.

The wall on the outer side was bordered by a ditch two hundred feet across; on the west side, however, the place of the ditch was taken by the Fleet River. Of old time the ditch not only was a defence, but also supplied most of the water and much of the fish used in the city. In Elizabethan times, however, it had become too filthy for such purposes, and was, moreover, encroached upon in many places, filled up with debris, turned into garden plots, and otherwise marred and displaced, much to the chagrin of the old historian Stow.

This relic of mediæval life had been of real service to the city in the time of Queen Mary, and actually formed an obstacle that turned to naught the ill-starred rebellion of Essex; yet, in spite of these facts, the wall was an obsolete and useless feature of London life. It was no longer necessary as a protection, and, in consequence, the city began to spread beyond the limits of its confines at the beginning of the reign of Elizabeth. By the end, the jurisdiction of the Lord Mayor extended over the adjacent ground north of the river in every direction for a distance varying from one to three-fourths of a mile. All this area, however, was not wholly occupied by buildings. On the east, running northwest from the Tower, was a single row of houses along the Minories. The same was true of much of the north side of the city; but in the immediate vicinity of the gates the populated portion extended along the high road for some little distance. There was, Stow tells us, a continuous line of houses along the river east of the Tower for half a mile or more; and the road from Bishopsgate was well occupied all the way to Shoreditch Church, which was well outside the city limits. Northwest of the city in the vicinity of Smithfield, and the church and hospital of St. Bartholomew's, a considerable hamlet had sprung into existence. The Strand was lined upon the south side with palatial residences all the way to Westminster, though the mayor's jurisdiction stopped then, as it does now, at Temple Bar. The north side of the Strand was built upon for the first time during the reign of Elizabeth.

The population of the city of that day cannot be accurately given; but a fairly trustworthy estimate can be obtained. The city contained in all likelihood not far from one hundred thousand people, with as many more in Westminster, Southwark, and the neighbouring suburbs to the north and west. It is interesting to note the foreign population at this time. In 1567 there were 40 Scots, 428 French, 45 Spaniards and Portuguese, 140 Italians, 2030 Dutch, 44 Burgundians, 2

Danes, and 1 Liegois. In 1580 there were 2302
Dutch, 1838 French, 116 Italians, 1542 English
born of foreign parents, and 664 not specified.

The increase of native population kept pace with
the foreign increase, a tendency the government
tried hard to interrupt. A proclamation of Elizabeth forbade the erection of any new buildings
upon hitherto unoccupied sites within three miles
of any of the city gates. The same proclamation
forbade more than one family to live together in
the same house. The noble persons were fast removing their mansions to new locations without
the walls, and the last mentioned provision of the
above proclamation was directed against the popular custom of turning the abandoned mansions into
tenement houses, crowded and filthy fosterers of
the plague. The reason given for this proclamation and some others of a similar nature, which,
however, were frequently violated, was to prevent
the danger arising from disease and disorder, both
important factors in the Elizabethan life ; but there
can be but little doubt that under the surface of
these building regulations lay a substantial jeal-
ousy, if not an actual fear, of the rapidly growing
wealth and power of the city corporation.

Within the area bounded by the old wall the
city was divided by a few grand thoroughfares,
but, for the most part, by narrow and filthy streets,

They were dark and dingy from the projecting upper stories of the gabled houses that shut out most of the light, and dirty under foot, while one in passing was not infrequently deluged with the house-maid's slops from an upper window. Most of the streets were poorly paved, or not at all, with a kennel half full of stagnant water in the centre. Sometimes there was no specially prepared foot-way; often such a convenience was little more than indicated by a low line of posts. The public streets were made the dumping grounds for all sorts of rubbish. Scalding Alley owned its name to the habit of scalding chickens there for sale in the neighbouring market of the Poultry. So little was the value of correct sanitation known that as late as 1647 the following permission is recorded in the official reports of the Royal Hospital: "No man shall cast urine or ordure in the streets afore the hour of nine in the night. Also he shall not cast it out but bring it down and lay it in the channel." It is not to be wondered at that the people often encountered the blue cross on a door-post, the sign of plague, or that statutes required every householder to build a fire opposite his house three times a week in order to purge the atmosphere.

The houses that lined these streets were of various kinds. There were still standing many of the

fine old mansions of the nobility that retained the
appearance, though no longer the reality, of stone
fortifications. One of the finest of these still
remains in part—Crosby Hall. The houses of
contemporary build were usually of brick and
timber, eked out with lath and plaster, and constructed on a less pretentious scale. The wood
work of the fronts was often grotesquely carved
and painted, and the roof usually gabled towards
the street, as is still to be seen in the Staple
Inn.

The windows were generally composed of small
panes of glass imbedded in lead, and opening case-
ment-wise; while each story of the house projected
several feet beyond the line of the story below.
Often a street of fair width on the ground showed
but a narrow sky line above, the house fronts being
so close together that people could shake hands
across the space. In addition, shop-keepers often
built pent-houses against their lower walls for the
display of goods, thus encroaching still further
upon the narrow passage.

One is particularly struck by three details in
connection with the houses of old London: (1) The
number of churches, to which allusion has already
been made. (2) The frequency of taverns. It
would be useless to attempt to catalogue the city
taverns. Besides the scores that are famous, there

were other scores and scores. Often and often
Stow finishes the description of an unimportant
street with the words, "containing many fair
houses and divers taverns." (3) The proximity of
shops of the same nature. Until quite recently
Holywell Street, Strand, presented an aspect typi-
cal of Elizabethan London. Both sides of the
street were lined with the shops of petty dealers
in second-hand books, one adjoining the other
throughout the whole length of the street. In
Elizabethan times this custom was carried out over
the whole city. Thus the pin makers were upon
London Bridge, the apothecaries in Bucklesbury,
the goldsmiths in Cheapside, etc. Only the ubiq-
uitous tavern possessed no local habitation.

Then as now the smaller streets were named in
connection with their proximity to larger streets.
As there were no numbers in use, each house
was indicated by a sign, and much ingenuity was
required to diversify them. These signs were
occasionally painted upon the house fronts, or
carved in the stonework; but more commonly they
hung out over the street, suspended from elaborate
wrought-iron brackets. Originally a sign had
indicated an individual shop-keeper's trade, but,
just as the number of a house remains to-day
unchanged with change of occupant, so the Elizabethan sign was generally permanent. Thus came

about the state of affairs that Addison ridicules in
The Spectator.

"I would enjoin every shop-keeper to make use
of a sign that bears some affinity to the wares in
which he deals. A cook should not live at the
'Boot,' nor a shoe-maker at 'The Roasted Pig,'
and yet for want of this regulation I have seen a
goat set up before the door of a perfumer and
the French King's head before a sword cutter's."

The streets of London were poorly lighted at
night, or not at all. Various acts provided that
householders should at regular intervals hang out
lanterns; but these lanterns did little or no good,
for they were only horn boxes containing a dim
candle. Even so, the acts were seldom obeyed, and
one of the common street cries was that of the
watchman reminding a delinquent householder
that his lantern was not in place.

The watchman, who was, too often, not at all
unlike Dogberry and his companions, went his
rounds armed with a huge halberd, and was about
as useless for the preservation of order as the
numerous "Statutes for Streets," which among
other things forbade persons to cry out at night,
to blow a horn after nine o'clock, to whistle, to
cause a disturbance, or to do a thousand and one
other necessary acts. From time to time special
attempts were made to improve the efficiency of

the police, especially in regard to the arrest of
" sturdy beggars," the pest of Elizabethan London. But, do what they could, the fact remained
that one always wore his side arms for protection,
and took his life in his hands, when he stirred
abroad after nightfall.

In connection with the streets of London one
might mention the water-supply of the city, since
so great a part of it was drawn from the public
conduits in the streets. Till the thirteenth century London depended for its water supply wholly
upon the neighbouring brooks and springs and
upon the Thames. With the growth of the city,
however, the smaller streams became polluted and,
in 1236, the citizens were given permission to
convey water in pipes from Tyburn to Cheapside.
In 1285 was commenced the great lead-lined cistern
with a castellated structure over it that was known
as the Great Conduit in Cheap, to which the water
was conveyed a distance of three and a half miles.

The conduits in Cheapside are described elsewhere in the present volume. There were in and
about London many springs and wells that were
turned to account in serving other conduits;
and there was also a system of pipes supplied
by a pump under London Bridge. Besides the
conduits in Cheapside, the principal conduits
throughout the city were as follows: the Tun upon

Cornhill, the conduit in Aldermanbury, the Standard in Fleet Street, the Standard without Cripplegate, the conduit in Gracechurch Street, the conduit at Holborn Cross, the Little Conduit at the Stocks Market, the conduit at Bishopsgate, the conduit in London Wall opposite Coleman Street, the conduit without Aldgate, the conduit in Lothbury, and the conduit in Dowgate.

An annual custom in connection with the conduits is thus described by Stow: " And particularly on the 18th of September, 1562, the Lord Mayor and others . . . rid to the conduit heads for to see them after the old custom (of annual inspection), and after dinner they hunted the hare and killed her, and thence to dinner at the head of the conduit . . . and after dinner they went hunting the fox."

The vehicles encountered in the streets were mostly the carts of costermongers, still more clumsy wagons, men on horse-back, chairs and coaches. The latter, however, were of infrequent use, having been but recently introduced. It was considered so effeminate as to be almost a disgrace for a man to be seen riding in a coach, unless it were the occasion of some civic or royal ceremony.

Stow in many places expresses his heartfelt enthusiasm for the city, such enthusiasm as a native Londoner born within sound of Bow Bells would feel. Elsewhere, however, the same Stow bewails the following state of affairs in the streets of his native city:

"But now in our time, instead of these enormities, others are come in place no less meet to be reformed, namely, purprestures, or encroachments on the highways, lanes, and common grounds, in and about this city; whereof a learned gentleman and grave citizen hath not many years since written and exhibited a book to the mayor and commonalty; which book whether the same have been read by them and diligently considered upon, I know not, but sure I am nothing is reformed since concerning this matter.

"Then the number of cars, drays, carts, and coaches, more than hath been accustomed, the streets and lanes being straightened, must needs be dangerous, as daily experience proveth.

"The coachman rides behind the horse tails, lasheth them, and looketh not behind him; the drayman sitteth and sleepeth on his dray, and letteth his horse lead him home. I know that, by the good laws and customs of this city, shodded carts are forbidden to enter the same, except upon reasonable cause, as service of the prince, or such like, they be tolerated. Also that the fore horse of every carriage should be led by hand; but these good orders are not observed. Of old time coaches were not known in this island, but chariots or whirlicotes, then so called, and they only used of princes or great estates, such as had their footmen about them; . . . but now of late years the use of coaches, brought out of Germany, is taken up, and made so common, as there is neither distinction of time nor difference of persons observed; for the world runs on wheels with many whose parents were glad to go on foot.''

The close crowding of the city and the timber framework of the buildings gave rise to the two great dangers of the Elizabethan city: fire and plague. People are prone to think of the great plague which DeFoe described as the only plague to which the metropolis has been subjected; but, as a matter of fact, this dread disease visited the city about once in thirty years. It was not an uncommon happening to have the court moved inland because of the danger of infection, and it furnished the cause of many of the brief closures of the theatres long before the Puritans carried their way on moral grounds. Camden asserts that in 1563 there were 21,530 deaths from plague in London alone.

The streets of Elizabethan London were proverbially noisy, not only from the busy, jostling traffic, but also from the innumerable street cries heard upon every hand. It was the custom for an apprentice to stand in the door of his master's shop and to solicit trade of the passers-by with the cry of "What do you lack?" A foreigner, who was likely to be ridiculed by the common people wherever he was met in those days, or any other person who examined articles without making a purchase, was liable to the sarcastic chaff of the disappointed 'prentice; and if the customer answered impudently he was likely to have the whole brotherhood down upon him with their clubs in a trice. Sir Walter Scott in *The Fortunes of Nigel* has given an excellent picture of the Elizabethan shop, the rude behaviour of the apprentices, and a subsequent riot.

In the days of Elizabeth they declare by act of common council that in ancient times the lanes of the open city have been used and of right ought to be used as the common highway only, and not for hucksters, pedlars, and hagglers to stand or to sell their wares in, and to pass from street to street, hawking and offering their wares. The preventive acts of Elizabeth, however, chiefly illustrate the abuses in full operation notwithstanding the violation of the law; hence we are not surprised to find a number of forbidden street cries alluded to in the old plays, among which are the following: "Old clothes, any old clothes"—"Buy, sell, or exchange, hats, caps, etc."—"Any kitchen stuffs,

have ye, maids "—(the latter was the cry of those
who collected refuse for the manufacture of soap
and candles). " Ballads, Almanacks," was the
frequent cry of the itinerant book-seller. Heywood, in *The Rape of Lucrece*, under the head of
cries of Rome, gives a series of amusing illustrations of the London cries of his own day. Many
others are to be found in the second act of *Bartholomew Fair*. Suffice it to say here that they
were of innumerable variety, representing nearly
every trade imaginable, and were heard like a
constant chorus in the streets.

The principal thoroughfares of London were as
follows: (1) From Newgate, across the city by
Cheapside to Aldgate. (2) From Bishopsgate,
south by London Bridge to the Surrey Side. These
were the only thoroughfares that crossed the city
completely. (3) From Ludgate to the Tower by
way of Candlewick Street, interrupted, however,
by the necessity of going through or around the
churchyard of St. Paul's. (4) Thames Street, that
ran parallel to the river from Blackfriars to the
Tower.

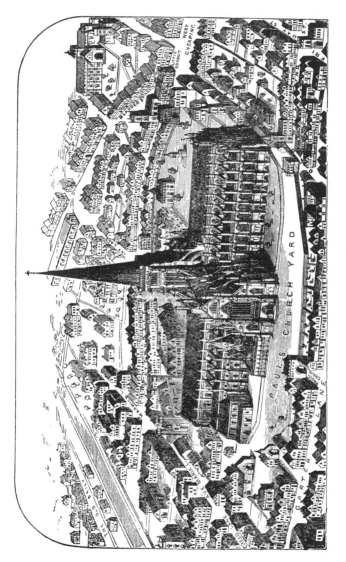

BIRD'S-EYE VIEW OF OLD ST. PAUL'S
(From drawings by E. B. Ferrey and F. Watkins)

CHAPTER IV

OLD SAINT PAUL'S

THE cathedral that met the eyes of the old Dutch traveller Hentzner towards the close of Elizabethan times was far different from the modern pile upon the same site, and far more magnificent as a piece of architecture. The ancient church was, in fact, the largest and most splendid cathedral in England. It had been long in building, and gave evidence of the many architectural styles that had obtained at one time and another since its origin; yet the different parts suited one another most harmoniously.

It was, however, essentially of two styles. The nave was Norman and the choir Early Decorated. It is not the purpose of this chapter to describe in detail the architecture of the old structure, inasmuch as the most careful drawings of the original building are now readily accessible, but rather to describe the customs and traditions that characterised it during the time of Elizabeth.

The cathedral stood in the centre of a churchyard that was surmounted by a wall, and occupied the area between Paternoster Row on the north, Old Change on the east, Carter Lane on the south, and Creed and Ave María Lanes on the west. Paternoster Row took its name from the paternoster or bead makers who used to dwell there of old time. Old Change derived its name from a former exchange for coinage of bullion that of old time stood upon the east side of the street. Carters from all parts of the kingdom resorted to the numerous taverns on Carter Lane, and text writers gave names to Creed and Ave Maria Lanes.

In the churchyard wall were six gates. The principal entrance was near the north end of Creed Lane, and formed part of the passage from Ludgate along Bowyer Row to the west front of the cathedral. Of the three gates in the north wall one opened into Paternoster Row by Paul's Alley, one by Canon Alley, and the third, known as the Little Gate, opened into Cheapside not far from the present statue of Sir Robert Peel. The Saint Augustine Gate was on the east side opposite Watling Street, said to be the oldest thoroughfare in London. The sixth gate was on the south side leading into Paul's Chain, a narrow alley that led south across Thames Street to the river at St. Paul's Wharf. It derived its name from the old practice of drawing a chain across the street to hinder traffic during the hours of divine worship in the cathedral.

There were numerous buildings in and about

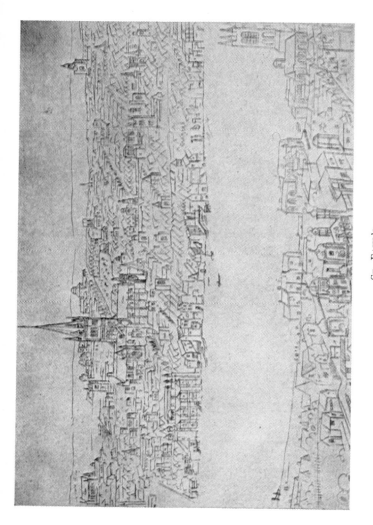

ST. PAUL'S
(From the drawing by Wyngaerde)

the enclosure. At the northwest corner stood the Bishop's palace. On the north were the college of petty canons, numerous small chapels, and the charnel house. The most famous structure of the northern precinct was Pardon Churchyard, which, though demolished shortly before the accession of Elizabeth, still lingered so distinctly in the neighbourhood memory of the people that it is worth while to quote its description by Stow.

"There is also one great cloister on the north side of this church, environing a plot of ground, of old time called Pardon Churchyard; whereof Thomas More was either the first builder, or a most special benefactor, and was buried there. About this cloister was artificially and richly painted the Dance of Machabray, or Dance of Death, commonly called the Dance of Paul's; the like whereof was painted about St. Innocent's cloister at Paris in France. The metres or poesy of this dance were translated out of the French into English by John Lydgate, monk of Bury, and with the picture of death leading all estates, painted about the cloister, at the special request and at the dispence of John Carpenter in the reign of Henry VI. In this cloister were buried many persons, some of worship and others of honour; the monuments of whom in number and curious workmanship, passed all others that were in the church.

"Over the east quadrant of this cloister was a fair library, built at the cost and charges of Walter Sherington, chancellor of the Duchy of Lancaster in the reign of Henry VI., which hath been well furnished with fair written books in vellum, but few of them do remain there.   In the midst of this Pardon Churchyard was a fair chapel, first founded by Gilbert Becket, portgrave and principal magistrate of this city in the reign of King Stephen, who was there buried.

"Thomas More, the Dean of Paul's before mentioned, re-edified or new built this chapel, and founded three chaplains there, in the reign of Henry V.

"In the year 1549, on the 10th of April, the said chapel, by commandment of the Duke of Somerset, was begun to be pulled down, with the whole cloister, the Dance of Death, the tombs and monuments, so that nothing thereof was left but the bare plot of ground which is since converted into a garden for the petty canons."

To the northeast stood Paul's Cross, where open air sermons were preached on the forenoon of Sundays unless dispensed with for some especial reason.   On the east side of the churchyard was Paul's School, founded in 1512 by Dean Colet for 153 poor men's children.   Its foundation is thus described by Erasmus:

PAUL'S CROSS
(From an engraving by Wilkinson)

"Upon the death of the father of Colet, when by right of inheritance he was possessed of a considerable sum of money, lest the keeping of it should corrupt his mind and turn it too much to the world, he laid out a great part of it in building a new school in the churchyard of St. Paul, dedicated to the Child Jesus; a magnificent fabrick to which he added two handsome dwelling houses for the two several masters, to whom he assigned ample salaries, that they might teach a certain number of boys gratuitously. He divided the school into four apartments. The first is the porch or entrance for *Catechumens* (or children to be instructed in the principles of religion), and no child is admitted there unless he can already read and write. The second apartment is for lower boys who are taught by the *Hypodidasculus* (or usher). The third is for those who are more learned (under the head master), which former parts of the school are divided from the other by a curtain which can be drawn or undrawn at pleasure. Over the master's chair is seated a figure of the Child Jesus, of excellent work, in the act of teaching; whom all the assembly, both at coming in and going out of the school, salute with a short hymn. There is also a representation of God the Father, saying: 'Hear ye him,' but these words were written there at my recommendation. The last apartment is a little chapel adopted to divine service. Throughout the school are neither corners nor hiding places, nor anything like a cell or closet. The boys have each their distinct forms or benches, rising in regular gradients and spaces one over another. Of these every class contains sixteen, and he who is most excellent in his class has a kind of small desk by way of eminence. All children are not to be admitted as a matter of course, but to be selected according to their parts and capacities. The most sagacious founder saw that the greatest hopes and happiness of the commonwealth was in the training up of children to good letters and true religion; for which purpose he laid out a great sum of money, and yet would not admit anyone to a share in the expense. . . . When he had finished all his arrangements he left the perpetual care and government of the establishment, not to the clergy, not to the bishop, not to the chapter, as it is called, nor to nobles—but to certain married citizens of honest report. On being asked the reason for it he replied that there was no absolute certainty in human affairs, but that he found these persons to be the least corruptible."

Just why Colet left the government of his school to married citizens is explained by Fuller: "It may seem false Latin that this Colet, being Dean of Paul's, the school dedicated to St. Paul, and

St. Faith's

(From an engraving by Hollar)

distanced but the breadth of a street from St. Paul's Church, should not intrust it to the inspection of his successors, the Dean and Chapter of Saint Paul's, but committed it to the care of the Company of Mercers for the managing thereof . . . who [Colet] had found by experience many laymen as conscientious as clergymen in discharging this trust in this kind; conceiving also that a whole company was not so easily to be bowed to corruption as any single person, how eminent and public soever."

Lilly, the grammarian and friend of Erasmus, was the first head master of the school, and the grammar that he compiled of the Latin language is still in use. Among the eminent sixteenth century scholars that were educated at St. Paul's were John Leland, the earliest English antiquary; Sir Anthony Denny, William Whittaker, and William Camden, the author of the *Britannia*.

To return to the buildings in the churchyard. North of Colet's school and not far from the pulpit cross stood the bell tower that was used by the Jesus Chapel and by the church of St. Faith, both structures underneath the cathedral. In the angle south of the nave and west of the south transept stood the cloister, notable for having a double ambulatory, one walk above the other. In the centre of the cloister yard was one of the most beautiful

chapter houses of the olden time. It was indeed
small—but 32 feet 6 inches internal diameter—but
carved and proportioned with extreme delicacy and
grace. The parish church of St. Gregory stood
south of the nave at its western extremity, built
quite against the wall of the cathedral. It was
then a not uncommon custom for a parish church
to be built in close proximity to the cathedral, as
may be seen to-day in St. Margaret's next to Westminster Abbey; but there seems to be no other instance of a parish church built directly against, as
if part of, the mother structure.

Perhaps the most remarkable adjunct to the
cathedral was what was commonly referred to as
St. Faith's under St. Paul's, which served mainly
as a place of worship for the stationers who dwelt
in the neighbourhood and carried on their business
within the cathedral grounds. It was a sort of
crypt under the choir and next to the Jesus Chapel,
both of which used the bells of the tower in the
cathedral yard.

The uninformed reader who for the first time
turns over the pages of *Every Man Out of His
Humour* is likely to ask the question: For what
was Saint Paul's used? The answer is brief and
in two words: for various purposes and for religion. The reason for the apparent inversion of
the proper order of these two details will presently

CHOIR OF ST. PAUL'S
(From an etching by Hollar)

appear. The desecration of the cathedral during
the sixteenth century forms one of the darkest
pages of its annals. Not only was the surrounding churchyard within the walls given up to buying and selling, to lotteries, and even to the public
execution of criminals, but the interior of the very
nave itself became a centre of vice, the city club,
so to speak, the resort of every form of influence
that was wicked and ungodly. During the joint
reign of Philip and Mary, when Catholicism was
the established religion of the realm, an act was
passed whose purpose it was to diminish this desecration. It complained of them who make "their
common carriage of great vessels of ale or beer,
great baskets full of bread, fish, flesh, and fruit,
fardels of stuff, and other gross wares, through the
cathedral church of St. Paul's, and some in leading
mules, horses, and other beasts irreverently and to
the great dishonour and displeasure of Almighty
God."

This act was fruitful of good results in so far
as it is probable that horses and mules were henceforth excluded from the nave and transepts; but
that in the main it failed of its intent is certain
from the fact that the following proclamation was
issued during the Protestant reign of Elizabeth:

"If any person shall make any fray, or draw
or put out his hand to any weapon for that pur-

pose, or shoot any hand gun or dagge, within the cathedral church of Saint Paul or churchyard thereto adjoining, or within the limits of the boundaries composing the same, they shall suffer imprisonment for two months. Any of Her Majesty's subjects who shall walk up or down, or spend the time in the same, in making any bargain or other profane cause, or make any kind of disturbance during the time of divine service, shall incur the pain of imprisonment and fine, the fine to go to the repair of the church."

Elizabeth's threats, however, turned out to be idle thunder. The desecration not only continued, but also vastly increased, though the iniquity was inveighed against by all the reformers, and also held up to ridicule upon the public stage.

" The characters," says Milman, " which old Ben [Jonson], though a coarse not usually irreverent writer, scruples not to assemble in the church is the most vivid illustration to which the abuse had grown ; nor does this comedy so far as I can trace appear to have given any offence."

Let us look for a moment more closely into the details of this malpractice. The passage from north to south through the body of the cathedral by the transepts had become little more than a common alley across the holy precincts. The middle aisle of the nave, which was thrown open to the same usages, was familiarly known as Paul's Walk, and gave rise to the term, a Paul's man, meaning one of the dissolute roisterers about town. Here came every day between the hours of eleven and one the city gallants to take a few turns up and down in order to gossip, meet a friend or vainly exhibit their new clothes; or, perchance, to pick quarrels and draw the ever-ready sword in violation of the royal proclamation. Assignations with lewd women were more frequently made in Paul's Walk than in any other part of London save in the Bankside Stews. It was the Elizabethan Burlington Arcade *par excellence.* The foot of each great column of the nave was turned to its particular use. About one lawyers knelt, writing upon knee as they took notes of a client's case. About another men and boys stood waiting for hire as they did at a country fair upon quarter day. This one and that one was each given up in a well understood way to a different profession. Tailors stood behind one to take note of the newest fashions, or to display samples of cloth, lace, and gold points; while about and among the crowd went all sorts of petty hawkers, crying out their wares in shrill voices among the echoing arches of the church.

Perhaps the greatest desecration of all was the fact that this is only half the story. Had the

cathedral been wholly abandoned to such purposes
it would not seem half so bad. It is possible to
understand the spirit that would turn a noble remnant of the Catholic faith into a stable for Puritan
horses; but it is much more difficult to understand
how the scenes already described could be carried
on within eye- and ear-shot of the holy service
actually being performed simultaneously. Yet
this condition of affairs was common, the every-day
occurrence, for public worship was carried on with
all the devotion of to-day, and more. If a man
entered the choir from the Walk with his spurs on
spur-money was demanded of him, partly as a fine,
partly as a joke to relieve the serious tone of worship. It was the choristers' privilege to collect it,
and one of the good contemporary sports was to
heat the pennies paid as tribute so that the choir
boys would cry out and interrupt the service. Furthermore, houses were commonly built against the
outer walls, not at St. Paul's alone, however; it was
the common custom about any church of size.
There is a tradition that one of these was even
used as a play-house. Perhaps the tradition is not
true, having grown out of the custom of the choir
boys performing plays at the chapter house; but
it is not inconsistent with the customs of the time.
For a small fee the bellman used to allow boys to
climb the bell tower in the yard for the purpose

of dropping things upon the head of passers below.

The first lottery in England of which there is any record was held in the open space of the churchyard about the cathedral in 1569. There were 400,000 ten shilling lots, and a pardonable aspect was given by authority to the whole affair by applying the proceeds to the patriotic purpose of repairing the harbours throughout the kingdom. There was another great lottery held in 1586, and another in 1612, and many later, some of which were auctioned within the church itself. The Losely Manuscripts give a very circumstantial account of the first one, which is curious and interesting for its light upon social customs.

The greatest and most excellent prize was estimated at 5000 pounds, of which 3000 pounds were to be paid to the lucky adventurer in cash, 700 pounds in plate, the remainder in hangings and linen cloth. The lots, however, were somewhat tardily disposed of, and the lottery was not " read," as the saying was, till January 11, 1568-9; when the reading took place in a building erected for the purpose just outside the door of the cathedral. The reading continued day and night till the following May. Though the price of each lot was ten shillings, a lot was often divided into shares, and sometimes as many as ten clubbed to-

gether to make a single share. Great pains were
taken, it will be seen, by the government to "provoke" the people to adventure their money in this
voluntary mode of taxation.

The lottery was announced to the public by a
chart printed for the most part in black letter. It
was a long and narrow handbill with the royal
arms at the top, the city of London, a picture of
the cathedral to make it more respectable, and representations of the prizes of plate that were on exhibition at a shop in Cheapside. Then followed
numerous directions about the apportionment of
lots and other necessary details for the information
of a greedy public as eager to get rich in those
days as in ours.

"A very rich lottery general," it begins, "without any blanks, containing a great number of good
prizes as well of ready money as of plate, and
certain sorts of merchandises, having been valued
and priced by the commandment of the Queen's
most excellent majesty, by men expert and skilful;
and the same lottery is erected by her majesty's
order, to the intent that such commodity as may
chance to arise thereof, after the charges borne,
may be converted towards the reparation of the
havens and strength of the realm, and towards
such other public good works."

Then follows a list of the prizes. The first has

already been mentioned. The second was 2000 pounds in money, 600 pounds in plate, the rest in hangings. The thirteenth prize was 140 pounds, part money, part plate, and tapestry. Then followed 12 prizes of 100 pounds; 24 of 50 pounds; 64 of 25 pounds; and so on, increasing in numbers as they decreased in size till we find 9418 prizes of 14 shillings in money; and then, "all the rest to the accomplishing of the aforesaid number of lottes, shall be allowed for every adventure at the least two shillings and six pens in ready money."

The chart sets forth all sorts of extra inducements. Persons may resort to the lottery agents in various towns for "seven whole days, without any molestation or arrest of them for any manner of offence, saving treason, murder, pyracie, or any other felony, or for breach of her majesty's peace, during the time of their coming, abiding, or return." Extra prizes were allowed to those who took above a certain number of shares, or to those whose tickets were read out three, four, five, or more in succession.

Lots, however, were not taken up with sufficient rapidity. On January 3 appeared a royal proclamation that began: "Whereas in the chart of the lottery lately erected amongst other things devised for the advantage of the adventurers, there was a limitation of three months within the compas whereof, whoso adventured money into the said Lotterie, should be partakers of divers profits and advantages more than others that should adventure their money after the said three months ended . . . for divers reasons her majesty is pleased that the 'advantage of the said three months now expired shall be enlarged and prorogued to all manner of persons that have or shall adventure their money into the said Lottery, for three months longer, etc." The proclamation further informs the public that in case of any adventurer's death before the reading of the lottery his prize, if he draw one, shall go to his heirs. It is needless to particularise further as to the correspondence that followed, save to say that every inducement was made to persuade people to venture in the lottery, and that the list was not made up soon enough to enable the reading to begin before January 11. Each man when he put in his lot put in a posy or verse that was publicly read or proclaimed at the drawing, hence the term "reading the lottery."

So much for this unusual purpose to which the cathedral was put. Perhaps the worst desecration of all to which St. Paul's was ever subjected was the use of its precincts as a place of public execution. John Felton, who posted the bull of Elizabeth's excommunication upon the door of the Bishop of London's palace, was hanged on a gallows set up in front of the said palace. On January 30, 1606, some of the Gunpowder conspirators were executed, and, later, the celebrated Jesuit intriguer, Father Garnet. The tale is pitiful of how he was given opportunity to speak to the people, after which he asked for leave to pray and how long they would allow him. They told him that he might pray as long as he wished. " But," says an eye-witness, " he was so excited, either by the fear of death or the hope of pardon that he could not pray, but kept looking constantly in every direction, but could not compose himself to prayer." Indeed, as we read his last exhortation and hope " that the Catholics may not fare worse for my sake," we may well wonder what he thought of the new religion that made such use of the cathedral house of God.

A characteristic feature of the life about St. Paul's was the bookshops and stationers' stalls that thronged the churchyard more thickly than any other part of the city. Mr. Arber has furnished a careful list of booksellers and printers in London between 1556 and 1558. For the former year he lists thirty-two, of whom fifteen lived in Paul's churchyard, and five in the immediate neighbourhood. John Kingston had his shop at the

west door. Richard Jugge built against the north
door and marked his house by the sign of the
Bible. This Jugge was a famous printer who had
been educated at Eton and Cambridge. Over seventy books bear his imprint, most of which are
Bibles of remarkably fine press-work, especially
noted for the elaborate initial letters. In January,
1550, he received from the government the sole
licence to print New Testaments in English. On
the accession of Elizabeth he was joined by John
Cawood as queen's printer at a salary of six pounds,
thirteen shillings, and four pence per annum.

The widow Toy kept her shop at the Bell in the
churchyard; Henry Sutton at the Black Boy;
Reginald Wolfe at the Brazen Serpent; John
Turk at the Cock; and William Seres at the Hedge-
hog. The list is too long for insertion here; but
to this menagerie might be added the Lamb, the
Red Lion, the Swan, and the White Horse, all of
which had stalls about the cathedral. Enough has
been said to suggest how the book trade monopo-
lised the vicinity. And it was a busy monopoly,
for in those days placards were as frequent as to-
day, people also lounged and gossipped in the book
shops, and even managed occasionally to read a
book through, and thus save the purchase price, by
successive peeps on different days.

" To dine with Duke Humphrey " was a prover-

bial expression of the day that came into existence
through a curious custom connected with St. Paul's.
One who had dined with the duke had in reality
gone without his dinner. At the foot of the second
column of the northeast corner of the nave stood
the tomb of Sir John Beauchamp, constable of
Dover Castle and son of Guy Beauchamp, sometime Earl of Warwick. Through popular misin-
formation this tomb was believed by the common
people to be that of the good Duke Humphrey of
Gloucester. Before this tomb it was the custom
for penniless men to walk up and down in the hope
of catching sight of some kind-hearted and liberal
friend with a ready invitation to dine. And when,
as often happened, the expectant sponge went
hungry he was said to have dined with Duke
Humphrey.

Strype thus describes another custom in connection with the same tomb: " He is by ignorant people
misnamed to be Humphrey, Duke of Gloucester,
who lieth honourably buried at St. Albans, twenty
miles from London. And therefore such as merrily profess themselves to serve Duke Humphrey
are to be punished here and sent to St. Albans to
be punished again for their absence from their
master as they call him.

"In idle and frivolous opinion of whom some
men of late time have made a solemn meeting at

his tomb upon St. Andrew's day in the morning (before Christmas), and concluded on a breakfast or dinner, as assuring themselves to be servants, and to hold diversity of offices under the good Duke Humphrey.

"Likewise upon May Day tankard bearers, watermen, and some others of like quality besides, would use to come to the same tomb early in the morning and (according as the other) have delivered serviceable presentation at the same monument by strewing herbs and sprinkling fair water on it, as in the duty of servants, and according to their degrees and charges in office. But as Master Stow has discreetly advised such as are so merrily disposed, or simply profess themselves to serve Duke Humphrey in Paul's, if punishment of losing their dinners there daily be not sufficient for them, they should be sent to St. Albans, to answer there for their disobedience and long absence from their so highly well deserving lord and master, because in their merry disposition they please so to call him."

In the northeast corner of the churchyard stood the famous pulpit structure known as Paul's Cross. It was a cross of timber mounted upon stone steps and surmounted by a conical roof of lead. It was the place whence government delivered its public sayings. The whole battle of the Reformation

was fought over in little from this oracle, as well as
the later contest between the Reformed Faith and
Papacy on the one hand and stiff-necked Puritans
on the other. The questions were submitted to the
public by a series of divines, the list of which contains the names of all those most famous in the
annals of church history. Ridley, Latimer, Far-
rer, Gardiner, Bonner, Coverdale, Sandys, Jewel,
Grindel, Pilkington, and Laud, not to speak of a
host of other scarcely less famous men, have up-
held their various faiths from the open air pulpit
of Paul's Cross. Before it Bishop Stokesly burned
Tyndall's translation of the Bible. The Pope's
sentence on Luther was publicly read from the cross
in the presence of Cardinal Wolsey. During the
whole time of the divorce proceedings Henry's
agents were busy announcing ideas from the cross
that subservient England was supposed to believe
like gospel narrative. When Henry finally con-
summated his revolt from the see of Rome he caused
a proclamation to be read at the cross stating that
orders be taken "that such as preach at Paul's
Cross shall henceforth continually from Sunday to
Sunday, teach and declare unto the people that he
that now calleth himself the Pope, and any of his
predecessors, is and were, only Bishops of Rome,
and have no more authority or jurisdiction, by God's
law, within this realm than any other bishop had,

which is nothing at all." Before this cross knelt in shame the Holy Maid of Kent with her confederates beside her, while her confession was read aloud, the Bishop of Bangor setting forth in his address the heniousness of her offence. Four years later the famous Boxley Rood was exhibited and the machinery by which it worked miracles laid open to the scoffing view of multitudes. During the reign of Mary Protestants were continually abused from Paul's Cross. Gardiner lauded King Philip as "the most perfect prince"; and a few years later the same most perfect prince was held up from the same cross as a merciless tyrant and agent of the devil. From it people were exhorted to give thanks for the defeat of the Armada, while a gaudy streamer taken from one of the captured galleons waved defiantly over the preacher's head.

It was from this cross that the May-pole, from which the church of St. Andrew Undershaft derives its name, was denounced as an idol by the narrow-minded curate of St. Catharine Cree. Here recantations were made, royal victories, marriages, proclamations of peace, etc., announced with a blare of trumpets and a prayer. Here the memory of Elizabeth's "darling," the Earl of Essex, was blackened by command in a Sunday sermon. Enough has been said to show that Paul's Cross was the government oracle for the guidance of the people.

After Elizabeth came to the throne the people looked in vain for some weeks for an official delivery. The usual succession of Sunday sermons was, however, interrupted; and when the silence was at last broken the people heard only noncommittal judgments from the mouthpiece of the wily Queen. She had not yet made up her mind concerning the policy of her religion, a subject she never for a moment decided upon conviction. When at last she was ready to have a sermon delivered the keys of the cross had been lost. The Lord Mayor found it necessary to set in motion the official machinery of the city corporation in order to commission a locksmith to force the entrance; and then the pulpit was found so fouled by birds as to be unfit for immediate use. The birds are still there and daily fed at the expense of the city, but the cross is long since a thing of the irrevocable past.

Two or three memorable occurrences during the reign of Elizabeth deserve a passing notice. One of the glories of the old cathedral was the spire and its weather-cock. "This steeple," says Stow, "was repaired in 1462, and the weather-cock again erected. Robert Godwin, winding it up, the rope brake, and he was destroyed on the pinnacles, and the cock was sore bruised; but Burchwood (the King's plumber) set it up again; since the which time, needing reparation, it was both taken down and set up in the year 1553; at which time it was found to be of copper, gilt over; the length from the bill to the tail being four feet, and the breadth over the wings three feet and a half. It weighed forty pounds. The cross from the bowl to the eagle (or cock) was fifteen feet and six inches of assize; and the length whereof athwart was five feet and ten inches, and the compass of the bowl was nine feet and one inch."

Its new splendour, however, was to be of short duration. In 1561 a terrible storm burst over London. A flash of lightning fired the church of St. Martin next to Ludgate, and soon afterward the spire of St. Paul's was discovered to be ablaze. It burned fiercely, creeping slowly downward, melting the lead and crumbling the stone. Every effort was made to stay the progress of the conflagration, which spread along the roof of nave and choir, and both the transepts, till the whole mass fell, filling the body of the church with debris. Only the walls were left intact when the fire finally burned itself out. The destruction of the cathedral was looked upon as a national misfortune. Contributions for its reconstruction flowed in from every hand. Even the parsimonious Queen gave a

St. Paul's Nave

thousand marks in gold, and an equal value in timber from the royal forests. With phœnix-like rapidity St. Paul's rose from its ashes to enjoy another century of splendour. Yet it was somewhat shorn, for its tall and graceful spire was never replaced, and the pictures drawn towards the close of the sixteenth century and afterward show only a mutilated stump.

On May 15, 1570, all London rose as one man in rage, for during the night an unknown person had posted on the door of the Bishop of London's palace the bull of Pius V. excommunicating England's Maiden Queen. The tempest of anger spread like a whirlwind. The country was filled with ballads hawked about the streets, vituperative of Pope and Catholics; and the storm was not allayed till the people's wrath was appeased by the public execution of the culprit Felton, who had posted the bull, an execution that took place within sight of the door he had defamed.

To St. Paul's on Sunday, November 24, 1588, came a great procession headed by the Queen, surrounded by all her court and the dignitaries of the city, with meek and humble hearts to render thanks unto God for the miraculous dispersion of the Armada. St. Paul's, desecrated as it was, was yet the religious centre of the capital of England. It was to the merchants and citizens of London above

all else that England owed the strength that enabled her to cross swords successfully with her powerful rival, and it was indeed fitting that the Queen
should choose as the scene of her thanksgiving not
the court, or Westminster, but the cathedral church
of St. Paul.

CHAPTER V

THE WATER FRONT

ONE who entered the city through the famous prison of Ludgate would, at the gate of St. Paul's, turn to the right along Creed Lane and Puddledock, or St. Andrew's Hill, to reach Thames Street, which from Blackfriars to the Tower constituted the rear frontage of the river buildings. It bordered the rear of Baynard Castle, one of the great river palaces that figures in Shakespeare's *Richard III.;* the wharves abutted upon it; it contained the approach to London Bridge; and Billingsgate, then a respectable landing place for general goods, not yet celebrated for its fish and dialect.

In approaching Thames Street we have passed on our left Carter Lane, which formed the southern boundary of Paul's churchyard. It was a narrow, crooked street, then famous for its taverns, still more famous now because of its literary associations. It contained the dwelling place of the merry cobbler of Tarlton's *Jests* and the Hart's Horn Tavern, one of the plotting places of the Gunpowder conspirators. It was from the Bell

Inn in Carter Lane that Richard Quiney in 1598 directed the only extant letter addressed to Shakespeare; and Thomas Creed at his house in Carter Lane printed in 1600 the first edition of the *Chronicle History of King Henry the Fifth.*

At the corner of Carter Lane and St. Andrew's Hill, opposite a narrow passage towards the Shakespeare play-house, on the site of the present Wardrobe Court, stood a building of great importance to the Elizabethans. The ancient building was erected in 1359 by Sir John Beauchamp, the good man whose tomb in St. Paul's was mistaken for that of Duke Humphrey. The house was subsequently converted into an office for the Master of the King's Wardrobe, an officer whose duty it was to look after the King's wearing apparel, and to provide proper furnishings for the royal family at coronations, funerals, marriages, and other ceremonials. He had also to furnish beds, hangings, etc., for the houses of foreign ambassadors, for the Prince of Wales, for the Lord Lieutenant of Ireland, and many other public officers.

Another building on one of the side streets in this neighbourhood deserves mention before we pass to Thames Street and the water front proper. South of the Wardrobe was the church of St. Andrews, from the churchyard of which Knightrider Street extended east parallel to Thames Street. It

contained the Stone House, the original shelter
of the College of Physicians. The history of
this organisation, the rivalry and petty feuds
of its factions, is not only interesting, but also
amusing.

The records of the barbers as well as of the surgeons extend back almost to the beginning of the
fourteenth century. The guild of surgeons, then
the aristocrats of the profession, was a small select
body, doubtless never over twenty in number, and
sometimes as few as ten or a dozen. While they
were still young, the barbers, having more or less
skill at such minor operations as bleeding and dressing of wounds, aspired to the practice of surgery.
Being of more humble pretensions, these barber-
surgeons could afford to charge less than the regular surgeons, and therefore became immensely popular. Both the guilds of barbers and of surgeons
continued to exist side by side as distinct and generally rival bodies for many years.

As a result of this rivalry the barbers were
granted a charter by Edward IV. in 1462. The
interesting detail of this charter is that it has much
to say about the practice of surgery and, though
granted to the barbers, nothing about barbery.
There is among the records at the Barber Surgeons' Hall an agreement dated thirty years later,
which shows that at that time the rival organ-

isations were upon friendly terms. We are not surprised, then, to find that half a century (1540) was sufficient to bring them close together in a union that lasted till 1745. Concerning this step, the editor of the Annals and Papers of the Company says: "The union, therefore, was not a joining of barbers with surgeons (that had existed from earliest times), but was the consolidation of the 'Guild of Surgeons' with another body of surgeons that was incorporated and practised under the name of barbers in conjunction with actual working barbers; and as the act provided what the surgeons should and should not do, and the like as to actual barbers, limiting their operations also, most if not all difficulty and apparent incongruity in the union seems to vanish."

The dead bodies of four malefactors were assigned to the new company annually for dissection. The dissection of these bodies gave rise to the "Public Anatomies," which took place in the company's hall, and it was illegal to dissect elsewhere. They became semi-public exhibitions to which every member of the company was compelled to attend at the risk of being fined for absence; and on each day so long as the dissection lasted there was a great feast at the company's expense. Occasionally bodies obtained in other ways were dissected under the name of "private anatomies."

Attendance upon these demonstrations was not compulsory, but by invitation. The company also possessed a skeleton, probably but one, which was mounted for exhibition, and may have formed a part of a public museum, inasmuch as a " case of weynscote " was ordered for it in 1568.

The following extract, quoted in Aiken's *Memoirs of Medicine*, illustrates the state of medical practice at the time:

" I remember," says Gale, " when I was in the wars at Mittrel [Montreuil] in the time of that most famous prince, King Henry VIII., there was a great rabblement that took on them to be surgeons; some were sow gelders, and some horse gelders, with tinkers and cobblers. This noble sect did such great cures, that they got themselves a perpetual name; for like as Thessalus's sect were called Thessalians, so this noble rabblement, for their notorious cures, were called Dog-leeches; for in two dressings they did commonly make their cures whole and sound forever; so that they neither felt heat nor cold, nor no manner of pain after. But when the Duke of Norfolk who was their general, understanding how the people did die, and that of small wounds, he sent for me and certain other surgeons, commanding us to make search how these men came to their death; whether it were by the grievousness of their wounds, or by the lack of knowledge of the surgeons; and we, according to our commandment, made search through all the camp, and found many of the same good fellows, which took upon them the name of surgeons; not only the name but the wages also. We, asking them whether they were surgeons or no, they said they were; we demanded with whom they were brought up, and they, with shameless faces, would answer, either with one cunning man or another, which was dead. Then we demanded what chirurgery stuff they had to cure men withal; and they would show us a pot, or a box, which they had in a budget; wherein was such trumpery as they did use to grease horses' heels withal, and laid upon scabbed horses' backs, with rewel, and suchlike. And others that were cobblers and tinkers, they used shoemaker's wax, with the rust of old pans, and made therewithal a noble salve, as they did term it. But in the end this noble rabblement was committed to the Marshalsea, and threatened by the Duke's Grace, to be hanged for their worthy deeds, except they would declare the truth what they were, and of what occupations; and in the end they did confess as I have declared unto you before."

William Clowes, an eminent member of the profession who lived in the latter half of the sixteenth century, wrote as follows: "Where the learned

physician cannot be had for counsel, I am herewith
to admonish the friendly reader to take heed and
not to commit themselves into the hands of every
blind buzzard that will take upon them to let blood,
yea, to the utter undoing of a number. For
many in these days being no better than runagates
or vagabonds, do extraordinarily, yea, disorderly
and unadvisedly intrude themselves into other men's
professions, that is to say, not only in letting of
blood, but also do take upon them to intermeddle
and practise in the art, wherein they were never
trained or had any experience: of the which a great
number be shameless in countenance, lewd in disposition, brutish in judgment and understanding
as was their unlearned leader and master, Thessalus, a vain practitioner, who, when his cunning
failed, straightway sent his patients to Lybia for
a change of air. . . . This their grand captain was by profession a teazler of wool and also
the fore-runner of this beastly brood following:
which do forsake their honest trades, whereunto
God hath called them, and do daily rush into
physic and surgery. And some of them be Painters, some Tailors, some Weavers, some Joiners,
some Cutlers, some Cooks, some Bakers, and some
Chandlers. Yea, now-a-days it is apparent to see
how Tinkers, Tooth-drawers, Pedlars, Ostlers, Carters, Porters, Horse-gelders, and Horse-leeches,

Idiots, Apple-squires, broom-men, bawds, with witches, conjurers, Sooth-sayers, and sow-gelders, Rogues, rat-catchers, runagates and proctors of Spittle-houses, with other suchlike rotten and stinking weeds which do in town and country without order, honesty or skill, daily abuse both physic and surgery, having no more perseverance, reason or knowledge in his art than hath a goose, but a certain blind practice without wisdom or judgment, and most commonly useth one remedy for all diseases, and one way of curing all persons both old and young, men, women, and children, which is as possible to be performed or to be true as for a shoe-maker with one last to make a shoe to fit every man's foot, and this is one principal cause that so many perish."

It was in order to put an end to such corrupt practices that Henry VIII., in the tenth year of his reign, founded the Royal College of Physicians. It was to this organisation that Dr. Linacre, its first president, and one of the six specified in the original charter, presented the above mentioned Stone House in Knightrider Street.

"In the year 1518," says Dr. Johnson, "when Linacre's scheme was carried into effect, the practice of medicine was scarcely elevated above that of the mechanical arts; nor were the majority of its practitioners among the laity better instructed than the mechanics by whom these arts were practiced."

For a long time physics and surgery were kept distinct, surgeons not being allowed to give inward treatment. The remedies of the former, like all the prescriptions of the sixteenth and seventeenth centuries, contained "amongst a few efficacious articles, many which are foreign, if not useless, to the purpose for which they are designed." (Munk: *Roll of the Royal College of Physicians.*) Much advantage, however, was derived from the institution of the college. It had supervision over all the practitioners of medicine in the kingdom, except regular medical graduates of Oxford and Cambridge; and in 1556 we find the college actually engaged in a quarrel with one of the universities for granting a degree to a coppersmith unsuited by study for the proper practice of medicine.

In the twenty-fourth year of Elizabeth Richard Caldwell and Lord Lumley, whose house was upon Tower Hill, endowed a surgery lecture in the college that was afterward occupied by Harvey at the time he expounded his famous theory of the circulation of the blood.

With such men as Gales, John Halle, and Clowes about the same time, not to speak of Linacre and many others, it is no wonder that the medical profession improved wonderfully during the sixteenth century and early years of the seventeenth. It was no longer possible for any one who chose to practise the art and mystery of surgery. Mr. Darcy Power thus describes the process by which one obtained rank in the profession:

"The easiest way to understand this is perhaps to follow the course of a boy whose father was anxious that he should attain a high position as a surgeon in London towards the end of the reign of Edward VI., or whilst Mary or Elizabeth was on the throne. Such a boy would be taught to read and write in one of the grammar schools then recently founded in London. He had learnt, too, a little arithmetic and some Latin, but his knowledge of Greek would be of the scantiest. About the age of fourteen he would leave school when his father had found some member of the Barber-Surgeons' Company who was in need of an apprentice. Terms being agreed upon, the boy, his father, and the barber-surgeon would meet at the Barber-Surgeons' Hall in Monkwell Street, where the candidate for apprenticeship was duly presented to the court or council of the company to show that he was sound in wind and limb and that he had received a sufficient education. If he were approved the clerk of the company made out his indentures, which were then taken to the Guildhall to be registered. The lad was bound to his master **for**

seven years, which in some cases was extended to
eight or even nine years. The master received a
lump sum of money, in return for which he undertook to find the apprentice 'meat, drink, apparel,
lodging, and all other necessaries according to the
customs of the city.' Each master was allowed to
take three or four apprentices, according to his
position in the united company, and if he died the
apprentice was turned over to another master.
During his indentures the apprentice remained the
slave of his master, who might whip or starve him
into submission, or might even have him imprisoned in the city compter. The boy, however, had
a right to appeal to the Barber-Surgeons' Company, which he sometimes exercised, though more
often he revenged himself by a thousand impish
tricks, for he was constantly in hot water. Usually,
however, things came right in the end and the apprentice was admitted to the freedom of the company by servitude, upon the recommendation of
his master, and he thus obtained a licence to practice surgery within the city of London.

"The licence was granted in two forms. The
one after a comparatively simple examination,
when the candidate was allowed to practise in a
definite place for a definite number of months or
years, at the end of which he was told to appear
again before the company that his further profi-

ciency might be ascertained; secondly, the grand diploma was granted to those who had submitted themselves to a more severe test. It entitled its owner to be called a Master in Surgery and Anatomy and allowed him to practise his art anywhere and during the whole of his life. . . .

"The education of the surgeon did not end with the granting of his licence; indeed, it only now began, and to the end of his life he was bound to attend the lectures and demonstrations given at the Barber-Surgeons' Hall, unless he chose to stay away and pay a fine. The company taught especially surgery and anatomy; surgery by lectures, anatomy by lectures and demonstrations."

Let us now return from the region into which this digression about medicine has led us. We find ourselves back in the neighbourhood just southwest of the cathedral. There is a wall on the right hand side of the street that leads down to the cathedral, that bounds the precinct of the Blackfriars. We shall hurry past the gate down the decline. St. Andrew's Hill, otherwise known as Puddledock Hill, conducts us to the Puddle Dock. According to John Stow, the Elizabethan Baedeker, the place derived its name from the habit of leading horses down to water. Directly east of the Puddle Dock, with a frontage for some distance upon the river, stood one of those prominent landmarks of a past age. In Elizabethan times the residents of great palaces had for the most part quitted London and moved westward to airier and sunnier sites. One, however, was still left to ruffle it bravely among the greasy costermongers and tawdry shops of Thames Street. This was Baynard Castle, a huge stone structure crowned with gables and turrets, whose lower walls were washed by "the silver streaming Thames." It was built in 1428 by Humphrey, Duke of Gloucester, on whose attainder it reverted to the crown. During the Wars of the Roses the Duke of York was lodged there, and the place is frequently mentioned by Shakespeare. Henry VII. enlarged it and made it more of a palace than a castle. It was there that on July 19, 1553, "the council partly moved with the Lady Mary's cause, partly considering that the most of the realm was wholly bent to her side, changing their mind from Lady Jane, lately proclaimed queen, assembled themselves, where they communed with the Earl of Pembroke and the Earl of Shrewsbury; and Sir John Mason, Clerk of the Council, sent for the Lord Mayor, and then riding into Cheap, to the Cross, where Garter King at Arms, trumpet being sounded, proclaimed the Lady Mary, daughter of Henry VIII. and Queen Katharine, Queen of England." (Stow.)

Let us leave this so-called palace, in appearance

the most gloomy of all those riverine mansions, and
pass on a few yards to a steep narrow passage from
the river to the cathedral.   On the east side of this
Paul's Wharf Hill stood the College of Heralds,
one of those organisations that represent the very
life and blood of the English nation.   The college
of arms received its first charter as early as the
time of Richard III., who gave them Poultney's
Inn, "a right fayre and stately house" in Cold
Harbour.   They were dispossessed of this property by Henry VII., when they removed to the
Hospital of Our Lady Rounceval at Charing Cross,
where now stands Northumberland House.   They
next removed to Derby or Stanley House, on St.
Benet's Hill (Paul's Wharf Hill).

The service of the pursuivants and of the
heralds, and of the whole college, was used in
marshalling and ordering coronations, marriages,
funerals, etc.   Also they took care of the coats of
arms and the genealogies of the nobility and the
gentry.   "Anciently the Kings-at-arms were sol-
emnly crowned before the sovereign, and took an
oath; during which the Earl Marshal poured a
bowl of wine on his head, put on him a richly embroidered coat of arms, a collar of Esses, a jewel
and gold chain, and a Crown of Gold."   (Cham-
berlayne's *Magnæ Britainniæ Volitia.* 1726.)

The college consists of three kings—Garter,

Clarenceux, and Norrey; of six heralds—Lancaster, Somerset, Richmond, Windsor, York, and Chester; and of four pursuivants—Rouge Croix, Blue Mantle, Portcullis, and Rouge Dragon. The Court of Honour, as the Earl Marshal's office was called, was situated here. It was so named because one of its duties was to take cognisance of words that reflected upon the nobility. In this court Sir Richard Grenville was fined for saying that the Earl of Suffolk was a base man. Here also used to meet the College of Antiquaries, founded by Archbishop Parker in 1572, and to which belonged such memorable scholars as Camden, Cotton, and Stow.

One cannot leave the Herald's College without a word concerning its greatest member, an Elizabethan, and the chief ornament of his time in the world of letters. William Camden was born in a house in the Old Bailey, May 2, 1551. His father, Sampson Camden, was a common painter, and it is worth recording that in after years when Camden became Clarenceux King-at-arms, and was known all over Europe as the foremost antiquarian scholar of the day, he never became too proud to acknowledge his humble birth or the calling of his father.

At the age of twelve he sickened of the plague, but fortunately recovered and was sent to St. Paul's School. It was in later years while a student at

Oxford that he began to develop his bent towards antiquarian affairs. On leaving Oxford about 1571 he took up his residence at London. He soon became known throughout an ever widening circle of friends, who implored him to write a history of Great Britain in the ancient times. For years the magnitude of the task deterred him, but as his fame increased the pressure grew, and at last he succumbed.

Ten years were spent in preparation, during which time he overcame herculean difficulties. He travelled, corresponded with scholars on the continent, and searched the ancient records. As the result of his study of place names he came to the conclusion that he could do nothing further until he had mastered the ancient British language. The absence of text-books and teachers made this no easy task, but he accomplished it thoroughly at last. Once again his work was laid aside while he took time to master the Saxon language. So much painstaking labour could not but be crowned with success. In 1586 appeared the first edition of the *Brittannia*, dedicated to his dear friend, Lord Burghley, and the work to this day is the starting point of all study of ancient Britain.

In 1597 died Richard Lee, and Camden was elected in his place Clarenceux King-at-arms, one of the chief offices of the College of Heralds. In

1600 he produced an historical account of Westminster; in 1603 a volume of English historians, dedicated to Fulke Grevile; and in 1607 an account of the Gunpowder Plot, written in Latin. All these latter books, however, were the product of his spare hours. His main time after the completion of the *Brittannia* was devoted to the composition of his great history of the reign of Elizabeth. In 1589 he had published a part of it, which was so well received that he was encouraged to proceed. In 1617 the whole was finished, constituting his second monumental work for all time.

With the history of Elizabeth his life work ended. He died November 9, 1623, and on the 19th was interred at Westminster Abbey, opposite the grave of Chaucer, where a monument of white marble bears his effigy, holding a book on which is inscribed the word " Brittannia."

A little further east, on the south side of Thames, was Queenhithe, an ancient landing place that shared the importance of Billingsgate in the days before it became exclusively a market for fish. From 1600 to 1625 it was the headquarters of the London watermen. This important fraternity was not pretentious. It used to hold its meetings in an alehouse by the riverside, namely The Red Knight, and its most glorious member set out thence upon a penniless pilgrimage about the country. This

was John Taylor, familiarly known as the Water
Poet.   He was born in 1580 of humble parentage.
He found the "learning" of Gloucester grammar
school beyond his ambition if not his attainment,
and was sent in consequence to London, where he
was apprenticed to a waterman.   He was impressed
into the navy, a fact that accounts for his presence
at the siege of Cadiz, where, doubtless, he acquitted
himself with no particular credit.   After varied
experiences he returned to London to the quiet calling of waterman.   An accident in 1622 by which
he was stripped of certain perquisites that he had
received from the Tower induced him to attempt
to increase his diminished earnings by the construction of poetry—God save the mark!   Though not
suited by nature or education to the production of
literature, he managed to pen innumerable verses
that brought him what Dogberry might have called
posterior fame; for to us they are a mine of social
information, though of no literary value.   In *The
Sculler* (1612) he ridiculed the great traveller
Thomas Coryat, who appealed to "superior pow-
ers" to defend him.   Taylor grew popular, and
Ben Jonson, not to speak of lesser lights such as
courtiers and statesmen, patted him fondly on the
head for his rollicking verse.   He was an erratic
genius in act as well as in verse.   He delighted in
eccentric feats that would astonish the reader when

made into literature. For instance: he once set out with another rattle-brained companion to make a voyage from London to Queensborough in a brown paper boat with two stockfish tied to canes for oars. The boat collapsed, but the poet escaped drowning. Each similar adventure was followed by a printed account. His most famous lark was a trip he undertook, setting out from London, with empty pockets, an expedition that is now known to us as *The Penniless Pilgrimage, or the Money-less Perambulation of John Taylor.* The Water Poet died in 1654, far away from the river front and Thames Street, in Phœnix Alley, Long Acre, where he kept the Crown.

All this part of old London was crossed by narrow filthy streets that descended to the river over very steep hills. Dowgate, one of the steepest of them all, was the scene of an accident that, though it seems almost impossible, has the authority of Stow. "The descent of this street is such," he says, "that in the year 1574, on the fourth of September in the afternoon, there fell a storm of rain, where through the channels suddenly rose, and ran with such swift course towards the common shores, that a lad of eighteen years, minding to have leapt over the channel near to the same conduit, was taken with the stream and carried from thence towards the Thames, with such a violence, that no man with staves or otherwise could stay him, till he came against a cart wheel that stood in the same water gate, before which time he was drowned and stark dead."

All youthful readers of *Henry VI.* and *The Last of the Barons* have wondered where the great king-maker, "that centre shaking, thunder-clap of war," resided when in town. Warwick's palace was of old time known as Erber House, and stood on the east side of Dowgate Hill, next the church of St. Mary Bothaw. In subsequent years it was occupied by "false, fleeting, perjured Clarence"; and when Shakespeare wrote was the town house of the most famous of all the Elizabethan navigators, Sir Francis Drake.

In the neighbourhood of Dowgate wharf Robert Greene the dramatist died in 1592. He was living in the house of a shoemaker at the time, and died indebted to his landlord for the mere necessities of life. Customs were sometimes collected at Dowgate, and it was the chief place whence water was carried to be peddled about the city. It was then a common sight to see the water carriers, usually called "cobs," going from house to house with their tankards upon their shoulders. These were wooden vessels, wide at the bottom and narrow at the top, bound round with iron hoops, and capable of holding three gallons each.

East of Dowgate was the Steelyard, occupied by the merchants of the Hanseatic League, who kept Bishopsgate in order in return for certain trading privileges. Next came a block of ramshackle buildings that took its name from a structure demolished in the time of Stow. Cold Harbour was noted in the time of Elizabeth as a neighbourhood of bad repute. Sir Walter Scott's description of Alsatia at a slightly later date as readily applies to Cold Harbour. But little imagination is needed to conjure up the scene. In the very centre of the river front of a densely populated city, on one of the filthiest streets, surrounded by miserable tenements, Cold Harbour was the haunting place of every kind of vice. It undoubtedly possessed that traditional or empirical kind of sanctuary that was attributed in common with it to Suffolk Place in Southwark, to St. Martin's le Grand, and to Alsatia. Cold Harbour Stairs was known throughout all London as the place to be watched for embarking debtors and criminals of all sorts who found even the sanctuary too hot for them. What is perhaps an unfamiliar fact even to Londoners is that in the early years of the seventeenth century Cold Harbour was the place *par excellence* for irregular marriages, such as the Fleet afterwards became.

One who continues east along Thames Street to-

day passes under London Bridge, and comes immediately to the church of St. Magnus the Martyr
at the corner of Fish Street Hill. This street was
the approach to the old London Bridge, which stood
a short distance east of the present structure. The
street was narrow and dangerously steep of old
time, and occupied mainly by the shops of fishmongers, and the ever present tavern. "These fishmongers," says Stow, "have been jolly citizens,
and six mayors of their company in 24 years."
King's Head Court just below the monument marks
the site of King's Head Tavern, frequented by
roisterers and famous for its wine. Diagonally
opposite is Bell Yard, where once stood the Black
Bell, a tavern that further back in its history was
the residence of Edward, the Black Prince.

East of the bridge lay a small ward that took
its name from Billingsgate, which was long one of
the principal city wharves. From Stow's list of
commodities landed at Billingsgate one can see that
it had not yet become especially noted for its fish,
a distinction it did not gain till the time of William
III., when, in 1699, by an act of Parliament, Billingsgate was made a free port for fish with a market every week day. On the east side of Billingsgate was Smart's Key, where was located a famous
den of vice, known as the cut-purse school.

"One Wotton," writes Fleetwood to Burleigh in

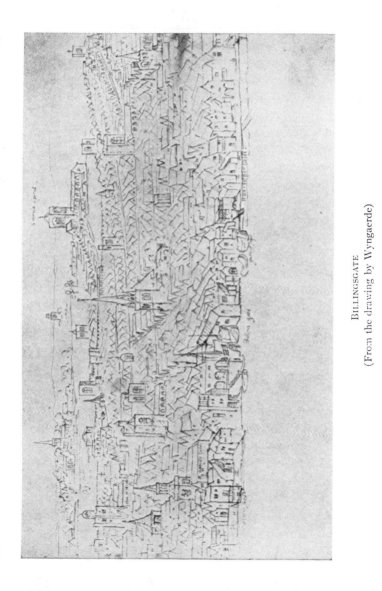

BILLINGSGATE

(From the drawing by Wyngaerde)

1585, " a gentleman born and sometime a merchant of good credit, who falling by time into decay, kept an ale-house at Smart's Key near Billingsgate, and after, for some misdemeanour being put down, he reared up a new trade of life, and in the same house he procured all the cut-purses about the city to repair to his said house. There was a school-house set up to teach young boys to cut purses. There was hung up two devices, one a pocket, the other a purse. The pocket had in it certain counters and was hung about with hawk's bells, and over the top did hang a little scaring bell; and he that could take out a counter without any noise was allowed to be a public hoyster (pickpocket), and he that could take a piece of silver out of the purse, without the noise of any of the bells, he was adjudged a judicial nipper (cut purse.)"

We have now traversed almost the entire river front, and have arrived close to the Tower. In the lower part of Thames Street were a number of wharves belonging to private persons, landings whose names changed from time to time with the change of occupant. The only building of note was the custom-house. This was, in reality, the busiest part of the frontage on the river. Here congregated merchants from every part of the world, in their outlandish dress, arguing their du-

ties, buying, selling, cheapening till the air became
a bedlam like Lombard Street before the building of
the Exchange.   There was a good business done
in those days.   In 1572 a report to Elizabeth shows
an average collection of customs amounting to
65,000 pounds.   For all that, the duties were so
carelessly collected that a report dated the ninth of
her reign estimated that the leakage since her coronation had amounted to 96,000 pounds ; whereupon
Edward Matthews was appointed commissioner for
the concealment of customs, but he was menaced
with destruction if he should proceed with his in-
vestigations.   In order to save the expense of
operating the custom-house Elizabeth farmed out
the office in 1590 for 20,000 pounds a year, and it
was soon discovered that she lost 10,000 pounds
annually by the new arrangement.   A rare old
print of the building published by Wilkinson
shows it to have been a massive structure of three
stories, with a huge gate near the east end.   It
faced a large paved court that stood between it and
the river, where congregated the merchants who
daily turned it into a sort of mart for the transac-
tion of business.

Towards the east end of Thames Street, in a
turning towards the north, stood the Bakers' Hall.
The building itself is of no particular interest, but
a list of rules and regulations pertaining to the

CUSTOM HOUSE

(From an engraving by Wilkinson of a print dated 1663)

company's affairs is so charged with the obsolete restrictions that were exercised by the paternal city governments of those days that it is worth insertion almost complete.

"First that no manner of person or persons shall keep a common bake-house in cities or corporate towns, but such persons as have been apprenticed unto the same mysteries, and brought up therein for the more space of seven years, or else otherwise skilful in the good making and true sizing of all sorts of bread; and shall put his own mark or seal upon all sorts of his man's bread, which he or they shall make or sell, as before is mentioned.

"Item, that no baker, or any other person do make, bake, utter and sell any kind or sorts of bread in the Commonwealth, but such which the statutes and ancient ordinances of this realm do allow them to bake and sell: that is to say, they may bake and sell Symnel bread, and Wastel, White Wheaten, Household and horse bread, and none other kinds of bread, to put to sale unto her majesty's subjects.

"Item, they must make and bake farthing white bread, half-penny white, penny white, half-penny wheaten, penny household, and two-penny household loaves; and none of greater size, upon pain of forfeiture, unto poor people, all such great bread which they or any of them shall make to sell of greater size (the time of Christmas always being excepted).

"Item, they shall not utter or sell to any innholder, or victualer, either in man's bread or horse bread out of size and not by law allowed), except worth for 12d without any poundage or other advantage.

"Item, they shall sell and deliver unto innholders and victualers in horsebread but three loaves for a penny, and 13 penny worth for 12d (as aforesaid) every one of the same three horse loaves weighing the full weight of a penny white loaf, whether wheat be good, cheap, or dear.

"Item, that no baker, or other person or persons, shall at any time or times hereafter, make, utter, or sell by retail, within or without their houses, unto any of the Queen's subjects, any spice cakes, buns, bisket, or other spice bread, (being bread out of size and not by law allowed), except it be at burials, or upon the Friday before Easter, or at Christmas; upon pain of forfeiture of all such spice bread to the poor.

"Item, whereas there are in cities and corporate towns, common bakers using the misterie of baking there, and within the same town bakers which come unto the market with their bread to be sold; they shall not only bring with them such kinds and sorts of sized bread as the law and ordinances do allow to be made and sold as aforesaid; but shall also keep and observe this order in the sale of their bread, as hereafter followeth.   Because the said foreigners do not bear and pay within the same cities and towns such scot and lot as the bakers of the same towns do.

"First the foreigners' half-penny white loaves shall weigh half an ounce more in every loaf than the bakers of the same towns half-penny white loaves do.   And so in similar proportions for other sorts and sizes of bread."

CHAPTER VI

THE TOWER OF LONDON

IT matters little whether it is to-day, or yesterday, or any day these eight hundred years past that one visits London—he finds the Tower one of the great sights of the town. All familiar with Shakespeare know that the Elizabethans attributed its foundation to Julius Cæsar. For this tradition there is no historical basis beyond the fact that the Tower was built upon a portion of the old Roman wall demolished for the purpose. The Tower, which was begun by William the Conqueror about 1087, was merely a single keep, a fortress erected for the main purpose of maintaining London in a wholesome state of awe, incidentally to protect it against an hostile attack. William was too new in his acquired property to feel that safety which led in later times to the abandonment of the Tower as a royal residence. He wished a safe place on which to rest the uneasy head that wore the new-earned crown. The structure was added to by William Rufus, and again and again by later sovereigns till it began to assume its present appearance. By the time of

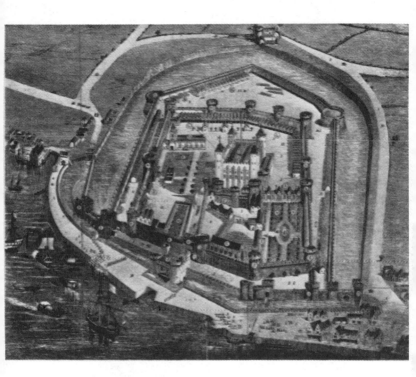

TOWER OF LONDON IN THE TIME OF ELIZABETH

INNER WARD—(A) White tower; (B) Wardrobe tower; (C) Cold Harbour; (D) St. Peter's Church; (E) Block on Tower Green; (F) Officer's house; (G) Lieutenant's house; (H) The Garden; (I) Queen's apartments; (K) Queen's garden; (L) Gunners' quarters.

ON THE WALL—(a) Beauchamp tower; (b) Prisoners' walk; (c) Belfry; (d) Raleigh's walk; (e) Bloody tower; (f) Lantern; (g) Salt tower; (h) Broad Arrow tower; (i) Constable tower; (k) Martin tower; (l) Northumberland's walk; (m) Brick tower; (n) Bowyer tower; (o) Flint tower; (p) Develin tower.

OUTER WARD—(1) Postern; (2) Middle tower; (3) Byeward gate; (4) Gateway under Bloody tower; (5) Hall tower; (6) Great hall; (7) Queen's stairs; (8) Traitor's gate; (9) St. Thomas' tower; (10) Cradle tower; (11) Well tower; (12) Galleyman tower; (13) Iron gate; (14) Brass mount; (15) Legge mount; (16) Soldiers' quarters.

Elizabeth the main lines of the Tower as it exists to-day had been laid down.

There was a narrow strip of wharf, guarded by the Tower, yet isolated from it and open to the public, which extended along the whole river frontage. There were cannons here for defence, and cranes for landing all sorts of goods belonging to the Queen and to others. An interesting bill of complaints directed against one of the Elizabethan Lieutenants of the Tower speaks thus in the quaint language of the time concerning the abuse of this landing-frontage to the fortress.

" That command had been given by their honours, that no great ordnance should be shot off at any time upon the Tower wharf, or about the Tower, except it were only for the Queen. Notwithstanding they continue to shoot from time to time great pieces, which pieces were to be sold or lent to divers persons, with the Queen's own powder, conveyed by them out of the Tower in barrels. That this shooting utterly marred the wharf, being sore worn and shaken already, brake the glass windows, and losed the tiles of houses newly repaired.

" That they did receive and discharge upon the same wharf divers men's stuffs, as timber, logs, billots, faggots, rubbish, hay, straw, and all other things, and carry and recarry the same with cars and carts; which did greatly decay the wharf and wear the Queen's cranes."

In a covered channel that passed under this wharf was the entrance known as the Traitors' Gate, so-called, says Stow, " of conveying prisoners for treason that way." It passed under the castellated tower of St. Thomas, thence beneath a roadway that divided the inner and outer walls, and arrived at the Bloody Tower. Here the unfortunate prisoner would alight and mount the stairs, the top of which were within the strongest part of the gloomy fortress. It was at the head of these steps that the Princess Elizabeth sat down in the rain and refused to go further. How the furious fickle wheel of fortune swept round before she returned after her imprisonment to sleep in the Tower the night before her coronation!

But those who visited the Tower voluntarily arrived in a different way and from a different direction. Every Tower visitor to-day must pass through a little office where he performs a most important act. If he or she wear a bag, no matter if it be too small more than to contain a handkerchief, the wearer must leave it behind. These great stone walls, venerable and massive as they are, are not able to withstand the force of powder. In the eyes of the Tower authorities dynamite is the accursed thing and must be

PART OF TOWER OF LONDON

watched for like the first signs of plague. Yet, if this seems to be over-carefulness, it is well to remember that it has the authority of centuries of custom behind it. Something very like was the custom in Elizabethan days. It was then all open ground upon Tower Hill, and one who rode across the green fields in the immediate neighbourhood was compelled to alight and give an account of himself. At the postern, which in position very nearly coincides with the office of to-day, he showed his passport and gave up his arms. Thence he passed along a narrow causeway with the moat upon either side to the strong auxiliary fortification in the very centre of the moat that was known as the Middle Tower. Through this ponderous gate he must pass, still upon the causeway, before he reached a still stronger place of defence, the Byeward Tower. From within this massive structure one exit gave upon the wharf before the Tower, the other gave entrance to the inner ward.

Let us imagine an attack. After the three gates already mentioned had been taken by force, the attackers would find that their work was hardly begun in earnest. The Tower enclosure was surrounded by a moat one hundred and twenty feet wide and more than three thousand in length measured along the outer side. It enclosed an area a little in excess of thirteen acres. The inner side was bordered by a heavy wall protected at the angles by fortifications. Within this was another stone rampart with no less than twelve large towers of defence at the various angles. The space between these two walls was known as the outer ward, and is where we have now arrived. It contained little more than gardens, playgrounds, and soldiers' quarters. It was not difficult to obtain permission to enter the outer ward, but permission to enter the inner ward was a privilege indeed.

To take advantage of it one had to pass along between the outer and inner walls to the gateway in the Bloody Tower which was midway in the front of the enclosure and immediately above the water entrance already described. Once within this we are within the precincts proper of the Tower. Yet the armed force bent upon mischief would not yet be within striking distance of success. There was still the original keep built by the Conqueror to be won. Whoever is familiar with the structure of the ancient castles knows that this was no easy undertaking. The White Tower, before the days of gunpowder, was impregnable to all but strategy.

There was but a single narrow entrance, only wide enough to permit one man to pass through

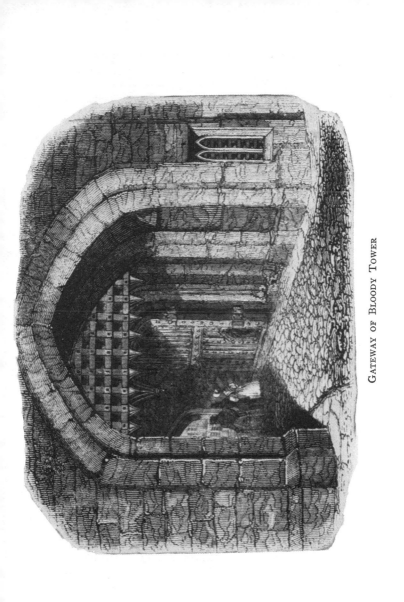

GATEWAY OF BLOODY TOWER

with ease at a time. Access above and below the floor of the entry was by means of a spiral stair within the massive walls that measured from ten to fifteen feet in thickness of solid masonry. There were four tiers in all. The lowest was of dungeons, and entered only from above. The two upper floors contained the banquet hall, the court-rooms and the chapel, one of the three existing Norman churches in the vicinity of London. This was the final stronghold. Not till the White Tower, which originally stood alone as the complete fortress, was won could it be said that the Tower was taken. Yet the word Tower implied all the group of buildings within the moat. There was the great hall on the south side, the King's palace for use when not in danger of attack, many gardens and walks, play-grounds, and the church of St. Peter, which faced the place of execution.

Stow thus enumerates the uses of the Tower in his day: "This Tower is a citadel to defend or command the city; a royal palace for assemblies or treaties; a prison of state for the most dangerous offenders; the only place of coinage for all England at this time; the armoury for warlike provision; the treasury of the ornaments and jewels of the crown; and general conserver of most records of the king's courts of justice at Westminster." Stow, however, does not mention

another use that, if not so important, was at least
more popular at the time than all the others put
together: namely, the use of one of the Tower
courts as a place for wild animals. In fact, the
Tower lions were considered one of the great shows
of the city, to which all foreign visitors of distinction were at once introduced.

It will be noticed that the Tower was no longer
a place of residence. Whitehall had become the
palace, and the fortress of London the principal
prison for those guilty of treason. Hence the
person in charge was a man of great importance,
and upon whose honesty the government must risk
great stakes.

From very early times the Tower had been
under the command of a constable. His office was
of such power and dignity that Elizabeth thought
fit to discontinue it. The constable's duties, however, were in every way performed by the Lieutenant, whose office was of almost equal dignity and
power. Elizabeth's first election to this important
post was Sir Edward Warner, who was deprived of
his office in 1562 for conniving at secret meetings
between the Earl of Hertford and the Lady
Katharine Grey. His successor, Sir Owen Hopton, retained his office till 1590, when he gave place
to Michael Blount, Esq. Sir Owen's long tenure
was not, however, a bed of roses. A series of com-

plaints preferred against him in 1572 has been already quoted in connection with the Tower wharf. A few more will be inserted for the sake of the vivid light they throw upon the customs and usages of the day.

" That the said Lieutenant showed the wardens that they were perjured if they did not first show him all treasons, conspiracies, and any other like matters that they should know or hear of, before they uttered the same to any of her majesties council. Whereupon he took oath of all such yeomen as came of late to serve there under him.

" That there should be seven score gunners belonging to the Tower, whereof there wanted a great number; and that the most part of them that took wages were unskilful. So that, if the Queen's Majesty should stand in need of servants she should be disappointed and besides that many of them are Papists.

" That the clerk of the ordnance is a very earnest Papist.

" That there wanted the most part of such warders as ought to watch and ward and lie within the Tower; and the hamlets did neither watch and ward according to their bounden duty. For if the Tower ditch should be frozen, considering there should be no better care taken for the defence of the same, and considering the state of

the time, and if need should require it it might
be in great danger. Wherefore all the yeomen
should be commanded to wait and to lie within the
Tower every night, for the preservation of the
same, seeing the watches of London and St. Katharine were not kept as of late, but now most need-
ful until this time be past.

"That they made a common highway with all
manner of carriages, from St. Katharines leading
to the Minories: by reason whereof the way is
greatly decayed; the banks of the Tower ditch
sunken, and the ditch filled with earth and filth,
whereas it was wont to be chained between two
great posts. And likewise by the Tower Hill there
was another chain and two great posts by the Bul-
wark gate, for the restraining of all carriages saving only for the Queen. By reason whereof the
banks there are greatly decayed and the ditch
overcome with earth by the sufferance thereof."

In the Bell Tower Elizabeth was confined as
a prisoner. The Beauchamp Tower was for
many years used as the principal prison of state.
Here, amongst others of less note, were confined
Anne Boleyn, John and Guilford Dudley, sons of
the Duke of Northumberland, Lady Jane Grey,
Edmund and Arthur Poole, the great-grandsons
of George Duke of Clarence, Philip Howard, Earl
of Arundel, and many others. Within the Tower

INTERIOR OF BEAUCHAMP TOWER

were executed Anne Boleyn, Katharine Howard,
Sir Thomas More, Protector Somerset, Lady Jane
Grey, and the Earl of Essex.

The immediate neighbourhood of the Tower was
for centuries the constant object of dispute, both
the Lord Mayor and the Lieutenant claiming the
supreme jurisdiction. That part of the city that
bordered the ditch east of the Tower was known
by the name of Little Tower Hill; while the high
ground adjoining the ditch west of the city wall
was known as Great Tower Hill. Here was set
up the scaffold for such prisoners as were not
condemned to suffer the death penalty privately
within the walls.

As had been hinted in the complaints preferred
against Sir Owen Hopton, affairs on Tower Hill
were not going to suit the public. In the following words Stow records the fact of building
encroachments, at the same time admitting a ray
of light in the character of the houses that were
eating up the time-honoured open space about the
Tower.

"For the Tower Hill, as the same is greatly
diminished by the building of tenements, and
garden plots, etc. So it is of late, to-wit in the
year of Christ 1593, on the north side thereof
and at the west end of Hog Street, beautified by
certain fair alms houses, strongly built of brick

and timber, and covered with slate for the poor,
by the Merchant Tailors of London, in place of
some small cottages given them by Richard Hils,
sometime a master of that company, one thousand
loads of timber for that use being given by
Anthony Radcliffe, of the same society, alderman.
In these alms houses, fourteen charitable brethren
of the same said Merchant Tailors yet living, have
placed fourteen poor sole women, who receive each
of them of their founder sixteen pence, or better,
weekly besides 8*l* 15*s* yearly, paid out of the
common treasury of the same corporation for
fuel."

From the western side of Great Tower Hill
started the important thoroughfares of Thames
and Tower Streets; and Barking Alley that ran
northward by the church of Allhallows Barking
was a favourable place for viewing the public executions on Tower Hill. Higher up, near the way
leading to Aldgate, stood the residence of a very
famous Elizabethan gentleman, John Lumley,
Lord Lumley. His house was at the south end of
Woodruff Lane, where it joined Tower Hill, and
was built by Sir Thomas Wyatt, the father, upon
a part of the grounds formerly belonging to the
Crossed Friars.

Stow merely mentions the fact that Lord
Lumley's house stood in this neighbourhood, but

he was a man of sufficient importance to merit more than a passing notice. He was born about 1534, and his father, George Lumley of Thwing in the East Riding of Yorkshire, was attainted of treason in 1537 for taking part in Ask's rebellion. On the death of his grandfather Lord Lumley got possession of the family estates by virtue of an arrangement made before his father's execution, and on petition to Parliament was restored in blood in 1547 and created Baron Lumley.

At Queen's College, Cambridge, he became the friend of Henry Fitz Alan, Lord Maltravers, whose sister he soon married. In 1553 he was made K. B. At the coronation of Mary, his wife, dressed in crimson velvet, sat in the third chariot of state. He was one of the peers who sat in judgment on Henry Grey, Duke of Suffolk, and was also present at the condemnation of Dr. Rowland Taylor at St. Saviour's; and at the accession of Elizabeth was one of the lords appointed to attend her from Hatfield. He was throughout a strong adherent of Arundel and deeply implicated in the Ridolfi plot for the marriage of his brother-in-law, the Duke of Norfolk, to Mary Queen of Scots. He was imprisoned for this complicity, and on release at once resumed negotiations with the Spanish ambassador in the interests of Mary. He was, however, not con-

cerned in her efforts to escape and had no sympathy with the plots of her adherents against the
life of Elizabeth. In 1586 he was one of the
commissioners for the trial of Mary. He was at
this time the owner of Nonesuch, which he conveyed
to Elizabeth in 1590, and in 1591 he entertained
her magnificently at Lewes. At first he sided with
the unfortunate Essex, but did not go so far as to
countenance the insurrection that brought the brilliant earl to the block. Lord Lumley died at his
house on Tower Hill, April 11, 1609.

He was a man of good parts, a skilful artist,
and an ardent lover of learning in all its forms.
He had a splendid library, which was bought
at his death by the King for Prince Henry, and
which eventually passed with other gifts of
George III. to the King's Library in the British
Museum.

East of the Tower lay the Hospital of St.
Katharine, originally founded as a monastery by
Matilda, wife of Stephen. It was then and so
continues under the special patronage of the Queen-
consort. The site is now covered by St. Catharine's
Docks and the immediate neighbourhood, the hospital itself having been removed to the neighbourhood of Regent's Park.

North and east of Little Tower Hill was called
East Smithfield, so called to distinguish it from

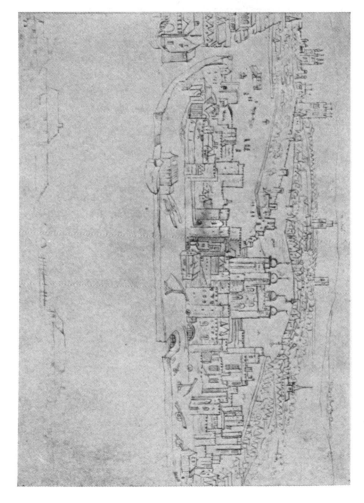

Tower of London
(From the drawing by Wyngaerde)

West Smithfield near Newgate. It possessed an annual fair of fifteen days' duration, beginning on the eve of Pentecost; but most of the familiar associations connected with the name of Smithfield relate to the market place in the neighbourhood of Newgate and St. Bartholomew's the Great.

From the Tower to Aldgate, parallel to the town ditch and only a few yards east of it, was a street that still bears the name of the Minories, commemorative of the site of an abbey of the same name. After the Dissolution the abbey fell into various hands, amongst others, those of Henry, Duke of Suffolk. Soon afterward the abbey buildings were removed and occupied by storehouses for naval goods, workshops, and bakeshops for the supply of bread to the royal navy.

East of the Minories lay Goodman's Fields, the scene of rapid changes during the latter half of the sixteenth century. The name then applied to the district may still be seen upon the map, but the scene which greets the eye of the visitor is huge buildings, railroad tracks, and crowded streets. Far different was it in the days of Elizabeth. It is hard to fancy that then, an arrow, shot from the corner of the Tower of London, would fall in the pastures of the open country. Such, however, was the case.

"Near adjoining this abbey," writes Stow,
"on the south side thereof was sometime a building belonging to the said nunnery; at which
farm myself in my youth have fetched many a
half penny worth of milk and never had less
than three ale pints for a half penny in the
summer, nor less than one ale quart for a half
penny in the winter, always hot from the kine,
as the same was milked and strained. One Trolop,
and afterwards Goodman, were the farmers there,
and had thirty or forty good kine to the pail.
Goodman's son being heir to his father's purchase,
let out the ground first for the grazing of horses,
and then for garden plots, and lived like a
gentleman thereby."

Northeast of Little Tower Hill was Hog
Lane, so called of driving hogs through it to
the neighbouring marshes to feed. (It is now
called Rosemary Lane.) At the west end were
the Merchant Tailors' alms houses already spoken
of and erected in the reign of Elizabeth. Southward from Tower Hill through East Smithfield was Nightinguild (now Nightingale) Lane,
which led to a gut or inlet of the Thames where
a recluse had once taken up his abode. There is
nothing of interest recorded of this place or of
its tenant, nor is there any record of the spot ever
having been built upon by any religious institu-

tion. It has, however, for centuries been called the Hermitage, and probably because of its dreary situation by the riverside was long used as the place of execution for pirates, whose bodies were left there hanging in chains.

CHAPTER VII

THE MAIN HIGHWAY

IN Elizabethan times there was but one continuous passage across London from east to west. It was known throughout this distance by many names, one of which is the name of the most notable street of the city of old and ancient times, namely Cheapside, or West Cheape, as it was originally called. The walk is a long one, more than a mile in length, in places as narrow as of old, everywhere crowded with interesting associations and memorable buildings. Let us traverse it in an orderly and methodical manner, pausing wherever necessary to examine the local habitations that have become world famous.

The present Newgate Street includes what was in Elizabethan times known as Newgate Street (to a short distance beyond Warwick Lane), Newgate Market (to the present King Edward Street), St. Nicholas Shambles (almost to St. Martin le Grand), and Bladder Street (to the junction with Cheapside of to-day).

This street, or succession of streets, as it should be called, was lined upon both sides with houses

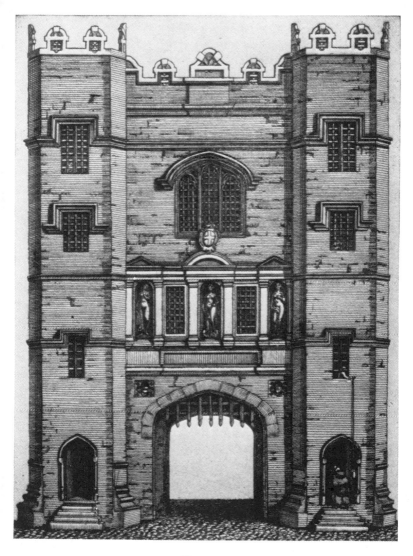

NEWGATE

of substantial build. At the left just beyond the great towered gate, the earliest of all, and which gave the name to the street, was a tavern marked "Ye Swanne" in an interesting map drawn as early as 1617. Next to it on the north side was Goldsmith's Rents, then St. Bartholomew's Brewhouse, and "Ye Bridge-House Rents." Between the last two houses was the "Stone Gate" that gave entrance to the dissolved monastery of the Greyfriars, known in Elizabeth's time by the name of Christ's Hospital, and in our own time by the more familiar appellation, the Blue Coat School. From the Stone Gate one could reach both the great and little cloisters or, by turning to the right, the church itself. Just beyond Warwick Lane was another gate directly by the west end of the church.

The street in this part was divided down the centre by a notable row of buildings much like the Butchers' row that characterised the Strand almost to our own day, and which served the same purpose and went by the same name. Butchers' Row, or the Shambles, were originally the tiny sheds set up in the midst of the street in days when Cheapside and its continuation in either direction was the principal market of the city. Each kind of vender had his particular neighbourhood allotted to him, and the dealers in meat were

lodged in the Shambles. The origin of the buildings date back to many years before the time of
Elizabeth. By the end of the sixteenth century
the old sheds had all disappeared and their place
was taken by permanent buildings known as above.
The passage to the north of them was familiarly
called St. Nicholas Flesh Shambles, or just the
Shambles, and the passage south, the Back Side
of the Shambles.

A habit in close connection with the butchering
of cattle, namely the sale of bladders, gave rise
to the name applied to the next section of the
street: Bladder, or more commonly Blowbladder
Street, where they were exposed for sale. Stow,
always with his amusing attention to details that
would seem out of place in Baedeker, but that are
of great interest to the student of antiquities,
after having spoken of the origin of Blowbladder
Street, thus adds a note on the other name by
which the rear of the Shambles was known: "Then
behind the butchers' shops be now divers slaughter
houses inward, and tippling houses outward. This
is called Mountgodard street of the tippling houses
there, and the goddards mounting from the tap
to the table, from the table to the mouth, and
sometimes over the head. This street goeth up
to the north end of Ivie Lane.

"Before this Mountgodard street stall boards

were of old time set up by the butchers to show
and sell their flesh meat upon, over the which stallboards they first built sheds to keep off the weather;
but since that, encroaching by little and little, they
have made their stallboards and sheds fair houses,
meet for the principal shambles."

Cheapside is that part of the Main Highway
that extended from the east end of Blowbladder
Street to the Poultry near the Bank of England.
At the junction of the former and Paternoster
Row, which bordered St. Paul's on the north,
where the statue of Peel now stands, was formerly
the church of St. Michael le Querne, against the
east wall of which was placed the Little Conduit.
This is the first of the four structures that stood
in the midst of the street and are perhaps the most
often met with locations in the records of old time.
At the opposite end of the street was the Great
Standard, another public fountain that contrib-
uted largely to the water supply of the city.
Intermediate between the two stood the Standard
and the Cross.

Almost from time immemorial there was a market
in Cheapside. Few persons stop to think that
the names which the streets in that vicinity bear
to-day are the result of the christening they received from the customs of this old market of days
before the Fire, if not almost before the Flood. The

fishmongers, for instance, all stood in a row, hawking fish from their tiny booths, and hence we still
walk along Friday Street. Wood Street, Bread
Street, Milk Street—they all owe their names to
the same origin. As might be expected, the neighbourhood of a public market would not be the most
splendid part of a great city; the assertion is both
true and untrue of the Elizabethan thoroughfare.
At that time the north side was furnished with
rather mean-looking houses of the timber gabled
variety, set close together, very regular and
monotonous in appearance, and occupied by petty
dealers with their clumsy booths projecting into
the street from the ground floor. The opposite
side of the street, however, contained several rows
of finer buildings, one of which, Goldsmiths' Row,
was considered the most spectacular, the grandest
building in the city, rivalled only by the Royal
Exchange.

The taverns in Cheapside were always numerous. The Nag's Head was there, and the Mermaid. Many people are of the opinion that the
Mermaid was in Friday Street; and so it was, yet
it is the same tavern as that in Cheapside; the
truth of the matter being that it stood back some
distance with an approach from three directions,
each from a different street; hence the confusion
of allusion. Here gathered those Elizabethan

CHEAPSIDE

(From an engraving by Wilkinson)

wits who made it as notable almost as the Apollo, and here was the mind of Keats when he thought of Elysian Fields and good mine host.

Cheapside was important not only for its market, but because, being a part of the only continuous passageway across the city, it took part in every public show and civic parade. In fact, to mention a city pageant is to mention Cheapside. Then as now the Lord Mayor always made his progress along Cheapside, as did all royal progresses from the Tower to Whitehall on the day of a coronation. On these occasions the street was cleared as well as could be and the surface strewed with fresh gravel. The custom was necessary then, because, though paved, it was so poorly paved that it was seldom in the condition for the touch even of a monarch's horse. The custom is still religiously carried out, though no longer necessary; yet this sentimental adherence to an old custom upon Lord Mayor's Day is one of the pleasantest features of the festivity. Seditious books were publicly burned in Cheapside, not for the purpose of advertisement, but for suppression. Prisoners were given painful notoriety by being whipped along Cheapside at the tail of a cart, and royal edicts were proclaimed in this street. No wonder that it is associated more than any other street with the public records of the corporation.

The water supply of London was mainly drawn
from the public fountains in the streets. The
tankard-bearers would gather in crowds and wait
their turns at the conduit, whence they set out in
every direction peddling the pure water that was
piped from one place and another. So general
was this custom that one of the regularly assumed
duties of an indentured apprentice was to fetch
water from the conduit. Two of the most important conduits of the city were in Cheapside;
namely, that at the end of St. Michael's Church,
and the Great Conduit opposite Mercers' Hall. In
appearance the latter was a long low stone building with battlements on the top, enclosing a lead-
lined cistern from which the water fell into a
square stone basin at the eastern end. The less
conspicuous Little Conduit was, however, much
more convenient, inasmuch as it had a stream of
water flowing from each of three sides. The
Standard already mentioned was another fountain
which stood opposite the end of Honey Lane. It
was by this structure that seditious books were
burned and offenders punished.

Of these four erections in the midst of the street
itself, by far the most famous was the Cross.
When Queen Eleanor, consort of Edward I. died,
her body was brought to be interred at Westminster Abbey. Wherever on the way the body rested

her devoted King and husband subsequently erected a stone cross. There were two of these in London. Charing Cross is still standing, but Cheapside Cross has long since disappeared.

The building of crosses in the olden time was a distinct and important branch of architecture; and this one of more than usual importance. Not only was it a graceful example of the art, with the Queen's arms and image carved thereon; it was also used in later times as a place of execution, and the place *par excellence* for reading public proclamations. Stow tells us that in the year 1599 "the timber of the cross at the top was rotted within the lead, the arms thereof bending, were feared to have fallen to the harming of some people, and therefore the whole body of the cross was scaffolded about, and the top thereof taken down, meaning in place thereof to have set up a piramis; but some of Her Majesty's Honourable Councillors directed their letters to Sir Nicholas Mosely, then Mayor, by her highness's express commandment concerning the cross, forthwith to be repaired and replaced as formerly it stood, &c; notwithstanding, the cross stood headless more than a year after; whereupon the councillors in great number, meaning not any longer to permit the continuance of such a contempt, wrote to William Ryder, then Mayor, and by virtue of her highness's said former

direction and commandment that, without any
further delay. . . . After this a cross of timber
was framed, set up, covered with lead, and gilded,
the body of the cross downward cleansed of dust,
the scaffold carried thence. About twelve nights
following the image of Our Lady was again de-
faced by plucking off her crown and almost her
head, taking from her her naked child, and stab-
bing her in the breast."

This attack was due to a spirit of opposition that
grew up in the later years of Elizabeth's reign.
Owing to the fierce religious feeling of the time
certain narrow-minded persons took it upon themselves to stir up the belief that the crosses which
adorned certain places were a relic of Popish
superstition. No feeling of reverence for age or
tradition affected them any more than it did years
later when the Puritans rivalled the savages of
antiquity in vandalism. The Cheapside cross was
almost destroyed by unknown persons on a night in
June, 1581, when the images of the Resurrection,
the Virgin Mary, Christ, and Edward the Confessor were miserably mutilated. It was not repaired till 1595. Four years later occurred the
incident above, and when further improvements
were demanded the next year the city went so far
as to consult the universities on the propriety of
replacing the crucifix. As a result the cross was

rebuilt " surmounted with a plain crucifix, but without the dove."

Just opposite Wood Street was the Goldsmiths' Row, to which allusion has already been made as the most splendid block of houses in London.   It should be remembered in connection with this building that banking in the time of Elizabeth had not yet become a separate profession, but was carried on as an avocation by the goldsmiths, who usually kept a shop and sold plate as well.   Further reference to this custom is made in connection with Lombard Street in the next chapter, the chief abode of the London bankers.   Stow, giving a very minute description of the building, is quoted here, as has been done many times elsewhere in this volume where it is possible to give the words of the interesting historian of the Elizabethan city to whom we owe so much of our knowledge.

" Next to be noted, the most beautiful frame of fair houses and shops that be within the walls of London, or elsewhere in England, commonly called Goldsmiths' row, betwixt Bread Street end and the cross in Cheape, but is within this Bread Street ward; the same was built by Thomas Wood, goldsmith, one of the sheriffs of London, in the year 1491.   It containeth in number ten fair dwelling-houses and fourteen shops, all in one frame, uniformly built four stories high, beautified towards

the street with the Goldsmiths' arms and the like-
ness of woodmen, in memory of his name, riding
on monstrous beasts, all which is cast in lead,
richly painted over and gilt: these he gave to the
Goldsmiths, with stocks of money, to be lent to
young men having those shops, &c.   This said
front was again new painted and gilt over in the
year 1594; Sir Richard Martin being then mayor,
and keeping his mayoralty in one of them, serving
out the time of Cuthbert Buckle in that office from
the 2nd of July till the 28th of October."

When the traveller to-day in passing down
Cheapside towards the bank pauses to look at the
Guildhall he should know in reality what a puzzle
is before him.   In Elizabethan times the building
was not thus visible, but had to be approached by
one or the other of two narrow and dirty alleys:
Lawrence Lane or Ironmonger's Lane.   But the
construction of King Street has thus laid bare to
Cheapside eyes the heart of London.   Yet, is it
proper to apply the word heart to an institution
whose origin, development, and early function are
wholly blank upon the page of history?   In reality
the façade of the Guildhall shrouds a riddle, and
one steps through the grand portal into the very
mouth of the silent Sphinx.

In the second chapter of this volume allusion has
been made to a distinction between the guilds and

the companies of London. Always in popular estimation, and sometimes in what should be more learned works, the two terms are confused and often treated as synonymous. Nothing has been said heretofore in detail concerning the guilds, because they were all suppressed before the accession of Elizabeth. Their early existence is known, but their early history is not. The fact that as they passed away their affairs in many instances were administered by the city Livery Companies is probably the origin of the confusion of terms.

To what guild did the Guildhall belong? That is the Sphinx riddle of London. There are some reasons for the belief that the early governing guild of the city was a sort of cosmopolitan or union guild composed of members of all the others; perhaps there is even more reason to believe that it was composed of a group of wealthy and aristocratic citizens of great influence who had got possession of the city government. There is little enough in support of either hypothesis. We may even be content to say, with Mr. Loftie, that the main invincible proof of the guild's existence is to be found in the existence of the Guildhall. There is the Guildhall, there must have been a guild for it to belong to. Yet we may in this connection remember that Jack Cade's father was a bricklayer, a fact Shakespeare supports by citing the existence of a chimney whose bricks are alive to testify to this day of his skill in laying them.

However interesting and unprofitable is the historical search into the origin of the Guildhall and its early occupants, it is certain that it passed gradually, with the passing of the guilds, into the possession of the city and became its city hall. In it were kept the courts of the corporation, the records, and there were held the great state banquets that were almost the *raison d'être* of the ancient guilds and companies. Then, too, at times, the hall was turned into a court of justice on a more pretentious scale. The Earl of Surrey, the poet, was tried in Guildhall, as were Lady Jane Grey and her husband, Sir Nicholas Throgmorton, and the Jesuit Garnet, whose execution took place in Paul's churchyard.

The two giants, Gog and Magog, that now adorn the great hall, were carved and set up in 1708. They are successors, if not copies, of two far more ancient and famous statues that used always to be borne prominently in the civic processions.

"In 1554, when Philip and Mary made their public entry into London, two images, representing two giants, the one named Corineus and the other Gogmagog, stood upon London Bridge, hold-

ing between them certain flattering Latin verses;
and when Elizabeth passed through the city, the
day before her coronation (January 12, 1559),
these two giants were placed at Temple Bar,
holding between them a political recapitulation,
in Latin and English, of the pageants that day
exhibited." (Fairholt.) "Here (in Guildhall)
are to be seen the statues of two giants, said to
have assisted the English when the Romans made
war upon them; Corineus of Britain and Gogmagog of Albion. Beneath, upon a table, the
titles of Charles V., Emperor, are written in letters
of gold." (Hentzner, 1598.)

Farther down the street is the Mansion House,
which now occupies the site of the ancient Stocks
Market. We are still in the neighbourhood of
the ancient Cheapside market place, but this name
comes rather from the stocks that were placed there
for the punishment of offenders than from any
commodity for sale, as is the case in so many other
place-names of this part of the city. It was for
years a place of punishment by the stocks, which
instrument of torture was situated in the middle
of the street, so that the culprit could be made to
suffer the ordeal of exposure to a greater concourse of people. The market-house which was
there in Elizabethan times was let out to butchers
and fishmongers, the rent being applied to the

repair and maintenance of London Bridge. It was rebuilt on a larger and more substantial scale at the beginning of the sixteenth century, with twenty-five stalls for fishmongers, eighteen for butchers, and sixteen chambers above. In the time of Elizabeth a stone conduit stood near the stocks, that came into existence as a result of the following petition to the Lord Mayor:

"Beseeching your Lordship and Masterships, the inhabitants dwelling about the *Stocks*, that by the space of five or six years past, a vent of water hath run by a pipe of lead beside the *Stocks*, which pipe of lead by reason that it is not closed, is daily hurt with horses and carts: It may therefore please your good Lordship and Masterships, and all our masters of the Common Council, to grant and give licence unto the said inhabitants, upon their own proper costs and charges to make or cause to be made, a little postern or stone with a cistern of lead therein: so that the said water shall be therein preserved and conveyed: and so be drawn out with cocks to the common weale of all the said inhabitants therein dwelling. Thus at the reverence of God, and in the way of charity."

In all probability the Royal Exchange, which fronted upon Cornhill, was the most conspicuous building next to St. Paul's of which London could boast. Sir Thomas Gresham, its founder, was a goldsmith who kept a shop in Lombard Street, and who also did a private banking business. He was, in fact, a man of note above most of his contemporaries, and probably did more towards the greatness of Elizabethan England than any other person except Lord Burghley. Gresham's genius was early recognised, and he was made the Queen's minister of finance. His duties in this office took him frequently to Flanders, and it was from the example of the Antwerp Bourse that he conceived the idea of a similar institution for London. Before that time the city merchants were used to meet in the open streets, in all sorts of weather, to transact their business. They eagerly welcomed the suggestion of Gresham, and helped him to put his plan into execution. Stow, in the following words, describes the preparation of the site:

" Then next is the Royal Exchange, erected in the year 1566, after this order, namely certain houses upon Cornhill, and the like upon the back thereof, in the ward of Broad Street, with three alleys, the first called Swan Alley, opening into Cornhill, the second New Alley, passing throughout of Cornhill into Broad Street Ward, over against St. Bartholomew Lane, the third St. Christopher's Alley, opening into Broad Street Ward and into St. Christopher's parish, containing in all four score households, were first purchased by the

citizens of London for more than three thousand
five hundred and thirty-two pounds, and were sold
for four hundred and seventy-eight pounds, to
such persons as should take them down and carry
them thence; also the ground or plot was made
plain at the charges of the city; and then the possession thereof was by certain aldermen, in name
of the whole citizens, given to Sir Thomas Gresham,
Knight, agent to the Queen's highness, thereupon
to build a bourse, or place for merchants to assemble at his own proper charges.   And he, on the 7th
of June, laying the first stone of the foundation,
being brick, accompanied with some aldermen,
every one of them laid a piece of gold, which the
workmen took up, and forthwith followed upon the
same with such diligence, that by the month of November, 1567, the same was covered with slate, and
shortly after fully finished."

This building was in the form of a quadrangle
with a large interior court with huge arched entrances from north and south.   On the outside of the
north entrance was a tall Corinthian column, topped
with a grasshopper, the crest of the Greshams.   It
is interesting to note that the existence of this immense column, which must have towered above its
surroundings much as the Monument does at present, is recorded nowhere except in a contemporary
print of the building.   It is barely possible that

the picture alluded to is from the architect's design
and that the column was never actually set in place.

Within the quadrangle was an arched walk or
cloister with a double row of shops, one above the
other.   In niches over the cloister were arranged
statues of the kings and queens of England, from
Edward the Confessor to Elizabeth.

The opening of the Exchange was an occasion
of great festivity, the Queen attending the ceremony in great state.   Gresham's hope of remuner-
ation, for the Exchange was built at his own
expense, was based upon the shops lining the quadrangle.   "A little before her majesty, attended
with her nobility, came from her house at the
Strand, called Somerset House, and entered the
city by Temple Bar, through the Fleet Street,
Cheape, and so by the north side of the bourse,
through Thread Needle Street, to Sir Thomas
Gresham's house in Bishopgate Street, where she
dined.   After dinner, her Majesty, returning
through Cornhill, entered the Bourse on the south
side; and after she had viewed every part thereof
above ground, especially the pawn, which was furnished with all sorts of the finest wares in the city,
she caused the same bourse, by a herald and trumpets to be proclaimed the 'Royal Exchange,' and
so to be called thenceforth and not otherwise."
(Stow.)

"After the Royal Exchange, which is now [1631] called the Eye of London, had been builded two or three years, it stood in a manner empty; and a little before her Majesty was to come thither to view the beauty thereof, and to give it a name, Sir Thomas Gresham, in his own person, went, twice in one day, round the upper pawn, and besought those few shopkeepers then present that they would furnish, and adorn with wares and wax lights as many shops as they either could or would, and they should have all those shops so furnished rent free for that year, which otherwise at that time was 40s a shop by the year; and within two years after he raised the rent unto four marks a year; and within a year after that he raised his rent of every shop unto £4:10s a year, and then all shops were well furnished according to that time; for then the milliners or haberdashers in that place sold mouse-traps, bird-caps, shoe-horns, lanthorns, and Jews-trumps, etc. There were also at that time that kept shops in the upper pawn of the Royal Exchange, armourers that sold both old and new armour, apothecaries, booksellers, gold-smiths, and glass-sellers." (Howes.)

For a while everything in the Exchange went well, except that the lower range of shops was always unpopular. Strype says that "the rent of the shops here brought in considerable gains to Sir

Thomas Gresham the builder. And about five or six years after the shops were all furnished with wares, Gresham constrained all the shopkeepers that had shops above to take shops below in the lowest vaults of the Exchange, where was an equal number of shops to those above. At which time every one paid four marks a year for every shop above; and he would have as much rent for every shop below or else they should not have a shop above. But after they had kept shop below a little while, what with the damp of the vault, the darkness of the place, and the unwillingness of the customers to buy their wares there, they were so wearied, that they agreed among themselves to give 4l a year for a shop above, so that they might be freed from keeping shop below; and so Sir Thomas should turn the vault to such other use as he would, either for merchants' goods, or otherwise. Which offer he accepted; and so the tenants only furnished the shops above. . . . And the vaults have been used now a long time for the stowage of merchandises, and chiefly pepper."

The great bell of the Exchange used to ring at noon and at six in the evening, when the merchants would assemble to consult, bargain, and arrange affairs. The Exchange, however, must not be looked upon as a place of meeting for a collection of sober and sedate city fathers; for, though given up twice a day to mercantile transactions on a large scale, the real character of the Exchange was that of a bazaar filled with petty shops, a permanent Bartholomew Fair, so to speak. The quadrangle and its occupants reminded one of the Globe Theatre and its pit, full of disorders, petty-hawkers, and graduates of the cut-purse school.

"On Sundays and Holy days the Exchange was enlivened during a portion of the year with the music of the city waits, who were ordered by the Court of Aldermen (April, 1572), to play on their instruments as they had hitherto been accustomed, at the Royal Exchange, from seven o'clock till eight o'clock in the evening up to the Feast of Pentecost, after which they were to commence playing at eight P. M., and 'to hold on' till nine P. M., up to Michaelmas. There is another circumstance connected with the same building that deserves a passing notice, which is that football used to be played within its walls, a game forbidden in 1576 to be played any longer there or in any of the city's wards." (Sharpe I. 502.)

When one reads with what haste the original building was erected one is not surprised to find it in constant need of repair. The following quaint "presentment" sets forth its condition less than fifteen years after it was completed:

"In most humble wise beseech your Lordships

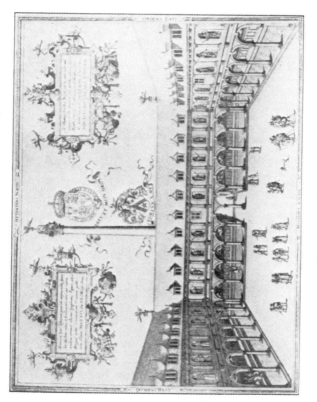

THE ROYAL EXCHANGE

(From an engraving by Wilkinson of a scarce contemporary print)

and worships, we the wardmote enquest of the ward
abovesaid, that whereas of long time the upper part
or arches of the Royal Exchange, being on the
south west and southern parts thereof within the said
ward, whereunto the merchants do commonly resort, have access, and do walk, being the charge of
reparation on [the] parte of the Lady Gresham to
be done, hath byn and is greatly by the insufficiency
of the workmanship thereof, and want of good stuff
greatly defective and very perilous to the walkers
thereunder.   In such as the main freestones of the
arches thereof have fallen, and a great part of the
same arches are ready to fall, to the great danger
of the lives of persons young and old, daily walking
thereunder and resorting to the same Exchange.
And whereas at a certain grate belonging to the
like charge of the Lady Gresham, being right over
against the south of the said Royal Exchange, in
the middle of the street, and common passage
thereof, is a great hole which of long time hath so
continued to the great danger and hurt, and loss of
life and limb, and maiming both of men and beasts,
and other common passers thereby—as namely, the
foot of a horse slipped lately therein, a man being
on horseback, to the great danger of the horse-leg,
and of the leg of the man by the fall of the horse.
Since which an ox-leg fell therein and was broke in
two.   So it is right honourable that divers of the

inhabitants of the said ward hath certified the same to the keeper of the Exchange, to certify it to the Lady Gresham, yet no reformation or consideration had thereof. May it therefore please your lordship and worships the premises tenderly considered of your goodness to take such speedy order therein as that the said arches and hole may be presently and out of hand amended, otherwise it will turn to the hurt and spoil of many." (To the Lord Mayor and Aldermen. 1581.)

It is almost needless to add that the original building was destroyed in the great fire, and its successor from the same cause in 1838. Though somewhat foreign to our particular subject, it is interesting to note that the only remnant of the original structure to survive both fires is the statue of Gresham.

CHAPTER VIII

THE MAIN HIGHWAY (Continued)

THE name of the thoroughfare that we have been traversing throughout the preceding chapter changed again at Gracechurch Street, east of which it was called Leadenhall Street, after the principal building upon it. There is much confusion in the pages of Stow concerning the early history of the Leaden Hall and Chapel. Later researches, however, establish the fact that it belonged to the city as long ago as the beginning of the fourteenth century. It was then, and continued almost to our own day to be, the great market for poultry brought into London from the outside. It may be doubted, however, whether the hall itself was ever actually given up to the poulterers. In 1445 Simon Eyre*, a draper and also mayor of London, erected a granary on the site at his own expense for the common use of the city. This is the building that is described by Stow as in existence in Elizabethan times. It had a chapel on the

---

*One of the characters in Dekker's *Shoemaker's Holiday.*

east side dedicated to the Holy Trinity, that was not taken down till 1812. However great the confusion of Stow between the manor and the hall of Leadenhall, we may trust the following account of what come within his own observation:

"The use of Leadenhall in my youth was thus:— In a part of the north quadrant, on the east side of the north gate, were the common beams for. the weighing of wool and other wares, as had been accustomed; on the west side of the gate were the scales to weigh meal; the other three sides were reserved for the most part to the making and resting of the pageants showed at the Midsummer Watch; the remnant of the sides and quadrants was employed for the stowage of woolsacks, but not closed up; the lofts above were partly used by the painters in working for the decking of pageants and other devices, for beautifying of the watch and watchmen; the residue of the lofts were letten out to merchants, the woolwinders and packers therein to wind and pack their wool."

The next object of interest, namely the Church of St. Andrew Undershaft, is important mainly in connection with the name of John Stow. The last chapter ended with a note upon the most important financial figure of the age; but a stone's throw further down the same thoroughfare is the church where lies buried the other most famous Elizabethan

of whom memories live upon the Main Highway.
The reader may have already asked the question
why John Stow of all others should have furnished
so many of the quotations that embellish the present volume. There is but one answer. He not
only wrote more about, but is almost the only contemporary writer upon Elizabethan London. In
fact, his famous *Survey of London* is the Baedeker of the day, full, complete, crammed with little
topographical details and descriptions of manners
and customs. It is the one book to which all
students of the Elizabethan city must go for much
of their material.

John Stow, himself a tailor and son of a tailor,
was born in Cornhill in the parish of St. Michael,
1525. His father, who followed his trade in this
street, was opulent enough to possess a garden in
Throckmorton Street near the Drapers' Hall, to
which he could withdraw for recreation. When
John Stow moved from Cornhill is not known, but
in the year 1549 he was dwelling near the well
within Aldgate, the bailiff of Rumford having been
"executed upon the pavement of my door where I
then kept house." Afterward he moved into Lime
Street Ward and dwelt in the parish of St. Andrew
till his death.

Stow loved the ancient in religion, Strype tells
us, as well as the ancient in history, and he became,

therefore, a suspected man. In 1568 his library was searched, and many books were found that related to Papistry. What resulted from this search we do not know, but two years later he was tried before the Ecclesiastical Commissioners; the charges against him were all false, and he escaped punishment.

"He was tall of stature," says Edmond Howes, his literary executor, "lean of body and face, his eyes small and chrystaline, of a pleasant and cheerful countenance; his sight and memory very good; very sober, mild, and courteous to any that required his instructions; and retained the true use of all his senses unto the day of his death, being of an excellent memory. He always protested never to have written anything either for malice, fear, or favour, nor to seek his own particular gain or vain glory; and that his only pains and care was to write *truth*. He could never ride, but travelled on foot to divers cathedral churches, and other chief places of the land, to search records. He was very careless of scoffers, backbiters, and detractors. He lived peacefully, and died of the stone collick, being four score years of age, and was buried the 8th of April, 1605, in his parish church of St. Andrew Undershaft; whose mural monument neere unto his grave was there set up at the charges of Elizabeth, his wife."

About 1560 Stow began to collect the antiquarian information that has made his name a by-word among historical students. His first book was the brief *Summary of the Chronicles,* in which he attempted and nearly achieved the task of bringing order out of the chaos of ancient historical records. The book first appeared in 1561, but was soon followed by an enlarged edition. The year 1598 saw the first edition of the *Survey of London,* and 1600, the *Annals* of English history.

Stow hardly needs a word of praise, nor is there need of any insistence on his value as a writer concerning the manners of the Elizabethan age. He spent forty years in indefatigable research among original sources, spending his patrimony in the purchase of books and manuscripts. In his old age he became ill and feeble, and a great sufferer from the gout. It is a crying shame to London that, when her great historian lay sick and stricken with poverty, she turned a deaf ear to his petition for a pension. He had "spent his patrimony and the best part of his estate in those studies and labours, useful to the city, and to the English nation, though not to himself." At the city's refusal to grant him help, he must needs fall back upon the King. James under his own hand and seal acknowledged that "John Stow, citizen of London, having, for the good of the Commonwealth, and Posterity to come,

employed all his Industry and Labour to commit to
the History of Chronicles, all such things worthy
of remembrance, as from time to time happened
within this whole Realm, for the space of five and
forty years, until Christmas last past (as by divers
large and brief Chronicles of his writing may appear) besides his great pain and charges in writing
his book, called his *Survey of London*, wherein he
spent eight years searching ancient records concerning the Antiquities both for London and Southwark, etc;" and in reward for his great labour the
despicable pedant from Scotland granted his "loyal
subject" a licence to beg. But, as Strype says,
Stow's memory has outlived that. Surely the inheritance in the good will of posterity possessed by
the humble student of the city's lore, honest and
upright as he was, is more to be envied than that of
the first of the English house of Stuart, albeit he
was a King. Stow died at the age of eighty, April
6, 1605, leaving a name now endued with a full
share of reverence and respect.

This *Survey of London* is an immortal book.
It appeared first, as has been said, in 1598, and soon
went into a new and enlarged edition. At regular
intervals it was republished, "with additions" by
one editor after another. Each new issue preserved
the same form and arrangement as the old, but with
increased number of documents and other illustra-

tions of the places and customs described. The last edition under such a name was that of Strype in 1720, published at London in two huge folio volumes, embellished with numerous engravings. The later issues of the book, however, are of little use to the reader whose mind is set upon Elizabethan London; for such a man as Strype, for instance, does not always make it clear to whom the personal pronoun relates. Thus I in one paragraph may mean Stow, in the next Strype. And furthermore, though called Stow's *Survey*, all the pictures and most of the descriptions apply to the time of the editor rather than of the original writer. In more recent times, however, the value of the work as written by Stow himself has been recognised. In addition to a cheap reprint of the original form, a carefully collated text of the two editions published during the lifetime of the author was published in London in 1876 under the able editorship of William J. Thoms.

It is to the *Survey* that people must go to get the most authentic description of the city of that day. To be sure, the book is not altogether adequate. In the first place it is loaded down with gloomy lists of the burials and monuments of every church in London and much antiquarian information of past ages. Stow, as were all of the prose writers of the time, was a man who could not

wield the pen with accuracy, to say nothing of
grace. Then, too, he has his likes and his dislikes.
He does not care for theatres, and one who is
interested in the Elizabethan drama is disappointed
to find that a bare allusion to two of them and a
passing note of the Bear Garden is all that the
strait-laced old antiquary has to say concerning
these evil institutions to which as a loyal citizen
of London he was bound to hold a grudge. Yet
in spite of all this, Stow is still Stow for all time.
His name is immortal, and the place where rests
his ashes is consecrated ground. Let us thank
the muse of topographical history that he lived
and died before the record-blotting Puritan rose
to play vandal in his might.

Duke's Place was near Aldgate, on the north
side of the street where formerly stood one of the
great religious institutions within the walls:
namely, the Priory of the Holy Trinity, founded
by Matilda, Queen of Henry I. It managed to
pass into the possession of the Duke of Norfolk,
and thus got the name by which it was known at
the end of the century. Stow tells us that it was
a very fair and large church, rich in lands and
ornaments, and passed all the priories in the city
of London or the shire of Middlesex. It was for
a while a place of great merriment and state. "I
find the said Duke," relates Strype, "anno, 1562,

with his duchess riding thither through Bishopsgate Street to Leadenhall, and so to Cree Church
to his own place; attended with 100 horse in his
livery, with his gentlemen afore, their coats
guarded with velvet; and four heralds riding
before him, viz., Clarenceux, Somerset, Red Cross,
and Blue mantle." When the duke was beheaded
his son sold the mansion-house and priory precincts
that had come into the family through his mother.
Land was valuable, and there happened what often
happened after the wholesale spoliation of the
monasteries, most of the buildings were taken
down and the material used for building. Pardon
Churchyard north of St. Paul's had thus been
turned into use by the Duke of Somerest. Much
of the great Reading monastic buildings were
turned into road metal; and we learn from Stow
the use to which the destroyed buildings of the
Holy Trinity were put.

"For the workmen, with great labour, beginning at the top, loosed stone from stone, and
threw them down, whereby the most part of them
were broken, and few remained whole; and those
were sold very cheap, for all the buildings then
made about the city were of brick and timber. At
that time any man in the city might have a cart-
load of hard stone for paving brought to his door
for six-pence or seven-pence, with the carriage.

The said Thomas Lord Audley built and dwelt on
this priory during his life, and died there in the
year 1544; since the which time the said priory
came by marriage of the Lord Audley's daughter
and heir unto Thomas, late Duke of Norfolk, and
was then called Duke's place."

In the slight representation of this place contained in Aggas's map of London, drawn towards
the end of the sixteenth century, we find how ex-
tensive had been the alterations and how generally
the place had been changed from the appearance
and character of a great monastic institution.   It
was triangular in shape, enclosed by several
buildings, extending from a square embattled gate
leading into the churchyard of St. Catharine
Christ Church, to Aldgate, where they form a
rounded wall.   Within the space behind the church
are several large edifices, with gardens beyond,
leaving a long narrow lane between it and the city
wall.   Another embattled gate leads into the gardens, and the portion of the triangle next the
Aldgate is cut off by a wall that encloses some
small buildings and a garden.   The south gate
of the priory was in existence for a long time and
forms the subject of one of Wilkinson's engravings.

Aldgate stood at the north-east corner of the
city just beyond Duke's Place (the present Duke

Street) and Poor Jewry Lane (the present Jewry Street), while the church of St. Botolph was just outside the gate. The gate was so called, say most historians, because of its antiquity. It was the custom in olden times to rent some of the gates as private dwelling-houses; according to which practice we learn that in 1374 Aldgate was leased for life to Geoffrey Chaucer. "This is one of the four principal gates," says Stow, "and also one of the seven double gates mentioned by Fitzstephen. It hath had two pair of gates, though now but one; the hooks remaineth yet. Also there hath been two port closes: and one of them remaineth: but the place of letting down is manifest." This gate was removed in 1606. At Aldgate Elizabeth, accompanied by two thousand horse, met Queen Mary in greeting at the time of her public entry to London before her coronation in 1553.

In Aldgate Street, a short distance within the wall, was a pump that long enjoyed a reputation for the sweetness of its water. It stood at the junction of Fenchurch Street near where the gibbet was sometimes erected. Close to the pump and beneath the houses separating Aldgate and Fenchurch Streets was the chapel or crypt of St. Michael, built about 1110. It has been suggested that this as well as several other houses of wor-

ship owed their subterranean location to the grad-
ual rise in level of the street surface due to re-
peated fires and rebuilding in the history of the
city.

The street beyond the gate as far as Whitechapel was called Aldgate High Street. It contained an inn, the Pye without Aldgate, in which
plays were occasionally acted, though it was not
one of the inns constantly used for that purpose.
Other inns in the same street were the Three Nuns,
the Bull, and the Saracen's Head. East of the
church of St. Botolph there were " certain fair
inns for receipt of travellers repairing to the city,
up towards Hog Lane end, somewhat within the
bars, a mark showing how far the liberties of the
city do extend.

" This Hog Lane stretcheth north toward St.
Mary Spitle without Bishopsgate, and within these
forty years had on both sides fair hedge rows of
elm trees, with bridges and easy stiles to pass over
into the pleasant fields, very commodious for citizens therein to walk, shoot, and otherwise to rec-
reate and refresh their dull spirits in the sweet
and wholesome air, which is now within a few
years made a continual building throughout, of
garden-houses and small cottages; and the fields
on either sides be turned into garden-plots, tenter
yards, bowling alleys, and such like, from Houndes

ditch in the west, as far as White Chappell, and further towards the east." (Stow.)

There was on the south side not far from the gate a conduit erected in 1535, Sir John Allen being mayor at the time. Strype's account of the difficulty met with in the use of this conduit and its reparation affords a graphic picture of one of the customary sights of the day.

" Here I may not omit to tell you, that, although this water conduit was very beneficial to the people inhabiting there round about, yet in regard to the situation, being upon the street's south side, and immediately descending down many steps or stairs of stone, it was troublesome to the poor people fetching water there, in coming up laden with their tubs, pails, and Tankards. Besides, until the turn of each party came by order and due course, their tankards, tubs, and pails, did greatly pester the passage about, and through the gate, endangering divers personal harms, and other great inconveniences which since then, at the taking down of the old gate, that a new might be builded in the same place, is exceedingly commendably amended, to the city's honour, their credit that had care for disposing of the work, and the great ease of the poor water bearers, and all passengers. For now there is a fair spacious court, wherein all the tankards and other vessels orderly stand (with-

out any annoyance to the street), and the descent
to the conduit is made very convenient, free from
offending one another in their labour, the passage
to and fro is so aptly ordered, and the room so
large for their attendance."

Northwest from Aldgate, following the line of
the wall towards Bishopsgate, was Houndsditch.

"From Aldgate, north-west to Bishopsgate,
lieth the ditch of the city called Houndsditch; for
that in old time, when the same lay open, much filth
(conveyed forth of the city), especially dead dogs,
were there laid or cast; wherefore of latter time
a mud wall was made, inclosing the ditch, to keep
out the laying of such filth as had been accustomed.
Over against this mud wall, on the other side of the
street, was a fair field, sometime belonging to the
priory of the Trinity, and since by Sir Thomas
Audley given to Magdalen college in Cambridge:
this field (as all other about the city) was inclosed,
reserving open passage thereinto for such as were
disposed. Towards the street were some small cottages, of two stories high, and little garden-plots
backward, for poor bed-rid people, for in that
street dwelt none other, built by some prior of
the Holy Trinity, to whom that ground belonged.

"In my youth, I remember, devout people, as
well as men and women of this city, were accustomed oftentimes, especially on Fridays, weekly

to walk that way purposely there to bestow their
charitable alms; every poor man or woman lying
in their bed within their window, which was towards
the street, open so low that every man might see
them, a clean linen cloth lying in their window,
and a pair of beads, to show that there lay a
bedrid body, unable but to pray only. This street
was first paved in the year 1503.

"About the latter reign of Henry VIII., three
brethren that were gunfounders, surnamed Owens,
got grounds there to build upon, and to inclose for
casting of brass ordinance. These occupied a good
part of the street on the field side, and in a short
time divers others also built there, so that the poor
bed-rid people were worn out, and, in place of their
homely cottages, such houses built as do rather
want room then rent; which houses be for the most
part possessed by brokers, sellers of old apparel,
and such like. The residue of the field was for the
most part made into a garden by a gardener
named Cawsway, one that served the markets with
herbs and roots; and in the last year of King Edward VI. the same was parcelled into gardens,
wherein are now many fair houses of pleasure built.

"On the ditch side of this street the mud wall
is also by little and little all taken down, the bank
of the ditch being raised, made level ground, and
turned into garden-plots and carpenter's yards,

and many large houses are there built; the filth
of which houses, as also the earth cast out of their
vaults, is turned into the ditch, by which means
the ditch is filled up, and both the ditch and
wall so hidden that they cannot be seen of the
passers by."

The prolongation of Aldgate High Street east
of the bars was called Whitechapel. "Also without the bars both sides of the street be pestered
with cottages and alleys, even up to Whitechapel
Church, and almost half a mile beyond it into the
open field, all which ought to be open and free to
all men. But this common field, I say, being
sometime the beauty of this city on that part, is
so encroached upon by buildings of filthy cottages,
and other purpressors, inclosures, and lay stalls,
(notwithstanding all proclamations and acts of
Parliament made to the contrary), that in some
places it scarce remaineth a sufficient highway for
the meeting of carriages and droves of cattle;
much less is there any fair, pleasant, or wholesome
way for people to walk on foot; which is no small
blemish to so famous a city to have so unsavoury
and unseemly an entrance or passage thereunto."
(Stow.)

In proceeding eastward along Cornhill and
Leadenhall we have omitted to mention Lombard
Street, which is south of and forming a sharp

angle to Cornhill. From the earliest times this street was the residence of all kinds of merchants, but especially the goldsmiths and money lenders. Price records the names of about seventy goldsmiths living in Lombard Street during the reign of Elizabeth, among whom was Gresham, the builder of the Royal Exchange.

In those days every shop had its sign, and the following, most of them goldsmiths' signs, were to be found in Lombard Street: Sun, Flower de Luce, Rose, Three Tuns, Mermaid, Plough, Blue Anchor, Black Lyon, Flying Horse, Morocco's Head, Red Cross, Spotted Dog, Feathers, Three Lions, Cup and Crown, Bible and Crown, Cock, Globe and Anchor, Hand in Glove, Oxford Arms, Royal Oak, Castle, Cradle, Hare and Crown, Golden Anchor, Phœnix, Hat and Harrow, White Swan, Queen's Head and Sun, Artichoke, Bellows and Ball, Adam and Eve, Unicorn.

At the corner of Mark Lane and Fenchurch Street, the continuation of Lombard Street, was Blanch Apleton, where lived Alderman Billingsley, the first translator of Euclid into English: "Said Blanch Apleton was granted by the king to be inclosed and shut up. This Blanch Apleton was a manor belonging to Sir Thomas Roos of Homelake, knight, the 7th of Richard II., standing at the north-east corner of Mart lane, so called of a privilege sometime enjoined to keep a mart there, long since discontinued, and therefore forgotten, so as nothing remaineth for memory but the name of Mart lane, and that corruptly termed Marke lane. I read that, in the third of Edward IV., all basket-makers, wire-drawers, and other foreigners, were permitted to have shops in this manor of Blanch Apleton, and not elsewhere, within this city or suburbs thereof." (Stow.)

CHAPTER IX

NORTH OF CHEAPSIDE

THIS chapter contains the description of a few scattered streets and places of interest that lie north of the main route just described. At the west end of Cheapside Saint Martins le Grand runs north between the buildings of the general post-office. The street takes its name from a collegiate church and sanctuary, the grounds of which are now covered by the post-office. It was founded in the eleventh century, and, though within the walls of the city, was a liberty to itself over which the corporation tried in vain to gain control. Prisoners on their way to execution from Newgate to Tower Hill often attempted to escape when they passed the end of the street, and claim sanctuary in the church. St. Martin's was one of the chief churches of the city, and its bell in mediæval times tolled the curfew which was the signal to close the city gates. At the Dissolution of the religious houses the college was demolished, and, because of its former privilege of sanctuary, a kind of Alsatia grew up upon the site, mainly inhabited by "strangers born," *i.e.*, foreigner

either in the literal sense of the word, or as those
not having the freedom of the city. Their principal vocation was the manufacture of all sorts of
counterfeit ware, the true ancestors of those who
"set in" old marks upon new pieces of silver
plate. Another article sold there, or probably its
counterfeit imitation, is alluded to in *Westward
Ho,* (1607). "You must to the Pawn (Exchange) to buy lawn; to St. Martin's for lace."
In Elizabeth's time there were many tailors among
its inhabitants. By a bond dated May 9th, 1562,
Nicholas Rowell and eight other tailors agreed
not to put more than a yard and three quarters
of kersey into any one pair of hosen, and to cut
the same so as to "lye close to the legges, and not
loose or boulstered as in auncient tyme."

At the end of the street was Aldersgate, north
of which ran the street of the same name. It was
built upon both sides with fair houses, and was the
main entrance to the city from the north-west, and
is compared by certain ancient writers to an Italian street for beauty. On the left near the gate
was the church of St. Botolph, beyond which Little
Britain led west to Smithfield. The Halfmoon
Tavern was in this street, and two doors south of
Barbican was the Bell, whence John Taylor the
Water Poet set out on his "Penniless Pilgrimage"
to Scotland. North of Barbican was Bridgewater

House, the magnificent seat of the Earl of Bridge-water, whose site is now marked by Bridgewater Square and Gardens. "Nobody" was the sign of John Trundle, one of the well known Eliza-bethan booksellers and printers, a printer chiefly of ballads.

If the restaurant in Crosby Hall affords the modern visitor to London a glance of the finest house within the walls during the reign of Eliza-beth, a visit to the Charter-House will show, much more nearly in its original condition, one of the fine old country houses of that time, for we must not forget that in passing Barbican we have left even the outskirts of the Elizabethan city behind.

The Charter-House was once a Carthusian mon-astery, destroyed like all the others at the Dissolu-tion. The ancient buildings date chiefly from the early part of the sixteenth century, though some-what modified in more recent times. The Great Hall is considered one of the finest specimens of a sixteenth century hall in London, and the main staircase is unequalled. This, with the Great Cham-ber upstairs (except the west window), is just as they were left by the Duke of Norfolk more than three centuries ago. Part of the original chapel remains, though rebuilt in 1500 and in 1612. The entrance gate is a simple work of the fifteenth cen-

tury, beneath which still hangs the ponderous leaves
placed there in happier days by the Carthusian
monks. It gives entrance to what was the outer
court of the monastery, but a glance at the surroundings is sufficient to show that this was not
the principal court. One must pass through the
entrance opposite to gain what was in monastic
days the little cloister, though all traces of the
cloister walk have long since disappeared. On
the north of this court was the great hall for the
entertainment of guests, and behind it the fratry
or refectory. On the west side were guests' apartments and a passage that led to the wash-house
court. This was the most frequent resort of the
monks, and was surrounded by what in later times
would be called the servants' quarters: bake-house,
larder, pantry, wash-house, brew-house, etc. A
corresponding passage on the east side gave
entrance to the Chapel Court, on the north side
of which was the church and chapter house, while
beyond that were the great cloister and the
gardens.

After the Dissolution the Charter-House was
used by Henry VIII. as a store-house for tents
and pavilions. It was then given to Sir Thomas
Audley, who sold it to Sir Edward North, who in
turn sold it to Dudley, Duke of Northumberland.
On his attainder in 1553 it was regranted by the

crown to Lord North, who died there 1564. It was here that Elizabeth held court for five days as she cautiously approached London at the time of her accession. In 1565 Roger, second Lord North, sold the Charter-House to Thomas Howard, Duke of Norfolk. Again the purchase turned out a bad omen, for Howard was executed for treason in 1572. Elizabeth subsequently granted it to Howard's second son, Thomas, afterwards Earl of Suffolk.

The Charter-House, which was famous in the middle ages as a great religious establishment, figured only as a private country residence throughout the whole reign of Elizabeth, becoming important in the political eye only once—during the conspiracy of Norfolk. The third period of its existence, that of a great public school, is more brilliant far than either of the others, but belongs to the history of the reign of James and his successors.

Guildhall seems so intimately connected with Cheapside that it was described in the last chapter. A building that stood near it has, however, been reserved for this place. Bakewell or Blackwell Hall stood on the west side of Bassinghall Street. "The same was built upon vaults of stone, which stone was brought from Caen in Normandy, the like of that of Paul's Church." Stow continues in his account to deny the popular belief that the building was originally a Jewish synagogue, by the argument that it is not at all like a church, "and therefore the best opinion in my judgment is that it was of old times belonging to the Bassings, which was in this realm a family of great antiquity and renown, and that it bore also the name of that family, and was called therefore Basingshaugh or hall; whereunto I am the rather induced for that the arms of that family were of old time so abundantly placed in sundry parts of that house, even in the stone work, but more especially on the walls of the hall, which carried a continual painting of them on every side, so close together as one escutcheon could be placed by another, which I myself have often seen and noted before the old building was taken down."

The old house was demolished and rebuilt in 1588. "Bakewell Hall was by the corporation converted into a ware-house or market place for all sorts of woollen cloth, and other woollen manufactures brought from all parts of the Kingdom, and by an act of Common Council, held August 8, 1576, this was to be the only market for such woollen manufactures, and none to be sold at London except at this place." (Hatton.)

Opposite French Lane in Threadneedle Street on the site afterwards occupied by the French church stood the free school of St. Anthony. The hospital was suppressed by Edward VI., "the school in some measure remaining," says Stow, "but sore decayed." The laws of the middle ages were exceedingly strict in regard to the sale of food. Stow relates a curious illustration of this fact in connection with St. Anthony's Hospital.

"And amongst other things observed in my youth, I remember that the officers charged with oversight of the markets in this city, did divers times take from the market people, pigs starved, or otherwise unwholesome for man's sustenance; these they slit in the ear. One of the proctors for St. Anthonie's tied a bell about the neck, and let it feed on the dunghills; no man would hurt or take them up, but if any gave to them bread, or other feeding, such would they know, watch for, and daily follow, whining till they had somewhat given them; whereupon was raised a proverb, 'Such an one will follow such an one, and whine as it were an Anthonie pig'; but if such a pig grew to be fat, and came to good liking (as ofttimes they did), then the proctor would take him up to the use of the hospital."

Though "sore decayed" in Stow's time, the school of St. Anthony had once been the rival of St. Paul's. "The scholars of this school used at certain times of the year to go in procession. Thus I find in the year 1562 on the 15th day of September, there set out from Mile End two hundred children of this St. Anthony's school, all well be seen, and so along through Aldgate, down Cornhill to the Stocks; and so to the Freer Austins, with streamers and flags, and drums beating. And after every child went home to their father and friends." (Strype.)

The house of the Austin Friars was in Old Broad Street. It was founded by Humphrey Bohun, Earl of Hereford and Essex in 1253. The site occupied the whole area north and west of Throgmorton Street and Old Broad Street in the parish of St. Peter Poor, and extended north to the city wall. At the Dissolution Henry VIII. bestowed the house and grounds upon William Paulet, first Marquis of Winchester. This was the famous Marquis of Winchester who was made Lord High Treasurer of England by Edward VI. and retained his office throughout the reign of Mary and Elizabeth till his death in 1571. On being asked how he kept his position through so many political changes, the wily statesman answered: " By being a willow and not an oak."

He pulled down or altered the buildings that had been given him and constructed a splendid mansion. It degenerated, however, during the occupancy of his son, who was forced to sell the monuments of noblemen for one hundred pounds. It soon afterwards passed into the hands of the drapers and became their hall.

Winchester's alterations, however, did not extend to the handsome church of St. Augustine, which was turned over for use of the Dutch refugees. It was entered through a passage from the south end, and, according to Stow, was "a large church, having a most fine, spired steeple, small, high, and straight." Stow does not record the fact, but at the time he wrote this beautiful structure was almost ready to collapse, as is proved by the following letter dated 1600:

" There hath been offered of late unto this court a most just and ernest petition by divers of the chiefest of the parish of St. Peter the Poor in London to move us to be humble suitors unto your lordship in a cause which is sufficient to speak for itself without the mediation of any other, viz, for the repairing of the ruinous steeple of the church sometimes called the Augustine Friars, now belonging to the Dutch nation, situate in the same parish of St. Peter the Poor. The fall whereof (which without speedy prevention is near at hand) must needs bring with it not only a great deformity to the whole city; it being for architecture one of the beautifullest and rarest spectacles thereof, but also a fearful eminent danger to all the inhabitants next adjoining. Your lordship being moved herein, (as we understand) a year since was pleased then to give honorable promises with hope of present help. But the effects not following according to your honorable intentions we are bold to renew the said suit again eftsoons craving at your lordship's hands a due consideration of so worthy a work as to help to build up the house of God, one of the chiefest fountains from whence has sprung so great glory to your Lordship's most noble descendency of the Paulets. Whose steps your lordship must needs follow to continue to all posterity the fame of so bountiful benefactions both to church and common wealth.

"So that I trust we shall have the less need to importune your lordship in so reasonable a suit, first because it does principally concern your Lordship, being the owner of the said spire or steeple, but especially by disbursing a small sum of money to the value of 50 or 60*l*., your lordship shall do an excellent work, very helpful to many, and most greatful to all, as well English as strangers."

A short distance west on Throgmorton Street was a house known as Cromwell's, which furnished an interesting example of the high-handed dealing of the time. Stow tells the story.

"On the south side, and at the west end of this

church, many fair houses are built; namely, in Throgmorton Street, one very large and spacious, built in the place of old and small tenements by Thomas Cromwell, master of the king's jewel-house, after that master of the rolls, then Lord Cromwell, knight, lord privy seal, vicar-general, Earl of Essex, high chamberlain of England, &c. This house being finished, and having some reasonable plot of ground left for a garden, he caused the pales of the gardens adjoining to the north part thereof on a sudden to be taken down; twenty-two feet to be measured forth right into the north of every man's garden; a line there to be drawn, a trench to be cast, a foundation laid, and a high brick wall to be built. My father had a garden there, and a house standing close to his south pale; this house they loosed from the ground, and bare upon rollers into my father's garden twenty-two feet, ere my father heard thereof; no warning was given him, nor other answer, when he spake to the surveyors of that work, but that their master Sir Thomas commanded them so to do; no man durst go to argue the matter, but each man lost his land, and my father paid his whole rent, which was 6s. 6d. the year, for that half which was left. Thus much of mine own knowledge have I thought good to note, that the sudden rising of some men causeth them to forget themselves."

Bishopsgate Street in the time of Elizabeth presented a far different appearance from that of
to-day and gave a view of magnificence unrivalled
elsewhere throughout the city. If one stood at the
south end near the corner of Threadneedle Street
by St. Martin Oateswich Church he would see a
narrowing vista of fine houses, alternating with
hostelries and cultivated gardens, and terminated
by the battlemented arch and two side wickets of
Bishopsgate. Not far in front of him, on the left
was Gresham House, the home of the builder of
the Royal Exchange. Almost directly opposite was
Crosby Hall, then in the zenith of its glory.
Beyond Crosby Hall was Ethelburga Church,
beside which a passage led to the church and dilapidated nunnery of St. Helen's. On either side
beyond were taverns as far as the gate.

Crosby Hall is the finest specimen of fifteenth
century domestic architecture left in London. It
was built at a time when the old single-court houses
were passing out of style, to be superseded by
those with two courts, the great hall forming the
division between the two quadrangles. Crosby
Hall is of this style, though it illustrates the rare
peculiarity of the courts being placed corner to
corner instead of end to end; the inner court lying
south-east of the outer court, one side of which was
near and parallel to Bishopsgate Street. The state

BISHOPSGATE STREET
(From an engraving by Wilkinson)

apartments, too, surrounded the outer court, which
was also unusual, but not unique. "This house,"
says Stow, "he (Sir John Crosby) built of stone
and timber very large and beautiful, and the highest at that time in London." In the reign of
Elizabeth Crosby Hall was still in the heydey of
its glory. It had been built by Sir John Crosby,
a grocer and woolstapler of London, in 1466, on
ground leased from the adjoining convent of St.
Helen's. About 1518 Sir Thomas More held
Crosby Place. In 1523 he sold it to his friend
Antonio Bonvivi, who later leased it to William
Roper, the husband of More's favourite daughter
Margaret. Crosby Place was seized, with Bonvivi's other property, by Henry VIII. in 1553,
but restored by Mary, shortly after her accession.

In 1560 it came into the possession of Germayne
Cioll, who with his wife resided here till May, 1566,
when the property was sold to Alderman William
Bond, a merchant adventurer. At this time and
later it was the custom to lodge ambassadors in
Crosby Hall, and the old chambers have rung to
many a state banquet in the days of Elizabeth.
Besides the Spanish and Danish ambassadors who
were lodged here, we hear of its being occupied
by the Duc de Sully in 1594, and by the Duc
de Boren in 1601. In 1594 it was bought by Sir

John Spencer, Knight, father-in-law of the first Earl of Northampton.

The present fame of Crosby Place is largely due to the fact, not that it was once the palace of the last of the Plantagenets, but because Shakespeare mentions the fact in *Richard III*. The poet was living close to Crosby Hall at the close of the six-teenth century, and was probably familiar with every detail of its history and appearance.

North of Crosby Hall was the nunnery of St. Helen's, or Black Nuns, belonging to the Benedic-tine order. Till a century ago there still existed very considerable remains of this splendid and spa-cious foundation. It consisted of a large collec-tion of buildings entered from Bishopsgate through an arch that gave upon the outer courtyard, a rec-tangle surrounded by the humbler offices of the establishment. From this there was a passage to the second or inner court, about which were grouped the more important buildings: the stewart's lodg-ing, counting-house, larder, the entrance to the hall and to the cloister. North of the cloister was a long building, the fratry, and on the east the lodging of the sub-prioress with its garden. On the east side near the lodging of the sub-prioress a door led to a small garden, beyond which were the pleasure grounds, the garden for kitchen stuff, a dove house, and a spacious wood-yard.

There were also tenements and a stable.   These buildings have been enumerated to show how great was the portion of the city, even within the walls, that was given up to the religious houses.   These buildings were bought after the Dissolution by the company of Leathersellers, and the nuns' hall made into a hall for the company.   Not till 1799 were the buildings removed, at which time they were demolished to make room for the present St. Helen's Square.   The records of St. Helen's show that in 1598 William Shakespeare was living in the parish.

Beyond Bishopsgate on the very bank of the ditch was the church of St. Botolph, one of many bearing the same name, and distinguished by the addition "without Bishopsgate."   Here was baptised in 1566 Edward Alleyn, play-actor, also founder of Dulwich College.   In 1600 an infant son of Ben Jonson was buried in St. Botolph; and in 1623 Stephen Gosson, who had published the *School of Abuse* in 1579.

By this church was a passage to Petty France, so called of the Frenchmen dwelling there.   It now goes by the name of New Broad Street.   Beyond was Bedlam, a hospital whose site is now covered by Liverpool Street and station.

"Next unto the parish church of St. Buttolph is a fair inn for receipt of travellers; then an

hospital of St. Mary of Bethelem, founded by
Simon Fitz Mary, one of the sheriffs of London, in
the year 1246: he founded it to have been a priory
of canons, with brethren and sisters. . . . It was
a hospital for distracted people. . . . The mayor
and commonalty purchased the patronage thereof,
with all the lands and tenements thereunto belonging, in the year 1546: the same year King Henry
VIII. gave this hospital unto the city; the church
and chapel whereof were taken down in the reign
of Queen Elizabeth, and houses built there by the
governors of Christ's Hospital in London. In this
place people that be distraight in wits are, by the
suit of their friends, received and kept as afore,
but not without charges to their bringers in.   In
the year 1569, Sir Thomas Roe, merchant-tailor,
mayor, caused to be inclosed with a wall of brick
about one acre of ground, being part of the said
hospital of Bethelem; to wit, on the west, on the
bank of Deep Ditch, so called, parting the said
hospital of Bethelem from the More field: this he
did for burial and ease of such parishes in London
as wanted ground convenient within their parishes."

By 1600 Bethlehem Hospital was considered one
of the sights of London. In Webster's *Westward
Ho!* while certain persons are waiting for their
horses to be saddled at the Dolphin without Bish-

opsgate, they go over "to Bedlam to see what Greeks are within." In the *Silent Woman* Bedlam is listed with the China Houses and the Exchange as among the sights of London.

For the accommodation of patients there were a parlour, kitchen, and larder below stairs and "twenty-one rooms wherein the poor distracted people lie, and above stairs eight rooms more for servants and the poor to lie in, and a long waste now being contrived and in work, to make eight more rooms for poor people to lodge where they lacked room before." The hospital was able to accommodate from fifty to sixty patients.

The treatment of mad people in the time of Elizabeth was cruel in the extreme, yet this very cruelty was a natural result of certain characteristics of the age. The Elizabethans, in fact, were at their wits' end concerning the treatment of madness. The condition perplexed them, and they did not know whether to treat it as a physical or moral malady. In general, insanity was considered to be evidence of the devil's presence in the patients. To maltreat the patient, therefore, was to maltreat the devil, the only way in which he could be successfully driven from his temporary dwelling place. Flogging, starvation, or solitary confinement of the patient, who was loaded with fetters in a pitch dark room, were some of the " cures " applied to lunatics.   A modern audience is likely to lose the point of the practical joke played upon Malvolio if they forget that the sanest man in the play is subjected to the customary treatment accorded a madman.

CHAPTER X

MILITARY COMPANIES

G ODDES instrument," as Bishop Latimore called the bow in his celebrated Sixth Sermon, was fast passing out of use as a weapon of defence: in fact, save in the eyes of an occasional enthusiast who loved the old order of things and deplored the new, archery had become a manly sport rather than a part of the art of war. Arthur's show, to which Justice Shallow refers with such naïve pride, was an exhibition held at Mile End Green near London, by one of the city shooting clubs. The society was visited and patronised by King Henry VIII., himself a skilful bowman, to whose love of the sport was due the peerage of Shoreditch. The Duke of Shoreditch, so frequently mentioned in contemporary writings, was a citizen named Barlow, who acquitted himself so well at one of these public exhibitions of archery that King Henry "was so exceedingly pleased, that he told Barlow that he should be henceforth called the Duke of Shoreditch, which appellation the Captain of the London archers enjoyed for ages after." (Maitland.) The various members of the Shore-

ditch peerage, such as the Marquises of Clerkenwell, Islington, Hoxton, etc., derived their titles
from other suburbs on the outskirts of London.

Though the practice of archery had degenerated
into a mere amusement that required encourage-
ment, there had developed as yet no regular military organisation for the defence of the city.
What little had been done in this direction consisted only in the temporary union of the "trained-
bands" in time of danger. Military education,
on the other hand, was not neglected. The youthful training of men in nearly every social rank
included the use of weapons. Even the London
'prentice boy was so skilful in the use of his staff,
which was so easily summoned into action by the
familiar rallying cry of "Clubs! Clubs!" that he
was a formidable antagonist, as every one knows
who remembers the sixteenth century riot that has
since been known as Evil May-Day.

The training of citizens in military affairs was
further provided for in a lecture founded by
Thomas Hood, to be read in the Chapel of Leadenhall. Though called a mathematical lecture, it
was largely given up to teaching the art of war
and the theory of defence. According to the practice of this school the city should appoint at least
forty captains, one of whom was to be chosen
governor, and twelve others assistants. There

were also to be 240 men specially chosen from the various wards of the city to be instructed in the duties of under-officers; and from their ranks new captains from time to time were chosen. Thus a body of nearly three hundred men was kept constantly trained as company officers. The actual organisation implied by this theoretical teaching was called into existence only when some danger threatened the city or country.

In all military affairs on land the individual company was the unit. An army was but a collection of companies temporarily under the command of a superior officer. The absolute power of a captain over his company, and the rivalry between the individual captains, often rendered an army far from effective, and accounts for the frequent desertion of small portions in the midst of a battle. The cashiering of a captain might throw his whole company, the members of which were often his, not the Queen's followers, into discontented inaction or open insurrection.

From *The Soldier's Accidence*, a work on tactics by a contemporary writer, Gervase Markham, we learn the principles upon which the trained-bands were organised. The company, which usually consisted of one hundred men, was divided equally into pikemen and men armed to shoot; of the latter, half carried muskets and half carried harquebuses.* The strongest and best men of the company were selected to carry the pikes. The pikemen wore Spanish morions, or close-fitting steel caps, lined with quilted padding to protect the head from the shock of a blow. They also wore cuirasses that were "at the least high pike proof," strong gorgets to protect the neck, and close-joined pieces for the thigh. The introduction of gunpowder had rendered the wearing of armour almost useless; and, though the Elizabethans had not yet fully realised the fact, full armour was no longer seen outside the tilting lists and public shows. Markham advises that all armour such as the members of the trained-bands wore should be russet, sanguine, or black. The pikes were made of sound ash, fifteen feet in length, exclusive of the steel head or point, and the shaft was protected with steel plates for four feet from the head. The pikemen also wore a broadsword and a girdle on which was an iron hook used to suspend the heavy morion when the soldier was not in action.

The musqueteers were similarly dressed, with slight additions. A broad leather band passed over the left shoulder and under the right arm,

---

* The harquebus was much like the musket, but lighter, and did not necessarily require a rest in taking aim. The harquebus by many was considered the more accurate.

to which were fastened by strings long enough to convey them to the mouth of the gun twelve or thirteen little cases of wood or horn, called bandileers, containing each a charge of powder. To the girdle were attached the rammer and priming iron, and bags to contain bullets, moulds, worms, screws, etc. For his right hand the musqueteer carried a rest. This was made of ash, shod with iron at one end and topped with a U-shaped prong in which the musket was rested at the moment of firing. On the march the rest was trailed upon the ground by a thong fastened to the wrist.

The harquebusers were likewise equipped, except that they carried no rest. The haldberdier was armed " at all points like the pikeman, only he shall carry a halberd, long, sharp, and well covered with plates . . . these halberds do properly belong to sergeants of companies." " The ensign, or bearer of captain's colours shall be full armed in every way, with a fair sword, and carrying the ensign." The lieutenant was armed like the ensign, and " his weapon shall be a fair, guilt partisan." Captains were likewise armed and habited; "but as much richer as they please: their weapons to lead with shall be feathersteaves: their weapons to encounter the enemy shall be partizans of strong, short blades, well gilt and adorned."

The company was divided into four corporal-

ships or squadrons, each squadron into files, and the
files into fellowships or comeradoes. The rows of
soldiers parallel to the front were called ranks; rows
at right angles were files. A corporal led the first
file, a lans-presado (or acting-corporal) another,
and "the most sufficient gentlemen" the others.
The corporal's chief duty was on guard at night
after the watch was set. He examined any one who
wished to pass, received the countersign, and made
sure that the arms of each soldier were in good
condition. He also taught the company the man-
ual and marching tactics.

The captain marched at the head of the troop,
the lieutenant in the rear, their positions, however,
being reversed in a retreat. On the march the
ensign's place was behind the captain; in action
he stood in the centre of the company surrounded
by the pikes. In square formation the drums and
fifes were placed in front of the right and left
wings; in extended formation, however, the eldest
drum marched between the third and fourth rank
of shot behind the captain, the second drum with
the ensign, and the third drum between the third
and fourth rank of shot in front of the lieutenant.
The eldest drum was considered a higher officer
than the sergeant. It was necessary for him to be,
not only a soldier, but also a linguist, for he served
in the capacity of interpreter in foreign cam-

paigns. Most of the commands now given by bugle were then sounded upon the drum.

The old firearms were clumsy and intricate, almost beyond modern comprehension. The following are the commands that indicate the necessary steps in the process of loading: Make ready—present—give fire for charging—clear your pan—prime your pan—cast off your loose corns—blow your pan—cast about your musket with both your hands and trail your rest—open your charge—charge your musket with powder—draw out your scouring stick—shorten your stick—ram in your powder—draw out your stick—charge with bullet—ram in your bullet—draw out your stick—shorten your stick and put it up—bring your musket forward with the left hand—hold it up with your right hand and recover your rest. Thirteen additional motions were necessary for firing the piece.

We are used to the fact that the front in battle is a place of greater honour and danger than any other. The Elizabethans, however, reduced the relation of honour to position to a science. Every one of the hundred men of a company was numbered. The first and second places were given to the end men of the front rank three and four were similar positions in the rear rank (next the enemy in a retreat). The front and rear ranks occupy

numbers 1-20; 21-40 are in the very middle of
the company, because on certain commands the
company opened into two parts with these ranks
exposed.   And so on for every person in the
company.

The trained-bands of London were so numerous
that they sent to a muster before the Queen at
Greenwich park 800 pikes, 400 harquebuses, 200
halberdiers, and 28 " whifflers."   In 1588, the year
of the Armada, the city furnished 10,017 men to
send to the camp at Tilbury. ₁

The favourite practice grounds of the trained-
bands were Finsbury and Moorfields, places north
of London that were also the haunt of motley
amusements of all kinds.   They were the place of
gamesters and fraudulent tricks.   They were the
great gymnasium of the capital, the resort of
wrestlers, boxers, runners, foot-ball players, etc.
" Here, too, I lament to say," writes Pennant,
" that religion set up its stage itinerant, beneath
the shade of the trees; and here the pious, well-
meaning Whitfield, long preached so successfully
as to steal from a neighbouring charlatan the
greater part of his numerous admirers."

West of Moorfields was another famous prac-
tice field, namely the Artillery Ground, where the
Honourable Artillery Company of the City of
London held its meets. This organization was dis-

tinct from the city trained-bands, with which it is
often confused.

Along with all this military business went a
good deal of parade and sentiment.   Though the
practice of heraldry had already begun to decay
into a mere sickly parade of vanity, strict heraldric
rules governed the choice of a captain's flag.   It
could consist of one colour mixed with a metal, and
a mistake in the choice of colours was considered a
great breach of honour.   Thus yellow or white
might be combined with blue, red, green, purple,
tawny, or ermine; but yellow and white could not
be combined, nor red and green.   A gentleman
captain chose his colours from his coat of arms;
but if he had none he chose to suit himself.   Each
colour had its special significance.   Yellow was
emblematical of honour, white of innocence, and
black of wisdom.   Scott made a poor choice of
colour for Marmion, inasmuch as blue represented
faith.   Red was the colour of justice; green, of
hope; purple, of fortitude; tawny, of merit; and
ermine of holiness.

CHAPTER XI

HOLBORN AND SMITHFIELD

A GLANCE at the interesting plan of London
drawn by Aggas about 1560 reveals the fact
that the region described in this chapter was then
in a transition state; it was neither city nor country. One could walk along Snow Hill and Holborn from Newgate to Gray's Inn Road and find
oneself between houses most of the way. Yet
an occasional peep would show that in many places
the houses were but one deep, a mere straggling
line that bordered the thoroughfare. To the north,
however, in the immediate vicinity of Smithfield,
a populous and thriving suburb had sprung into
existence.

Immediately without Newgate were two turn-
ings: that to the north was Giltspur Street (sometimes called Knightrider Street, but not to be confused with another of the same name north of
Thames Street), and led to Pye Corner, which was
on the south side of the open space known as West
Smithfield, or merely Smithfield.

Smithfield was famous in five directions: (1) as a
great horse and cattle market; (2) for the annual
fair of St. Bartholomew; (3) for its tilts and tour-

naments, a usage falling into decay during the
reign of Elizabeth; (4) as place for duels; (5) as
a place for executions. The Smithfield burnings
are proverbially associated with the Marian perse-
cutions, but as late as 1611 a person was burned
to death in Smithfield. The scene of these horrors
was opposite the main gate of entry to St. Bartholomew's priory.

Smithfield was an open space of some five or six
acres in extent, approached, as has been said, by
Giltspur Street. In the sixteenth century the
neighbourhood was held in bad repute. "And if
some *Smithfield Ruffian* take up some strange
going; some new mowing with the mouth; some
wrenching with the shoulder; some brave proverb;
some fresh new oath that is not stale but will run
round in the mouth; some new disguised garment,
or desperate hat, fond in fashion, or garish in colour,
whatsoever it cost, how small soever his living be,
by what shift soever it be gotten, gotten it must
be, and used with the first, or else the grace of it
is stale and gone." (Ascham, 1570.) Smithfield
preserved this reputation till 1615, when it was
subject to thorough improvement.

"And this Summer, 1615, the City of London
reduced the rude vast place of Smithfield into a
fair and comely order, which formerly was never
held possible to be done, and paved it all over, and

made divers sewers to convey the water from the
new channels which were made by reason of the
new pavement; they also made strong rails round
about Smithfield and sequestered the middle part
of the said Smithfield into a very fair and civil
walk, and railed it round about with strong rails
to defend the place from annoyance and danger,
as well from carts as all manner of cattle, because
it was intended hereafter, that in time it might
prove a fair and peaceable Market Place, by reason
that Newgate Market, Cheapside, Leadenhall and
Gracechurch Street were immeasurably pestered
with the unimaginable increase and multiplicity of
market folk. And this field, commonly called West
Smithfield, was for many years called 'Ruffians'
Hall' by reason it was the usual place of frays
and common fighting during the time that sword
and bucklers were in use. But the ensuing deadly
fight of Rapier and Dagger suddenly suppressed
the fighting with Sword and Buckler." (Howes,
1631.)

"You may have a fair prospect of this square
fellow, as you pass from the streights of Pie-
corner. This place is well stored with good harbours for passengers to put into: for flesh and
drink and fish it is admirable; but fish harbour
appears now but two days in seven above water.
Here, thrice in a week one may see more beasts than

men. Butchers that have money make this their
haven or rendezvous; men that are down fled, and
better fed than taught, may see many like themselves, brought here for the slaughter. Butchers
surely cannot endure cuckolds, because they kill as
many horned beasts; some, I suppose may be said
to buy themselves, such as traffic for calves. Though
the place be square, yet there is much cheating in
it; here land-pirates used to sell that which is none
of their own; here come many horsemen, like
Frenchmen, rotten in the joints; which are made
to leap, though they can scarce go. He that
lights upon a horse in this place, from an old horse
courser, sound both in wind and limb, may light of
an honest wife in the stews. Here's many an old
jade that trots hard for't, that uses his legs sore
against his will; for he had rather have a stable,
than a market or a race. I am persuaded that this
place was paved without the consent of the horse-
coursers company. This place affords those black
leather coats which run so fast upon wheels, they
shake many a young heir out of his stock and
means." (Lupton, 1632.)

Beginning at Pye Corner and making the circuit
of Smithfield towards the east, one passes the Hospital of St. Bartholomew, next to which stood the
church and priory of the same name. Between
these two institutions was Duck Lane, that ran

south-east towards Little Britain, by which passage one could reach Aldersgate Street. Opening out of the east side of Smithfield, and bordering St. Bartholomew the Great on the north, was Long Lane, which also led east to Aldersgate Street. The passage out of the north side continuous with Giltspur Street was closed by Smithfield Bars, which marked the limit of the city in that direction. In the north-west corner were the sheep-pens; and from the west side, opposite Long Lane, Cow Lane ran down to Holborn. Cow Lane was then the abode of booksellers and coachmakers as well as of " cunning men," a term applied by Ben Jonson in *Bartholomew Fair* to astrologers and their like. Hosier Lane and Cock Lane also turned out of the west side of Smithfield, the latter from a point very near Pye Corner.

Whatever call one makes upon his memory he finds that most recollections of the place turn upon Bartholomew: Saint, Priory, Hospital, or Fair. There was one Rahere who played the part of jester or court fool in the palace of King Henry I. As he grew older he became repentant for having lived a life of folly, and set out upon a pilgrimage to Rome for the benefit of his moral health. It was on his return that he fell asleep and dreamed of himself standing at the edge of a bottomless pit with no aid to prevent his destruction, when suddenly there appeared to him the form of Saint Bartholomew, who commanded him to build a priory and hospital at Smithfield near London. It was to fulfil the dictates of this vision that he obtained permission of the King, to whom the ground belonged, and set about the task of building a hospital in 1123. The priory, which was finished about the same time, he dedicated to the order of St. Augustine, and himself became first prior.

The hospital was the earliest institution of the kind in London, and, though subject in some things to the priory, had an independent constitution and estate. From the very beginning it was a hospital for the sick, not merely an almshouse, as were so many of the so-called hospitals.

The priory was suppressed in 1537, and the hospital refounded in 1544 at the petition of Sir Richard Gresham and others. The superintendence of the hospital was committed to Thomas Vicary, Sergeant, Surgeon to Henry VIII., Edward VI., Mary, and Elizabeth; he was also the author of *The Englishman's Treasure*, the first book on anatomy published in the English language. The nearest date that can be assigned for the origin of a medical school at this hospital is that it was previous to 1662, when we learn that students were in the habit of attending the medical and surgical practice.

East of the hospital across Duck Lane was the priory, the bounds of which can easily be traced on a modern map by the following description: The west wall began at the south-west corner of Long Lane and followed the boundary of Smith-field and Duck Lane to the South or Great Gate House, where is now the entrance of Bartholomew Close (so-called, says Stow, because closed at night). The southern wall ran east nearly half way to Aldersgate Street, then south for forty yards, and then east. The east wall was parallel to Aldersgate Street, and twenty-six yards west of it. The north wall followed the south side of Long Lane.

Within this wall was a magnificent church and chapel, cloisters, prior's lodgings, and all the other buildings connected with a mediæval establishment of this kind on a large scale. It was also famous for its mulberry garden. Though time has dealt harshly with Rahere's foundation, one splendid fragment still remains. The choir and transepts (the old nave occupied the site of the present graveyard) of the priory church are in use to-day as a parish church, and, though altered and re-stored, constitute the finest Norman remains in London, if not in England. Opposite the founder's tomb is the monument of Sir Walter Mildmay, Chancellor and Sub-Treasurer of the Exchequer in the reign of Elizabeth, and founder of Emmanuel College, Cambridge.

If our recollections of this neighbourhood cling about the name of Bartholomew, still more are they associated with the fair. No one needs a more accurate or complete guide, or is a more graphic picture of this institution extant, than that contained in Ben Jonson's comedy of *Bartholomew Fair*, upon which the present writer has depended chiefly for his illustrations.

Fairs were of common occurrence in olden times. Every village had its fair, and one at East Smithfield and another in Southwark vied in importance to Londoners with that held at West Smithfield. It derived its name from the fact that it originally began on the eve of St. Bartholomew's day and lasted three days, a period subsequently extended to a fortnight. For centuries it was the chief cloth-fair of England, but by the time of Elizabeth its character had altogether changed. It was no longer a fair in the old sense of the word, but a place of revelry and dissipation. Monsters were exhibited, all sorts of jugglers, mountebanks, and puppet-show men had their booths there. Every sort of article was found for sale. It was particularly famous for its roast pig and pickpockets. The fair was opened by the Lord Mayor at the entrance to Cloth Fair with the following proclamation:

"Oyez! Oyez! Oyez! All manner of persons may take notice that in the Close of St. Bartholomew the Great, and West Smithfield, London, and the lands and places adjoining, is now to be held a fair for this day and the two days following, to which all persons may freely resort to buy and sell, according to the liberties and privileges of the said fair, and may depart without disturbance, paying their duties. And all persons are strictly charged and commanded, in his Majesty's name, to keep the peace, and do nothing in disturbance of the said fair, as they will answer the contrary at their perils; and that there be no manner of arrest or arrests, but by such officers as are appointed. And if any persons be aggrieved, let them repair to the court of Pie-Powder, where they may have speedy relief, according to justice and equity. God save the King! and the lord of the manor."

The court of Pie-Powder was within the district of the fair, and was characterised by the speedy quality of its justice. Prisoners were summoned before it, tried, condemned, and punished in the stocks or at the whipping post within a couple of hours.

"It is worthy of observation," says Paul Hentzner in 1598, "that every year upon St. Bartholomew's Day, when the Fair is held, it is usual for the Mayor (attended by the twelve principal Aldermen) to walk in a neighbouring field, dressed in his scarlet gown. . . . When the Mayor goes out of the precincts of the City, a sceptre [mace], a sword, and a cap are borne before him, and he is followed by the principal Aldermen in scarlet gowns, with gold chains, himself and they on horseback. Upon his arrival at the place appointed for that purpose, where a tent is pitched, the mob begin to wrestle before him, two at a time; the conquerors receive rewards from the magistrates. After this is over, a parcel of live rabbits are turned loose among the crowd, who are pursued by a number of boys, who endeavour to catch them with all the noise they can make. While we are at the show, one of our company, Tobias Salander, Doctor of Physic, had his pocket pickéd of his purse, with nine crowns *du soleil*, which, without doubt was cleverly taken from him by the Englishman who always kept very close to him that the doctor did not in the least perceive it."

Plays of all sorts were acted at the fair. " O the motions that I, Lanthorn Leatherhead, have given light to in my time! Jerusalem was a stately thing, and so was Nineveh, and the City of Norwich, and Sodom and Gomorrah, with the Rising of the 'Prentices, and the pulling down the

bawdy-houses there upon Shrove Tuesday; but the
Gunpowder Plot, there was a get-penny! I have
presented that to an eighteen or twenty pence
audience nine times in an afternoon. For home
born projects prove ever the best, they are so
easy and familiar; they put too much learning in
their things now o'days." (Jonson: *Bartholomew
Fair.*)

"I have been at the Eagle and the Black Wolf,
and the bull with the five legs, and the dogs that
dance the Morris, and the Hare and the Taber."
(*Ibid.*)

"Each person having a booth paid so much per
foot during the first three days. The Earl of Warwick and Holland is concerned in the toll gathered
the first three days in the Fair, being a penny for
every burden of goods brought in or carried out;
and to that end there are persons that stand at all
the entrances into the Fair; and they are of late
years grown so nimble, that these Blades will extort
a penny if one hath but a little bundle under one
arm, and nothing related to the Fair." (Strype.)

"Sir, it stands me in six and twenty shillings,
besides three shillings for my ground." (Jonson:
Bartholomew Fair.)

The cloister was a very important situation during fair time. Both sides were taken up with the
shops of milliners and sempstresses who, while the

fair was in progress, turned them into raffling shops and houses of ill resort. " This is not an ark like Noah's, which received the clean and the unclean; only the unclean beasts enter this ark, and such as have the devil's livery on their backs." (*The Obesrver*, August 21, 1703.)

" Smithfield is another sort of place now to what it was in the time of honest Ben, who, were he to rise out of his grave, would hardly believe it to be the same numerical spot of ground where Justice Overdo made so busy a figure; where the crop-eared Parson demolished a ginger bread stall; where Nightingale of harmonious memory sung ballads; and fat Ursula sold Pig and Bottled Ale." (*Tom Brown.*)

Imagine the letter Y, with Holborn for the stem, lying east and west; the northeastern branch would be Cow Lane leading to Smithfield; the southeastern branch would be Snow Hill, a confined, circuitous, narrow, and steep road leading to Newgate. Where these three streets intersected was Holborn Conduit.

On the north side of Snow Hill stood the church of St. Sepulchre, where Ascham is buried. There was an interesting custom connected with St. Sepulchre's which should be related. Robert Dow, a merchant-tailor who died in 1612, bequeathed a large sum of money to provide for the tolling of

the bell when condemned prisoners were led out of
Newgate on the way to execution. His legacy also
provided for two admonitions to be read as follows: the first to the prisoner in Newgate the
night before his execution, the second to be read
as he was passing the church on the way to the
gallows.

"You prisoners that are within,
        Who, for wickedness and sin,
after many mercies shown you, are now appointed
to die to-morrow in the forenoon; give ear and
understand, to-morrow morning the great bell of
St. Sepulchre's shall toll for you, in form and manner of a passing bell, as used to be tolled for those
at point of death; to the end that all godly people,
hearing that bell, and knowing it is for your going
to your deaths, may be stirred up heartily to pray
to God to bestow his grace and mercy upon you
whilst you live. I beseech you for Jesus Christ's
sake, to keep this night in watching and prayer,
to the salvation of your own souls, while there is
yet time and place for mercy as knowing to-
morrow you must appear before the judgment
seat of your Creator, there to give an account of
all things done in this life, and to suffer eternal
torments for your sins committed against him,
unless upon your hearty and unfeigned repentance,
you find mercy, through the merits, death and

passion of your only mediator and advocate, JESUS CHRIST who now sits at the right hand of God, to make intercession for as many of you as penitently return to him."

The following was read by the bellman as the prisoner was passing under the wall of the church:

"All good people pray heartily unto God for these poor sinners who are now going to their death for whom the great bell doth toll.

"You that are condemned to die, repent with lamentable tears; ask mercy of the Lord for the salvation of your own souls, through the merits, death, and passion of JESUS CHRIST, who now sits at the right hand of God, to make intercession for as many of you as penitently return unto him.

"Lord have mercy upon you.
"Christ have mercy upon you.
"Lord have mercy upon you.
"Christ have mercy upon you."

Next to St. Sepulchre's was the Saracen's Head, a celebrated tavern on the north side of Snow Hill. It was removed in the construction of Holborn viaduct. The Saracen's Head was next the church and not on the site of the present tavern bearing the same name. From the records of the preparations for the reception of Charles V. in 1522 we learn that the tavern had thirty beds and stabling for forty horses. Two other inns in the list have equal stable room, but none so many beds.

"Do not undervalue an enemy by whom you have been worsted. When our countrymen came home from fighting with the Saracens, and were beaten by them, they pictured them with huge, big, terrible faces (as you still see the sign of the Saracen's Head is) when in truth they were like other men. But this they did to save their own credit." (Seldon's *Table Talk*.)

Though written long after the Elizabethan age, the following description by Dickens portrays the place previous to its destruction and the sweeping changes in the neighbouring streets. With the substitution of costermongers for cabriolets and omnibuses, and tap for coffee-room, one can easily imagine the ancient surroundings.

"Near to the jail, and by consequence near to Smithfield . . . . and on that particular part of Snow Hill where omnibus-horses going eastward seriously think of falling down on purpose, and where horses in hackney cabriolets going westward not infrequently fall by accident, is the coach yard of the Saracen's Head Inn; its portals guarded by two Saracen's heads and shoulders . . . frowning upon you from each side of the gateway. The inn itself, garnished with another Saracen's Head, frowns upon you from the top of

the yard. . . . When you walk up this yard
you will see the booking office in the left, and the
tower of St. Sepulchre's Church darting abruptly
up into the sky on your right, and a gallery of
bedrooms upon both sides. Just before you will
observe a long window with the words, ' Coffee
Room' legibly painted above it." (*Nicholas
Nickleby.*)

At the point of intersection of the three branches
of the Y stood, as has been said, the conduit, and,
some three hundred and fifty feet west of this
point Holborn Bridge spanned the Fleet River,
here scarcely more than a tiny brook. A little
further west one would pass St. Andrew's Church
at the corner of Shoe Lane, next to which was
Thavie's Inn, while opposite on the north side stood
Ely House, belonging to the Bishops of Ely. This
brings us almost to the open country in Queen
Elizabeth's time. There was Christopher Hatton's
house on the north side, the Bell Tavern, where tradition says Shakespeare acted in his own plays, and
its next-door neighbour, the Black Bull, which is
still standing. Brook Street marks the site of
Brook House, the mansion of Fulke Grevile, and
Holborn Bars crossed the street where stood, then
as now, the fine old mansion of Staple Inn.

Beyond Holborn Bars all was open country. One
passed north across the fields to Clerkenwell and

the Priory of St. John; and west through equally pastoral scenes to the country church of St. Giles in the Fields; while to the south all was open as far as the Strand, where a new line of houses was just beginning to rise upon its northern side.

CHAPTER XII

THE STRAND

IN very ancient times the only land passage from London to Westminster was by way of Holborn; but little by little the marshes about Thorny Island, as the site of Westminster was called, were reclaimed, and the Strand sprang into existence. Though poorly paved in the middle of the sixteenth century, and in reality nothing but a back-door thoroughfare, it was the principal land connection between London and the court.

From Ludgate to Temple Bar the continuation of this street bore the name of Fleet, which was due to the river of the same name that crossed the thoroughfare at right angles. All of Fleet Street, though without the wall, was within the city liberties, which extended as far west as Temple Bar. The street in the time of Queen Elizabeth was as famous as any other neighbourhood for its numerous taverns, and it boasted a number of printers and booksellers, but its reputation *par excellence* was due to its travelling showmen, mountebanks, puppet-shows and " motions." It was all the year round a vivid reflection of the St. Bartholomew neighbourhood in fair time.

Concerning the bridge and river of Fleet Stow says: "Fleete bridge in the west without Ludgate, a bridge of stone, fair coped on either side with iron pikes; on the which, towards the south, be also certain lanthorns of stone, for lights to be placed in the winter evenings, for commodity of travellers.   Under this bridge runneth a water, sometimes called, as I have said, the river of the Wels, since Turnemill brooke, now Fleet dike, because it runneth by the Fleete, and sometime about the Fleete, so under the Fleete bridge into the river of Thames.   This bridge hath been far greater in times past, but lessened, as the water course hath been narrowed.   It seemeth this last bridge to be made or repaired at the charges of John Wels, mayor, in the year 1431, for on the coping is engraven Wels embraced by angels, like as on the standard in Cheape, which he also built.   Thus much of the bridge: for of the water course, and decay thereof, I have spoken in another place."

Elsewhere in the present volume we have pointed out the numerous conduits from which was drawn most of the city supply of water.   One of the most notable of these conduits stood in Fleet Street.

"The inhabitants of Fleet street," says Stow, "in the year 1478, obtained licence of the mayor,

aldermen, and commonalty, to make at their own
charges two cisterns, the one to be set at the said
standard, the other at Fleet bridge, for the receipt
of the waste water; this cistern at the standard
they built, and on the same fair tower of stone,
garnished with images of St. Christopher on the
top, and angels round about lower down, with
sweet sounding bells before them, whereupon, by
an engine placed in the tower, they divers hours of
the day and night chimed such an hymn as was
appointed."

Among the Fleet Street taverns we find The
King's Head, The Horn, The Mitre and, most
famous of all, The Devil. The latter tavern stood
on the site of No. 2, and had for its sign a picture
of St. Dunstan pinching the devil by the nose.
The great room was called the Apollo, and here
met the Apollo Club, presided over by Ben Jonson.
The rules of the club, written in verse by the master of the Tribe of Ben, were prominently placed
above the great sculptured fire-place. None but
guests were to be admitted; dunces were to stay at
home; learned men should be invited; no offence
allowed to guests; no discussion of serious subjects; no itinerant fiddlers were allowed in the
sacred precincts; jests must be void of personal re-
flections; poets could not recite insipid verses; and
the transactions of the club must be kept a secret.

In spite of the last prohibition we know enough to wish that we could go back in time and witness the celebrated combats of wit that used to take place in the room guarded by the bust of Apollo over the door, where the author of *Sejanus* wielded the mallet and ruled the roost as king.

On the east side of the Fleet River stood the Fleet Prison. It was originally regarded as especially the prison for persons committed by the Star Chamber Court, though it was also used for persons committed by the Court of Chancery.

" The damned in hell never cease repining at the justice of God, nor the prisoners in the fleet at the Decrees of Chauncery." (The Lord Keeper to the Duke, Dec. 16, 1621. *Cabala*, p. 65.) Star Chamber prisoners were conducted to the Fleet by water through a gate similar to the Traitors' Gate in the Tower. The old method of punishing drunkards was by the stocks, from which, if they escaped, they were set for shame and scorn in a tub at the gate of the Fleet. The chief officer was called the warden, and certain limits in the neighbourhood where occasional prisoners were allowed to lodge outside the prison walls were under his jurisdiction.

Lord Surrey, the poet, who was confined in the Fleet, dubbed it a noisome place with a pestilent atmosphere. Bishop Hooper, the martyr, was con-

fined here and treated most outrageously. Keys
was here confined for marrying the sister of Lady
Jane Grey, as was Sir Anthony Shirley, the great
traveller, for having accepted the order of St.
Michael and St. George from Henry IV. of France,
without first having asked the permission of Elizabeth. " I will not," she said, " have my Sheep
marked with a strange brand, nor suffer them to
follow the pipe of a strange shepherd." Nash, the
poet, William Herbert, Earl of Pembroke, and Dr.
Donne were also imprisoned in the Fleet; one for
writing the *Isle of Dogs*, the second because he was
the seducer of one of Elizabeth's maids of honour,
and the last for marrying his wife without her
father's consent. The famous Fleet marriages are
of later date, the earliest on record being in 1613.

If one turns out of the south side of Fleet Street
along the present Whitefriars and Carmelite
Streets he traverses a region perfectly familiar to
every reader who has delighted in the romances of
the Wizard of the North. For here, with the
Thames on the south, Bridewell on the east, and the
Temple on the west, lay that famous den of iniquity
that sheltered Nigel in the time of his adversity.
Alsatia, says Strype, " was formerly, since its
building in houses, inhabited by gentry; but some
of the inhabitants taking it upon them to protect
persons from arrest, upon a pretended privilege

belonging to the place, the gentry left it, and it became a sanctuary unto the inhabitants, which they kept up by force against law and justice; so that it was sufficiently crowded with such disabled and loose kind of lodgers. But, however, upon a great concern of debt, the sheriff with the *posse comitatus* forced his way in to make a search; and yet to little purpose; for the time of the sheriff's coming not being concealed, and they having notice thereof, took flight, either to the Mint in Southwark, or some other private place, until the hurly-burly was over."

Hardly more need be said concerning the practices of Alsatia which are so familiar from the accurate description in Scott's *Fortunes of Nigel.* Another trustworthy delineation of the same place at a somewhat later date is to be found in Shadwell's *Squire of Alsatia.*

Of Temple Bar, which stood in the immediate vicinity, it is sufficient to say that the structure so familiar to every one through pictures illustrative of eighteenth century London was built subsequent to the Elizabethan Era. It doubtless consisted at first of a mere chain and posts such as Holborn Bars, Smithfield Bars, etc., that marked the city liberties. There was, however, some sort of a structure on this site that was worthy the name of a gate, as early as 1532.

The Strand
(From the drawing by Wyngaerde)

The Strand, as has been said, was little better
than a mud road in the middle of the sixteenth
century. It was bordered on the south side by a
line of splendid palaces, but their fronts were all
towards the river. The stable-yards and back
walls only abutted on the Strand. During the
reign of Elizabeth, however, the appearance of this
thoroughfare changed considerably. Most of it
was paved, a continuous line of buildings, some of
a very substantial character, was erected on the
north side, and it came into more general use as
a passage to Westminster. There were three
bridges over the Strand: Strand Bridge, between
Surrey Street and Somerset Place; Ivy Bridge,
between Salisbury Street and the Adelphi; and a
third bridge opposite the end of Essex Street.
Though greatly improved, the Strand remained
for many years in a very poor condition as to paving, as is shown by the following quotation:

" The 18th December [1656], J. Naylor suffered part: and after having stood full two hours
with his head in the pillory, was stripped and
whipped at a cart's tail, from Palace Yard to the
Old Exchange, and received three hundred and ten
stripes; and the executioner would have given him
one more (as he confessed to the sheriff) there being three hundred and eleven kennels, but his foot
slipping, the stroke fell upon his own hand which

hurt him much." (Sewel's *History of the Quakers.*) According to this account, there were at that time 311 open gullies crossing the road between Westminster and the Royal Exchange.

The first of that splendid line of palaces along the river, which was the pride of London and astonished foreigners, was Exeter House. It belonged to the see of Exeter in old times. It fell next into the hands of Lord William Paget, during whose occupancy it was known as Paget House. Its most famous occupant during the reign of Elizabeth was her favourite, the unscrupulous Robert Dudley. While he lived there many illustrious personages trod its halls. It was there, doubtless, that he directed the movements of his wicked minions, one of whom Sir Walter Scott has pictured so graphically in the character of Varney. Leicester House, as it was called during the ownership of Dudley, next became the property of Robert Devereux, Earl of Essex, and was rechristened Essex House. The site is marked by the present Essex Street.

> " Near to the Temple stands a stately place,
>   Where I gayned giftes and the goodly grace
>   Of that great lord who there was wont to dwell,
>   Whose want too well now feels my friendless case;
>   But, ah! here fits not well
>   Old woes,"

wrote Spencer of Essex House. From there the young favourite set out for that "commonwealth of woe," as Raleigh called Ireland, &.a expedition commemorated forever in the Prologue to *Henry V*. To Essex House he returned in an ill-starred moment of rash boldness, to defy the Queen's command.

The story of Essex's rebellion is too familiar to need repetition. Suffice it to say that it was conducted from Essex House; there he imprisoned the officers charged with investigation; thence he issued with his followers towards the city; and, when the gates of the city closed behind him, it was to Essex House he returned, a hunted fugitive, by boat upon the river. There he was besieged like a rat in a hole till surrender sent him to his trial and a well-merited execution.

Next on the west stood the old house of the Bishop of Bath, better known as Arundel House. It was rebuilt by Thomas Seymour, Lord High Admiral, and called Seymour House. Then it passed into the hands of the Earl of Arundel, Henry Fitzalan, who died in 1579, who was succeeded by his grandson, Philip Howard, Earl of Arundel, son of the Duke of Norfolk. Philip was attainted and died abroad in 1595. In 1603 it was granted to Charles, Earl of Nottingham, but again returned to the person of Thomas, son of Philip, who four years later was restored to the Earldom of Arundel. The names of some of its various owners are preserved in the streets that now mark its site: Arundel, Norfolk, Surrey, and Howard.

The Duc de Sully, who was lodged here, speaks of it as fine and commodious, but pictures of the building show it to be low and mean in comparison with its palatial neighbours; but the river view was unrivalled and its gardens were of considerable extent. Every one knows the story of Essex's ring, which, if tradition is to believed, might have saved his life. The hand of death fell upon the Countess of Nottingham while she lived in Arundel House, and so awakened her conscience that she sent for the Queen to confess her own part in suppressing the claim of the favourite's ring. Elizabeth never recovered the blow of Devereux's treachery nor could she bear to hear the subject mentioned without great agitation. The presence of death, till it appeared to herself, had no terrors for Elizabeth. At the news about the undelivered ring she caught the dying countess by the shoulder and fairly shook the life out of her, crying, "God may forgive you, but I never can."

The palace that stood between Arundel House on the east and the Savoy on the west was begun on a scale that was intended to make it the finest structure of the kind in London. It stood on the

Somerset House

(From an engraving by Wilkinson after the original at Dulwich College)

site of the present Somerset House, and was built by Protector Somerset, brother of Jane Seymour, and maternal uncle of Edward VI. Two inns belonging to the sees of Worcester and Litchfield were destroyed to make room for it. So was the priory church of St. John's, Clerkenwell, to furnish building stone. Not satisfied with this, Somerset carried his vandalism still further, in the search for ready-made building stone, and removed the great cloister in the north churchyard of St. Paul's about which was painted the Dance of Death. The Protector was beheaded in 1552, and the building, though nearly completed, was stopped. Just how much was completed at the time it reverted to the crown is not known. During a part of Mary's reign it was appropriated to the use of Elizabeth, who in 1596 granted it to her cousin, Lord Hunsdon, for life.

The site of the Savoy, which stood on the south side of the Strand, is sufficiently marked by the chapel which still remains, situated on the west side of Savoy Street. Even in Elizabethan times the glory of the Savoy was mainly traditional. The earliest record of it is in 1246, when the site was granted by Henry III. to his uncle, Peter of Savoy.

The limits of the original grant were the Strand, the river, Strand Lane (where is now the approach

to Waterloo Bridge) ; and on the west the house of
the Bishop of Carlisle, whose site is now covered by
the Beaufort Buildings. Peter of Savoy built,
presumably, a castle which he left to the friars of
Mountjoy in 1268, who in turn sold it to Queen
Eleanor in 1270. In 1284 Queen Eleanor granted
it to her son Edmund of Lancaster, who walled it
about in 1293. It was he who brought home the
first red roses to England from Provence, eventually to become the badge of his house through long
and bloody civil wars. In 1386 the old Savoy was
destroyed, and it remained mostly in ruins till
opened as a hospital by Henry VII. in 1517.

The new buildings, of which only the chapel now
remains, were on a very magnificent scale, and were
long considered one of the sights of London. On
the Dissolution it was surrendered to the King, and
all the movable furniture, except that belonging
to the chapel, went to enrich the new house of correction at Bridewell.

The Savoy hospital was re-established, but on a
smaller scale, by Queen Mary, and only escaped a
second dissolution at the accession of Elizabeth
because of its insignificance. It continued to jog
along with indifferent fortunes throughout the
Queen's reign. In 1560 Fleetwood, Recorder of
London, in a letter to Lord Burleigh, describes it as
" the chief nursery of all these evil people." It

was considered to possess the right of sanctuary,
and was long a disreputable harbourage for debtors
and disorderly persons, similar to Alsatia.

Opposite the Savoy, on the north side of the
Strand, was Burleigh House. Here lived the greatest Englishman of the age. To him is due the
expansion and prosperity of England in the sixteenth century; Elizabeth trusted him alone of all
her councillors, and though sometimes a quarrel
seemed imminent between them, she always realised
before it was too late that the whole strength and
safety of her ship of state depended upon the
great man whom she had put at the helm.

" The house of the Right Honourable Lord Burleigh," says Norden, " Lord Treasurer of England
and by him erected, standing on the north side of
the Strand, a very fair house, raised with bricks,
proportionably adorned with four turrets placed
at the four quarters of the house; within, it is
curiously beautified with rare devices, and especially the oratory, placed in an angle of the great
chamber. Unto this is annexed on the east a proper
house of the Honourable Sir Robert Cecil, Knight,
and of Her Majesty's most honourable Privy
Council." (The site of Burleigh and Cecil House
is marked by Burleigh Street. William Cecil's
son built a house on the south side of the Strand,
which he called Cecil House. Its site is marked by

Cecil Street. Thomas Cecil, Earl of Exeter, later occupied Burleigh House on the north side of the Strand. He re-named it Exeter House, which should not be confused with the same name formerly applied to Leicester or Essex House.)

The site of Durham House is now occupied by the Adelphi as far as Coutts's Bank. Just how or when the first house of the name on this site was built is not known, though the following reference in Stow is not to the original building. "Durham House, built by Thomas Hatfield, Bishop of Durham, who was made bishop of that see in 1345 and sat Bishop there thirty-six years." In the reign of Henry VIII. Durham House was part of a forced exchange in which Cuthbert Tunstall, then Bishop of Durham, was forced to accept in its place Cold Harbour and other houses in London. Henry seems to have granted it to the Earl of Wiltshire; in 1550 M. de Castillon, the French Ambassador, was lodged there; in the 2d of Edward VI. it was granted to the Lady Elizabeth (afterwards the Queen) for life. Elizabeth, however, never occupied Durham House. After the execution of Somerset the all-powerful Dudley, Duke of Northumberland, took it for himself and gave the princess Somerset House. It then became Dudley's principal residence. He was living here at the death of Edward, and it was the scene of the ill-starred marriages of his children. Mary at her accession restored it to Bishop Tunstall.

From the accession of Elizabeth to 1563 it was occupied by DeFeria, the Spanish ambassador, and was the centre of much Catholic and Spanish intrigue against the throne. From time to time after the expulsion of DeFeria it was lent for varying periods of time. Ambrose Cave was there in 1565; Sir Henry Sidney was there in 1567; Essex was living there when he set out for Ireland in 1573; and in 1583 it came into the possession of Sir Walter Raleigh, who held it till his fall.

Mr. Hume* thus describes the place at the beginning of Elizabeth's reign:

" With the evidence now before us we can form an approximate idea of the appearance of Durham Place at the time. The Strand was a rough, unpaved road, with a fringe of shops and taverns on the northern side, whilst on the south side were the back walls and outer courts of the riverine mansions. The principal land gateway of Durham Place stood exactly opposite the spot now occupied by the Adelphi Theatre. The English custodian, or porter, who was in the pay of the Queen, had his dwelling just inside the gate, where he could spy those who went in and out on the land side. On

* See the paper, *A Palace in the Strand,* in *The Year After the Armada,* by Martin A. S. Hume.

each side of the gate in the outer courtyard were stables and outhouses, and in and around the gateway in the street were benches where idlers and hangers-on sat and lounged through the day, gossipping in various tongues and boasting of the prowess of their respective countrymen. On the other side of the street nearly opposite was a tavern called the 'Chequers,' which drove a roaring trade with the men-at-arms, Court danglers, and servingmen who were constantly passing to and from Whitehall and St. James'. Opposite the gateway, across the large outer courtyard, was the door of the great hall, generally standing open for the neighbours to pass through it to the inner or smaller courtyard, in which stood a water-conduit fed by a 'spring of fair water in Covent Garden.' Beyond this inner courtyard stood the house itself at the bottom of the slope on the bank of the river at the spot now occupied by the arches that support Adelphi Terrace. It was a castellated structure with its water-gate placed in the middle of the curtain between two turrets, and leading not, as usually was the case, through a garden, but straight from the steps into the house itself by an enclosed penthouse doorway. The domestic offices, and probably the chapel, were on the ground floor, but the principal dwelling rooms were all up stairs and in the turrets. Aubrey, in his letters (vol. iii. 573),

RIVER GATE OF YORK HOUSE

thus speaks of Raleigh's occupancy of one of these turrets: 'Durham House was a noble palace. After he came to his greatness, he lived there or in some apartment of it. I well remember his study, which was on a little turret that looked into and over the Thames, and had a prospect which is as pleasant as any in the world.'

"The water-gate of the house was not the only approach to the river, as there was a space with trees on each side of the house, with a dwarf wall fronting the water, and a descent on one side by which the neighbours were allowed to get water from the stream for washing and similar purposes. It will thus be seen that the only really private part was the house itself between the inner courtyard and the river; the great hall and both the courtyards being practically open to the public under the supervision of the custodian at the outer gate, who was responsible only to the Queen, and was a constant source of friction with the foreign occupants of the house."

York House, which stood west of Durham House, was obtained by Heath, Archbishop of York, during the reign of Mary in exchange for Suffolk House in Southwark. It seems to have been let by the Archbishops of York to the Lord Keepers of the Seal. Francis Bacon was born in York House in 1560-1; and his father died here in

1579, as did Lord Keeper Puckering in 1596. Perhaps the most interesting remnant of this part of old London is to be found on the Thames Embankment; for there, in the midst of the Embankment Gardens, still stands in a perfect state of preservation the ornamental stone portico that once sheltered the river entrance to York House. It not only affords an interesting illustration of what the old river landings of these splendid places were like, but also marks the border of the Thames, then so much farther to the north than at present. (York House should not be confused with York Place, the old name for Whitehall when in the possession of Wolsey.)

Passing the village of Charing Cross, in Elizabeth's time a tiny cluster of houses that formed a hamlet distinct from Westminster, passing also Scotland Yard, we come to Whitehall, the palace of the kings of England from Henry VIII. to William III.

Of Queen Elizabeth's royal palace of Whitehall nothing remains. It was originally built by Hubert de Burgh during the reign of Henry III. He bequeathed it to the convent of the Blackfriars in Holborn, and they sold it to Walter de Grey, Archbishop of York, in 1248. From that time it was called York House until renamed Whitehall by Henry VIII. It occupied a

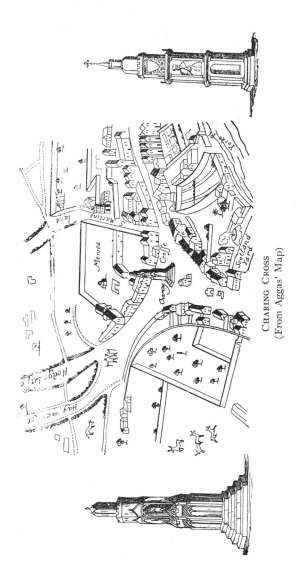

CHARING CROSS
(From Aggas' Map)

large space of ground fronting upon the Thames, with a front of a less pretentious kind towards St. James's Park. Scotland Yard was the northern boundary, and Cannon Row, Westminster, the southern. There was a public thoroughfare through the palace from Charing Cross to Westminster, spanned by two gates, one known as Whitehall Gate, the other as the King's Gate. Henry at once built a tilt yard and a cockpit, and additional buildings were added in succeeding reigns. Hentzner thus speaks of it in 1598:

"This palace is truly royal; inclosed on one side by the Thames, on the other by a park, which connects it with St. James's, another royal palace. . . . Near the palace are seen an immense number of swans, who wander up and down the river for miles in great security. . . . In the park is great plenty of deer. . . . In the garden adjoining to this palace is a *jet d'eau*, which while strangers are looking at it, a quantity of water forced by a wheel, which the gardener turns at a distance, through a number of little pipes, plentifully sprinkles those that are standing round."

"During several years," writes Mr. Wheatley, "of the reign of Henry VIII. Whitehall was the scene of many of those splendid jousts and revels in which he delighted till age and sickness had soured his temper. Here too passed before him those mighty musters of the citizens and train-bands which contemporary annalists describe with so much enjoyment. It was in Whitehall that at midnight, on January 25, 1533, the unfortunate Anne Boleyn was married to the wife-slaying monarch.

"Edward VI. held a parliament here, and here listened to the preaching of Latimer. At the outset of the reign of Mary Whitehall was attacked by a party of Wyatt's followers; and a few days after the Queen had the satisfaction of seeing the misguided rabble kneel in the mire in front of Whitechapel, with halters round their necks, and crave her mercy, which she, looking over the gate, graciously accorded, whereat they set up a mighty shout of 'God save Queen Mary.' Mary spent many solitary days here, and here her ecclesiastical adviser, Bishop Gardiner, died, November 15, 1556. Elizabeth restored to Whitehall its former splendour and festivity. She built a new Banqueting House and gave many magnificent feasts; held tourneys and jousts, where knights like Sir Harry Lee, Sir Christopher Hatton . . . kept the barriers against all comers; and saw grave tragedies and courtly masques, and sometimes baitings of bulls and bears and the performances of mimes and tumblers."

The great fabric of Henry VIII. and Queen

Elizabeth was not sufficient for James. Under his architect's care plans were drawn up for rebuilding the whole upon a stupendous scale. The present banqueting house, built upon the site of that erected by Elizabeth, was the only part of that plan ever put into execution.

Every volume must have a limit; and, as it is necessary to exclude many of the interesting London environs from the present volume, it is also necessary to look upon what was then the really distinct city of Westminster as outside our limits. Hence the briefest possible description will suffice.

"Thorney may be described as an island lying off the coast of Middlesex in the estuary of the Thames. It was very scientifically described for us about half a century ago by William Bardwell of Park Street, Westminster, one of the architects of the 'Westminster Improvement Company.' He says it is about 470 yards long and 370 yards wide, and is washed on the east by the Thames, on the south by a rivulet running down College Street, on the north by another stream which flows or flowed through Gardiner's Lane, the two being joined by the 'Long Ditch' which formed a western boundary, as nearly as possible where Prince's Street is now. Within the narrow limit thus described stand the Abbey and the Houses of Parliament and other familiar buildings." (Loftie's *Westminster Abbey*.)

Stow describes Westminster as extending on the east to Ivy Lane Bridge, west and south along the Thames, and westward from the Abbey for some little distance along Tothill Street. Besides Durham House and Whitehall, "then was there," says Stow, "an Hospital of St. Mary Rouncivall by Charing Cross [opposite the present Charing Cross Post-Office] (a cell to the priory and convent of Rouncivall in Navar, in Pampelion Diocese), where a fraternity was founded in the 15th of Edward IV., but now the same is suppressed and turned into tenements. . . . Near unto this hospital was a hermitage, with a Chapel of St. Katharine, over against Charing Cross; which cross built of stone was of old time a fair piece of work. . . . West of this cross stood some time an hospital of St. James. This hospital was surrendered to Henry VIII. the 23d of his reign; the sisters being compounded with were allowed pensions for the term of their lives; and the king built there a goodly manor, annexing thereunto a park, closed about with a wall of brick, now called St. James's Park, serving indifferently to the said manor, and to the manor or palace of Whitehall.

"South from Charing Cross on the right hand are divers fair houses lately built before the park,

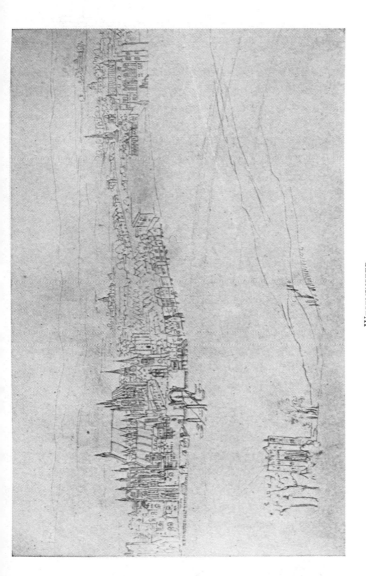

WESTMINSTER

(From the drawing by Wyngaerde)

then a large tilt-yard for noblemen, and other, to exercise themselves in jousting, turning, and fighting at the barriers.

"On the left hand from Charing Cross be also divers fair tenements lately built, till you come to a large plot of ground enclosed with brick, and is called Scotland, where great buildings have been for the receipt of the kings of Scotland, and other estates of that country."

Stow then goes on to describe Whitehall and Westminster Abbey. On rather legendary authority this establishment is said to date from *circa* 616. It is, however, plainly mentioned in a charter of Offa, King of Mercia, A. D. 785. The present Abbey was founded by Edward the Confessor and dedicated to St. Peter. It was consecrated on Innocents' Day, December 28, 1065, a week before the King died. Of this building very little remains beyond certain portions of the substructure of the dormitory and the dark cloister south of the south transept. Of the present church, Edward the Confessor's Chapel was built by Henry III., as were the choir and transepts. The four bays west of the transept (including the west end of the choir and the first bay of the nave) are of the time of Edward I. The remainder of the nave to the west door was built in the fifteenth century. Henry VII.'s Chapel was built by that king.

"Kings and queens crowned in this church," says Stow, "William, sur-named the Conquerer, and Matilde his wife, were the first, and since then all other kings and queens of this realm have been there crowned.   .   .   .

"In the year 1559, in the month of July, .   .   . Queen Elizabeth made the said monastery a college, instituting there a dean, twelve prebends, a schoolmaster, and usher, forty scholars, called commonly the Queen's scholars, twelve almsmen; and so it was named the Collegiate Church of Westminster, founded by Queen Elizabeth, who placed Dr. Bill, first dean of that new erection; after whom succeeded Dr. Gabriel Goodman, who governed that church forty years, and after Dr. Launcelet Andrewes." (Stow.)

"This church hath great privilege of sanctuary within the precinct thereof, to wit, the church, churchyard, and close, &c.; from whence it hath not been lawful for any prince or other to take any person that fled thither for any cause." (Stow.)

"The parish church of St. Margaret, sometime within the Abbey, was by Edward the Confessor removed, and built without for ease of the monks. This church continued till the days of Edward I., at which time the merchants of the staple and parishioners of Westminster built it all of new, the great chancel excepted, which was built by the abbots of Westminster; and this remaineth now a fair parish church, though sometime in danger of pulling down." (Stow.)

Westminster Hall was originally built in the reign of King Rufus. The present hall dates from 1399, when the old hall was considerably altered. The early parliaments were held in this hall, and it with its accompanying buildings constituted the palace from William the Conqueror till Henry VIII.

CHAPTER XIII

SOUTHWARK

SOUTHWARK, lying on the only approach to London from the south, had a separate existence from very early times, and was therefore a thorn in the side of the greater city across the Thames. Many and long were the complaints to the King concerning those criminals who executed their crimes in London and flew for safety across the bridge to the Surrey side. Edward III. granted to the city of London certain rights over Southwark which, however, proved insufficient. Henry IV. in the seventh year of his reign granted a patent to the city giving power to arrest robbers and other malefactors in the town of Southwark, and to bring them thence to the prison of Newgate, and to exercise almost every kind of jurisdiction there. Edward IV. granted further privileges, but the relation between the two towns remained in a state of confusion till the reign of Edward VI.

This sovereign granted to London divers properties and privileges, the most important of which are as follows: " All waifs, astrays, treasure-trove, goods and chattels of traitors, felons, fugitives,

outlaws, condemned persons, convict persons, and
felons defamed, and of such as be put in exigent
of outlawry, felons of themselves, and deodends,
and of such as refuse the law of the land: and all
goods disclaimed, found, or being within the said
borough, town, parishes, and precincts; and all
manner of escheats and forfeitures." That the
officers of London should have " the taste and
assize of bread, wine, ale, and beer, and all other
victuals and things whatsoever, . . . and the
correction and punishment of all persons there
selling" various commodities; " and that they shall
have the execution of the king's writ, and of all
other writs . . . as they should choose."

The grant goes on to state other details of the
local government of Southwark that were to be
undertaken by the city of London. " About a
month after the said Borough of Southwark was
granted by King Edward VI. to the Mayor, Commonalty, and Citizens of London; and that they
by the force of the said letters patent, stood
charged with the ordering, survey, and government of the same borough, and of all the king's
subjects inhabiting therein and repairing thither;
at a court holden before Sir Rowland Hill, Knight,
then Lord Mayor of London, and the aldermen of
the same city, in the Guildhall of London, on
Tuesday, the eighth and twentieth day of May, in

the said fourth year of the reign of King Edward
VI., the said town and borough was named and
called the Ward of Bridgeward Without: and Sir
John Ayliffe, Knight, citizen, and Barber-Surgeon of London was then also named, elected,
and chosen by the same court, to be alderman
of the same ward, albeit that before that time
there neither was any such ward or alderman."
(Strype).

With this reorganisation the reproach of iniquity somewhat abated; but Southwark remained
particularly famous in three directions: (1) for
its many noble residences; (2) for its taverns; (3)
for its brew houses, inasmuch as the taverns were
not allowed to brew their own ale.

The region roundabout was low, marshy, and
subject to all sorts of fevers and agues, as well
as to such diseases as were due to contaminated
water; for the sub-soil was extremely porous and
there were all sorts of percolations and leakages,
carrying the impurities of cess-pools and grave-
yards to the subterranean water-courses that
supplied the wells. Except along the streets, and
along the river bank on either side of the bridge,
the region now so thoroughly occupied by trade
was covered with woods or fields and gardens, and
intersected in every direction by streamlets crossed
by numerous bridges,

In the time of Stow the populated part of this
ward was shaped something like a cross, with the
centre at the Bridge-foot.   The houses included
within the ward extended along the bridge part
way, along the river half a mile in either direction,
and straight away south towards Newington for
nearly a mile.   The territory is described in the
following pages thus: (1) from the Bridge-foot
south to the extremity of the ward; (2) from
the Bridge-foot east; (3) from the Bridge-foot
west.

The ward extended north along the bridge as
far as the seventh arch from the south end, where
was the draw-bridge.   The shops between this
point and the Traitors' Gate, or tower over the
entrance, were occupied by Southwark folk.   The
houses constituted a solid mass of buildings, with
the bridge-way like an arcade running beneath.
Till 1577 the gate at the north end of the bridge
had been used as the principal resting place for
traitors' heads, but the gate, then falling into
decay, was no longer so used, and these dismal tro-
phies were removed to the south gate.   Beneath
the third arch, between the gate and the draw, was
a mass of sunken masonry that gave rise to the
name of the Rock Loch.   This *débris* was probably
deposited by a former accident when a part of
the bridge collapsed; at all events, it helped to

make the passage by boat more dangerous, which, at the best of times, was sufficiently risky.

The Traitors' Gate, with its massive doors, was the scene of many an ancient conflict and triumph. Here Sir Thomas Wyatt was stopped on his way to London, when the pretext of his insurrection was to prevent the marriage of Queen Mary to Philip of Spain. Soon afterward this same gate was the scene of a great triumph, as the royal pair returned to London from their wedding at Winchester. Here, too, thirty or more years later, in September, 1588, a great jollification took place over the defeat of this same Philip, on which occasion the flags captured from the "Invincible Armada" waved gloriously over the Traitors' Gate.

Standing at the very foot of the bridge and looking south, one had at his left Tooley Street, which led east along the Thames to Battle Bridge, where a road to the right led to Bermondsey Abbey; on one's right was a passage west towards Bankside; and directly in front was Long Southwark, the main street of the ward, which led to St. Margaret's Hill and Blackman's Street. From this point one could view the market-place in the midst of Long Southwark, the site of the annual fairs held in September. The last house at the Bridge-foot, on the observer's right, was the Bear

Tavern, which was anciently most popular because of its proximity to the river, whence a boat could be summoned to convey a passenger to any part of the river-front of London.

As we leave the Bridge-foot we pass Tooley Street on the left, and Pepper Alley on the right, which led behind the Bishop of Winchester's house to Bankside. We pass almost immediately White Horse Court, Checker Alley, and Boar's Head Court, which in later times marked the sites of three famous Elizabethan inns. One should not confuse this Boar's Head with the more famous tavern across the river in Eastcheap; and many so-called Shakespeare scholars have tired themselves in the attempt to prevent confusion and to establish correctly the relative facts. The following from Rendle and Norman's *Inns of Old Southwark* is interesting as an example of how small a seed of fact can give rise to a huge tree of dispute.

"In the map of 1542 prefixed to my account of Old Southwark and its people, in which many borough inns appear, the Boar's Head, although not actually named, is figured next the Ship and Black Swan, immediately north of St. Thomas's Hospital. In Eastcheap almost at the same distance from the city end of Old London Bridge as this was from the Southwark end, stood the Boar's

Head of Shakespeare's play. The city inn looked upon the burying ground of St. Michael's, Crooked Lane, as the other upon the Flemish burying ground in Southwark. At the former was laid the revelries of Prince Hal and his fat friend Sir John Falstaff—the latter was, curiously enough, the property of Sir John Fastolfe. In 1602 the Lords of Council, in a letter to the Lord Mayor, grant permission to the servants of the Earl of Oxford and Worcester to play at the Boar's Head in Eastcheap. The Southwark inns also were doubtless so used; the Boar's Head among the rest." With that uncertain word "doubtless" let the evidence end; we shall not continue the attempt to draw a comparison between the man named Falstaff and him named Fastolfe, men who, though quite unlike to other eyes, are as similar to the antiquarian lawyer as two bees in a bonnet.

Of the Checker Tavern it is enough to describe the origin of its sign. "During the Middle Ages," says Dr. Lardner, in his *Treatise on Arithmetic,* "it was usual for merchants, accountants, and judges who arranged matters of revenue, to appear on a covered banc (from the Saxon word meaning seat, hence our bank). Before them was placed a flat surface covered by a black cloth, divided by parallel lines into perpendicular columns, these again transversely by lines crossing the former, so as to separate each column into squares. This table was called an exchequer, from its resemblance to a chess-board, and the calculations were made by counters placed on its several divisions (something after the manner of a Roman abacus). A money-changer's office was generally indicated by a sign of the chequered board suspended. The sign afterward came to indicate an inn or house of entertainment, probably from the circumstance of the innkeeper following the trade of a money-changer, a coincidence still very common in seaport towns."

The latter surmise is, doubtless, quite correct, for in olden times nearly every kind of trade was carried on within the limits of a tavern.

Directly opposite the Boar's Head, on the west side of the street, was a butcher's shop kept by Thomas Harvard. Here in 1607 was born John Harvard, his son, the future founder of Harvard College, Cambridge, Mass. Continuing down the street, past the noble church of St. Saviour's, which stood back some distance on the right, we come to the Ship Tavern, the Black Swan, and St. Thomas's Hospital.

The latter institution fronted on Thieves' Lane (now St. Thomas Street), in those days an obscure by-lane leading to the meadows. The

buildings in the hospital were arranged in two
large quadrangles, with a burial ground opposite,
reclaimed from the marsh and surrounded with a
brick wall.   This institution was of early origin,
and was surrendered to the king in 1538 at the
Dissolution of the Monasteries.   For some time it
was neglected and fell into a sad state of ruin.
In 1552 it was bought by the city and turned into
a hospital.   Here was printed by one Nicholson
the first copy of Coverdale's Bible printed in
England, the earlier copies having been published
abroad and sent into the country.

Opposite St. Thomas's was Fowl Lane, and in
the midst of the street the pillory and the cage.
In close succession follow the King's Head tavern,
the White Hart, the George, and the Tabard.

The White Hart will always be remembered as
the headquarters in 1450 of Jack Cade.   Here his
lieutenants brought their captives to be judged
by the sturdy son of a bricklayer who struck his
sword upon London Stone, and who so nearly
made himself master of London town.   The White
Horse was one of the largest of the Southwark
taverns, capable of accommodating a hundred or
more guests, with their belongings, servants, and
horses.   It was approached by a long narrow
entrance guarded by a massive door with a lattice
for observation.   This precaution was the more

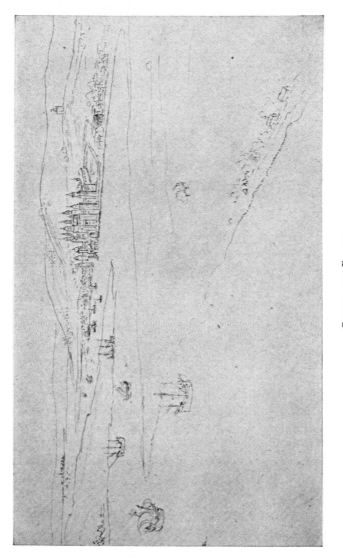

GREENWICH PALACE
(From the drawing by Wyngaerde)

necessary in those lawless times because guests usually held the landlord responsible for their property.

This neighbourhood was also, in the sixteenth century, a centre of the publishing trade. Nicholson's press was by St. Thomas's Hospital; Andrew Kempe, St. Margaret's Hill, was near the Tabard. He published *Amadis of Gaul*, Ovid's *Metamorphoses*, *Superstitious Jesu Worship*, etc., etc. Here Francis Faulkner issued Green's *Pandosto*, and *The Merry Devil of Edmonton*. An early manuscript gives eight as the number of printers in the neighbourhood, five of whom were on St. Margaret's Hill.

Next to the White Hart came the George, and next to that the Tabard, so-called of its sign, a sleeveless herald's coat. This was the most famous as well as the most ancient tavern in Southwark, built about 1306, some dozen years before the Bear at the Bridge-foot. It was here that Chaucer assembled his band of pilgrims before they set out on their way to Canterbury, a custom quite common then; doubtless there were many such assemblies in reality, but none has become so famous as the fictitious gathering of the poet.

Mr. Hubert Hall of the Public Record Office thus describes the old inn: "The arrangements of this inn about the middle of Elizabeth's reign would be much the same as those of any other hostel on the same scale. On the ground floor, looking onto the street was a room called the 'darke parlour.' This was probably the dining-room of the house, as it opened to the kitchen on the same level. Below the dark parlour was a cellar. On the first floor, above the parlour and the hall were three rooms—'the middle chamber,' 'the corner chamber,' and 'Master Hussyes chamber,' with garrets or 'cock-lofts' over them. Above the great parlour was another room. There were also rooms called the 'entry-chamber,' and the 'newe chamber,' the 'Flower du Luce,' and 'Mr. Russell's chamber,' of which the position is not specified. A warehouse, presumably under a separate roof, a coal hole, a double stable with an oat loft over it, and a similar stable with a half loft over it."

Speght's second edition of Chaucer, 1602, thus describes the condition of the Tabard at the end of Elizabeth's reign. "Whereas through time it hath been much decayed, it is now by Master J. Preston, with the Abbot's House [of Hyde] thereto adjoined, newly repaired, and with convenient rooms much increased for the receipt of many guests."

Opposite the Tabard was the site of St. Margaret's Church. Till 1540 it had been used as a parish church; but, at the Dissolution of the Monasteries, the magnificent church of St. Mary Overies became a white elephant on the borough's hands. Two parishes were united, one of which was St. Margaret's, and the monastic church given to them to be used as a parish church under the name of St. Saviour's. From this time the church of St. Margaret was used as a court-house, the churchyard as a market place, and the whole situation soon passes into obscurity through the confusion of records. The church was probably pulled down in 1546.

Between the Tabard and the next turning on the left, Long Lane, leading to Bermondsey Abbey, were the Salutation, the Goat, the Cross Keys, the Christopher, the Spur, and the Nag's Head,—all taverns,—the Marshalsea prison, the Mermaid and Half Moon taverns, the King's Bench prison, the White Lion prison, and St. George's Church.

The White Lion, Stow says, was of olden times a common hostelry. In 1569 a Mr. Cook was keeper, and it was then a criminal prison for Surrey, most frequently filled with religious prisoners who suffered for conscience' sake. Udal, one of the fiercest of the Marprelate men, died here in 1593, to be buried in St. George's churchyard; and from here John Rigby went to his death in 1599. The Marshalsea, sometimes called The

Epitome of Hell, was at the end of St. Margaret's Hill, opposite Maypole Alley; and the King's Bench half-way between it and St. George's Church.

This was the very centre of the region occupied by the booths of the great annual fair held in September. Like St. Bartholomew's Fair, held in West Smithfield, this fair was provided with a court of Pie Powder where offenders were caught, tried, and publicly whipped, or put in the stocks, within an hour.

At the end of St. Margaret's Hill toward the south, at the corner of Long Lane, was St. George's Church, once a beautiful edifice, but by 1600 falling into a state of great disrepair. Gower the poet left a bequest to this church; the Bishop of Winchester often held his court here, and sent many a Protestant to the stake during the Marian persecution. One curious punishment for less heinous offences, connected with this church, was that of standing in the porch, or in the middle aisle before service, dressed in a white sheet. The churchyard was mainly filled with the graves of prisoners from the neighbouring prisons.

Opposite St. George's Church once stood the magnificent house and park of Charles Brandon, Duke of Suffolk. In 1545 it came into the King's hands by purchase. He established there a royal

mint, and named it Southwark Place. The palace
was pulled down in 1557, and the neighbourhood
became a sanctuary for insolvent debtors, of evil
report, similar to Alsatia by the Strand.

From St. George's Church corner Long Lane
turned towards the left across the fields of Bermondsey Abbey. Not far from the church corner
Kent Street turned out of Long Lane to the south.
This street was formed on an embankment over
the marshy ground, and was part of the ancient
Roman road from Dover, through Canterbury, to
London. On it, not far from Long Lane, stood
the outermost house, called the Loke, a hospital for
lepers.

Let us return now to our starting point at the
Bridge-foot and set out along Tooley Street, eastward by the river side. On the north side of the
street, between it and the river, within a stone's
throw of the bridge stood the church of St. Olave's,
" a fair and meet large church, but a far larger
parish, especially of aliens or strangers, and poor
people: in which church there lyeth entombed Sir
John Bourchettur, Knight, 1466." (Stow.) These
strangers were chiefly Flemings and other con-
tinental refugees who had fled to England, bringing their trades and secrets with them to enrich
the country of their adoption. They were pretty
numerous in this part of Southwark, possessing

their own burying ground, and taverns where they especially congregated.

Almost opposite St. Olave's Church was Smith's Alley. Here was the back part of the Boar's Head that fronted on the High Street. There was also a local prison and the grammar-school of the church, founded by Elizabeth. Here was the Flemish burying ground, referred to above, and the town house of the Abbot of Lewes. Adjoining, in Tooley Street, was the cage, and then Walnut Tree Alley, from the walnut trees that grew thereabout.

In Tooley Street was the house of Sir John Fastolfe, who owned the Boar's Head tavern in Long Southwark. On the north side, east of the church, was Saint Leger House. It was originally the inn of the Abbot of St. Augustine (near Canterbury), and had passed into the Saint Leger family. It was sold in 1586 by Sir Richard Grenvile to George Fletcher. Next adjoining, on the east, was the Bridge House, " so called as being a store-house for stone, timber, or whatsoever pertaining to the building or repairing of London Bridge.

" This house seemeth to have taken beginning with the first founding of the bridge either of stone or timber; it is a large plot of ground, on the bank of the river Thames, containing divers large buildings for stowage of things necessary towards reparation of the said bridge.

"There are also divers large garners, for laying up of wheat, and other grainers for service of the city, as need requireth. Moreover, there be certain ovens built, in number ten, of which six be very large, the other four being but half so big. These purposely made to bake out the bread corn of the said grainers, to the best advantage for relief of the poor citizens, when need should require. Sir John Throstone, knight, sometime an embroiderer, then a goldsmith, one of the sheriffs in 1516, gave by his testament, towards the making of these ovens, two hundred pounds, which thing was performed by his executors. Sir John Munday, goldsmith, then being mayor, there was of late, for the enlarging of the said Bridge House, taken in an old brew-house, called Goldings, which was given to the city by George Monex, sometime mayor, and in place thereof, is now a fair brew house new built, for service of the city with beer." (Stow.)

William the Conqueror marked his last victory by the erection of Battle Abbey, and the abbot must have his town house. He chose to build it in Southwark, where so many famous inns were clustered close together.

"Next was the Abbot of Battailes inn, betwixt

the Bridge House and Battaile bridge, likewise on the bank of the river Thames; the walks and gardens thereunto appertaining, on the other side of the way before the gate of the said house, and was called the Maze; there is now an inn called the Flower de Luce, for that the sign is three Flower de Luces. Much other buildings of small tenements are thereon builded, replenished with strangers and other, for the most part poor people.

"Then is Battaile Bridge, so called of Battaile Abbey, for that it standeth on the ground, and over a water course (flowing out of Thames) pertaining to that abbey, and was, therefore, both built and repaired by the abbots of that house, as being hard adjoining to the abbot's lodging." (Stow.)

This brings us to the limit of the borough in Stow's time. The continuation of Tooley Street was an open lane, leading to the meadows and grazing ground called Horsedown. On the north side there was a spacious garden and vineyard, whence the locality obtained the name of the Vineyard.

Shortly before reaching Battle Bridge there was a turning out of Tooley Street to the southeast. At the beginning of this Bermondsey Street stood a cross belonging to the abbey of that name, to which the street led.

A short distance south-east of this cross, in the year 1082, Alwyn Child, a citizen of London, founded a monastery for monks of the Cluniac Order. Catharine, wife of Henry V., died there in 1437, as did Elizabeth, widow of Edward IV., in 1492. At the Dissolution the valuable property of Bermondsey Abbey passed to Robert Southwell, Master of the Rolls, who sold it to Sir Thomas Pope.

This Sir Thomas Pope was a man of considerable importance in his day. Though a Roman Catholic all his life, his consummate tact enabled him to remain unmolested through the reigns of Henry VIII., and of each of his three children. During Mary's reign Sir Thomas for a while was made keeper of the Princess Elizabeth, a task he executed with so much delicacy that he retained her good will after her accession. At the Dissolution of the Monasteries he was one of the persons principally concerned in the distribution of the spoils.

Though he became immensely wealthy during the process—at one time the owner of thirty manors—it must be said in his favour that he was the most nearly honest of all the men concerned in this game of national grab. It was said of him that he sailed as close to the wind of honesty as man could sail without crossing the line;

and every one knows that few of his colleagues seemed to know that there was a line in existence.

On receiving a grant of the Bermondsey property, he proceeded at once to tear down a part of the church and to use the materials in the construction of a mansion which he named Bermondsey House. At his death, which occurred January 29, 1559, of pestilential fever, he left much property in benefactions, having already endowed Trinity College, Oxford. He was buried with great pomp from the church at Clerkenwell.

Now let us return once more to our original starting point and glance at the district west of the bridge. Then as now the great glory of Southwark was the parish church of St. Saviour's, which had been a part of the magnificent monastery of St. Mary Overy. The priory church was built by Bishop Gifford of Winchester and others about 1106, when the Augustine priory was either established or reorganised by the Norman knights, William Pont de l'Arche and William Dawncey. The church passed through a varied history, but entered upon an entirely new era before the time of Queen Elizabeth.

"In October, 1539, the priory was suppressed, the canons were put out, and their place taken by secular priests, the property passing to Sir Anthony Brown, whose son became Viscount Mon-

SAINT MARY OVERIE
(St. Saviour's Cathedral)
(From an etching by Hollar)

tague. In 1540 the priory was made a parish
church—the little church of 'Marie Maudley'
(really a chapel attached to the chapel on the
south side of the choir) and that of St. Margaret's
(in the middle of the High Street) being united
with it." (Wheatley.)   The former was the
church of the parish of St. Mary Magdalen Overy.
It would be more correct to say that these two
parishes were united and both their churches superseded by the priory church which was handed over
to them under the new name of St. Saviour's.

So different is the present structure, through
much alteration and unhappy restoration, from
the original church, that I am fain to quote largely
from earlier records. "For a parish church it
had the longest vista of any—its full length a
little short of 300 feet—and the other parts were
in proportion. The plan: a nave, side aisles,
transepts and a choir. It is said that the Lady
Chapel was a part of an uninterrupted space of
about 240 feet long, a fine vista for the splendid
processions and ceremonial of the old church.
Proceeding from the east end, a small monumental
chapel was run out, known as the Bishop's Chapel,
from its being appropriated for the elaborate tomb
of Bishop Andrews. Some believe this to have
been the true Lady Chapel, that which has been
so called being in their opinion a retro-choir, a

continuation probably for processional purposes
of the internal space of the church visible through
the perforated screen of Bishop Fox. On the north
side of the choir was the chapel of St. John, afterwards the vestry; south of the choir, occupying
nearly its whole line, was the chapel of St. Mary
Magdalen, with its three aisles each way. It must be
recollected that the church was a priory church
and had buildings and cloisters. The site of the
cloister and conventual buildings was north of the
nave; this obtained the name of Montague Close—
close, from the cloisters—Montague from the
people who picked up the spoil at the Dissolution
of the Monasteries. . . . Some most important
buildings extended from the north transept some
100 feet direct toward the river. Probably these
had been a hall or refectory, and dormitories of
the priory. . . .

"The interior of the church: The nave is
marked by seven divisions of arches of the early
pointed style. The first division was of large
circular columns, with smaller ones at the cardinal
points. Other columns, octangular and circular
alternately, had smaller columns attached. The
small columns against the west wall had Saxon
bosses and capitals, hinting that the primary
building was probably of that order. . . . We
may imagine the effect of the whole when the

entire length from the altar screen, including the choir and the intersection of the transepts, was all open, the light from the windows of the tower streaming down; when the eye passed along the magnificent perspective of pillars below, and story upon story of arches above till it rested on the fine old western window at one extremity, nearly 250 feet distant; and looking from the west there was at the east end the beautiful screen of Bishop Fox. Take account also of the gorgeous vestments and rich implements at one time in the possession of the churches, used in solemn and imposing processions, with voices and bells ringing along the space. The picture of our old church in the Popish times may well overawe us, and strike us with some thought as to the present silent and undecorated contrast." * (Rendle.)

The boundary of St. Saviour's churchyard was Pepper Alley on the north, the High Street on the east, Fowl Lane on the south, and on the west the grounds of Winchester House. There were several chain gates to this enclosure; *i. e.*, open obstructions formed of posts connected with chains; and within them were many dwellings and shops.

* This nave was taken down in 1838 and replaced by a hideous structure. A restoration that is slowly proceeding gives hope that the church will eventually appear as it did in olden times.

Facing the churchyard on the south was the grammar school, like that of St. Olave's east of the High Street, a foundation of Elizabeth's.

To the north was Montague Close. Lord Montague and his family occupied what was anciently the prior's house, which remained for years a hot-bed of Papal disturbance. In 1606 it bore the name of Little Rome, and was subject to frequent searches and examinations by the government. The mansion consisted of a large irregular brick edifice, with two projecting wings, and a narrow centre containing a large doorway, surmounted by a very deep compass pediment enclosing a covered shell. The approach to the edifice was by a pair of semicircular stone steps. The whole of the building was lighted by transom casement windows, and with dormer attics in the roof. Within, the apartments were large and lofty, and long retained the remains of rich mouldings, with very spacious fireplaces.

The palace of the Bishop of Winchester which, as Stow says, was a " very fair house " was, in fact, one of the most magnificent of the old palaces. It possessed several courts richly laid out, and adorned with fountains and statuary among the trees. The great hall was 150 feet long and 40 across; and we are told that the east window was considered the finest in England. Next to it was the Bishop of Rochester's house, which, Stow tells us, " of long time hath not been frequented by any bishop, and lieth ruinous for lack of reparations."

From Pepper Alley a passage behind Winchester House led by a little bridge over a stream, where stood the ducking stool, to the Clink, " a gaol or prison for the trespassers in those parts; namely, in old time, for such as should brabble, fray, or break the peace, on the said bank, or in the brothel houses, they were by the inhabitants thereabout apprehended and committed to this gaol, where they were straitly imprisoned." (Stow.)

The brothel houses that furnished so large a proportion of the prisoners in the Clink stood next the river a little farther west. The Bordello or Stews was of old time openly licenced by government, under certain regulations quoted in full by Stow. They need not be inserted here, inasmuch as the Stews were suppressed, or, at least, legal protection and supervision was withdrawn from them during the reign of Henry VIII. " The pretence of these establishments," says Pennant, " was to prevent the debauching of wives and daughters of the citizens, so that all that had not the gift of continence might have places to repair to. Perhaps, in days when thousands were tied up by vows of celibacy these haunts might have been necessary; for neither cowl nor cape had virtue sufficient to annihilate the strongest of human passions. . . . The signs were not hung out but painted against the walls. I cannot but smile at one: *The Cardinal's Hat*. I will not give into scandal so far as to suppose that this house was peculiarly protected by any coeval member of the Sacred College."

West of these Stews stood the buildings that rise at once in everybody's mind in connection with Southwark in the days of Elizabeth. A narrow strip along the riverside, a quarter of a mile in length, was named the Bankside, and here were grouped those theatres the most famous of which was The Globe. The Bankside extended from the present Barclay's brewery to Bank End at the Castle and Falcon Taverns, near the present Blackfriar's Bridge. Here lived Kempe, the actor, Henslowe, Beaumont, Fletcher, Laurence Fletcher, the actor, Edmund Shakespeare, and Edward Alleyn. A special description of the London theatres is reserved for another place. Suffice it to say here that this is memorable ground. Here those great playwrights went about their daily affairs, attended service in St. Saviour's Church, laughed with Ben Jonson in the Falcon Tavern, furbished up old plays and produced new ones at the Globe and the Rose. Here came the wits and gallants

of the day eager for sport; here foreign ambassadors were brought to be entertained and to have
their secrets wormed out of them while they were
in a merry mood.

Indeed, nearly all of old Southwark has passed
away. One or two of the old churches are still
left, but St. Saviour's is shorn of much of its
ancient glory. The plays of the Elizabethan
dramatists, however, are alive and robust till this
day, a splendid monument of the Southwark of
three hundred years ago, a monument that age
cannot wither, that civilisation can not sweep
away.

CHAPTER XIV

THE THEATRES

I

AS early as the time of Henry VII. companies of players constituted a part of the households of the great noblemen of England. The players were attached to the musical part of the establishment and presented the interludes and morality plays that were the forerunners of the Elizabethan drama. When the service of the players was not needed by the master, they were allowed to wander about the country at will, performing on the village greens or in the tavern yards of the larger towns. On such journeys the players went by the name of My Lord So-and-So's Servants; and, as was natural, it was not long before the suburban districts were overrun with bands of rogues and vagabonds who, by calling themselves his servants, claimed the protection of some nobleman who may never have heard of them. To put an end to this practice a law was passed early in the reign of Elizabeth, which required every actor to obtain a licence. The power to grant these licences was given to certain noblemen, to the mayors of towns, to the Lord Lieu-

tenants of certain counties, and to two justices of
the peace resident in the neighbourhood where the
applicant resided.   This law, which inflicted the
penalty for vagabonds upon all unlicenced actors,
for a while put an end to the abuse of patronage.
For all that, even at a later time, a very loose connection existed between the members of a company
and its patron.

This restriction of actors occurred just at that
time in the reign of Elizabeth when the importa-
tion of foreign ideas and prosperity at home combined to develop the English nation with unparal-
leled rapidity.   So far as literature is concerned,
this remarkable development focussed on the drama.
No law was able to stop it.   So, after the temporary check produced by the requirement that all
actors obtain a licence, we find that the increased
number of players provoked further opposition.

During the years just previous to 1576 the London players produced their plays in the courtyards
of the city taverns.   The English tavern of those
days contained a central quadrangular courtyard,
entered through a door at one end.   About this
court were galleries, one above another at the level
of each story.   When a play was to be performed
the actors would build a temporary platform upon
trestles at the end of the court and extending beneath the first gallery.   From this gallery they

would hang drapery so as to convert the back part
of the platform and court into a dressing room.
The spectators of the play stood about in the open
court, or sat upon stools placed in the galleries.

Out of this manner of performing plays grew
the further opposition to the actors. Puritanism
had already taken root in England. The men who
later put a stop to bear-baiting, not because it gave
pain to the bear, but because it gave pleasure to the
spectator, could not abide the growing interest that
the nation was taking in the stage. To them the
drama was an abomination and a snare. Great was
the lamentation of the Puritans concerning the
brawls, the licentious conduct, the gambling, and
the numerous other evils that possessed the audience so frequently gathered about these inn-yard
scaffolds. But the Puritans were not yet masters
of England. To intrench their position they cou-
pled morality with expediency. They enlarged
upon the danger of spreading the plague which
would result from such large and frequent gather-
ings. This was a real danger. The Corporation
of London took up the cry. For a while the agitation was bitter. On one side stood the Queen, the
noblemen, and the actors; on the other side stood
the Puritans arm in arm with the city fathers. The
contest ended in a compromise. The companies of
actors were not disbanded, but they were compelled

to give their performances outside the jurisdiction of the Lord Mayor of London; that is, the limit of the city Liberties. They were prohibited from playing on Sundays, on holy days, and in Lent; but this part of the law was constantly violated. Furthermore, the players must receive an official approval of their productions from the Queen's Master of the Revels before they could put them upon the stage.

A year or two later—December 24, 1578—an order from the Privy Council limited the number of companies to six: The Children of the Royal Chapel, The Children of St. Paul's, The Servants of the Chamberlain, Warwick, Leicester, and Essex. From this time on the nobleman who figured as the patron of a company did little more in connection with his players than attend to the procuring of licences. The company derived a certain prestige from the use of his name, and frequently acted privately in his mansion, for which, however, they were paid extra. In later times there were other companies, the most famous of which was the King's Players, as Shakespeare's company was called after the accession of James. Material is not at hand, and probably never will be, from which can be written in any detail an accurate account of the Elizabethan companies. Certain it is that early historians of the drama have assumed a greater number of com-

panies than were ever in existence at one time. The
confusion is due to the fact that the same company
was often reorganised under a different name. The
published works of Mr. Fleay contain most of what
is known concerning this subject.

The contest between the players and the city resulted in the establishment of permanent theatres
on the outskirts of London. The first to be built
was The Theatre; The Curtain (so-called from the
plot of ground on which it was built) probably followed in the same year (1576). These were north
of the city, in Shoreditch. The principal Bankside theatres were The Rose, The Swan, The Bear
Garden, and The Globe. Built at a later date
north of the Thames were The Blackfriars, The
Fortune, and The Red Bull.

INNS USED AS THEATRES

The principal taverns thus used were: the Bull
and the Cross Keys, both in Gracechurch Street;
the Bell Savage on Ludgate Hill; Blackfriars and
Whitefriars are the names of inns so used, and
should not be confused with later theatres of the
same names; the Bull in Bishopsgate Street Within,
opposite St. Helen's Place; "Nigh Paul's" is an
inn frequently referred to, but about which nothing
is known; the Boar's Head, Eastcheap; the Boar's
Head without Aldgate was used for plays before

the accession of Elizabeth, but there is no record of plays having been acted there after 1558.

The Theatres

In speaking of Holywell Priory, Stow says: " The church being pulled downe, many houses have bene there builded for the lodgings of noblemen, of straungers borne and other; and nere there unto are builded two publique houses for the acting and shewe of comedies, tragedies, and histories, for recreation, whereof the one is called The Courtein, the other The Theatre, both standing on the southwest side towards the Field."

The Field was Finsbury Field, then a field indeed, open and country-like, with an unsavoury reputation for foot-pads and bad company. On the highroad all the way from London to Shoreditch was a double row of houses, in parts " pestered close together." In the immediate vicinity of the dismantled priory was a considerable cluster of houses with garden plots, some of which were in the possession of Giles Allen shortly before the building of the Theatre. The plot on which the Theatre was built was enclosed by a brick wall, the usual entrance being from the north. In this direction in plain sight was the well of Dame Agnes le Clear; westward, beyond the enclosing wall, lay the open fields, across which one could easily see the build-

ings of Finsbury Manor. It was a pleasant walk
from London by way of Moorgate, for the fields
were carpeted with soft grass, as we know, inasmuch as 40s fine was levied for injuring it at the
removal of The Theatre in 1599. These fields
abounded in wild flowers, and were frequently used
as military practice grounds. To the northwest
stood three windmills that are plainly shown on
Aggas's map, and which gave the name of Wind-
mill Hill to the neighbourhood.

James Burbadge, first a joiner and then a member of Leicester's company of players, leased a portion of the ground west of the priory of Giles Allen,
on April 13, 1576. Upon this plot of ground, near
the present National Theatre, Burbadge built his
new theatre. Inasmuch as The Theatre was enclosed by a brick wall, with probably no entrance
save from the north, it became necessary to make a
more convenient entrance to the site. A gate was
built in the west wall and the path across Moorfields thus became the common approach from London to its earliest theatre. This fact is alluded to
in Tarleton's *News out of Purgatory*, where one
sees "such a concourse of people through the
Fields" after a performance at The Theatre.

Of the construction of the play-house practically
nothing is known. No picture or detailed description of it is extant. Doubtless it was built wholly

of wood, a material likely to be selected by its owner, who was originally a carpenter; wood and timber are frequently mentioned in the account of its removal to Bankside. Furthermore, the contemporary description of its demolition shows that it could not have been built in a very substantial manner. This inference is practically proved by the fact that the Lord Mayor, writing to Walsingham in 1583, mentions among other dangers from stage plays at The Theatre, "the peril of ruins of so weake buildings." Upper and lower galleries are mentioned by Fleetwood. Beyond this, nothing is positively known of its structure. Its neighbour, The Curtain, was open to the sky. An engraving of The Rose, the earliest of the Bankside theatres, hints what the form of the theatre may have been, but further details are conjured up only by aid of the imagination.

The Theatre, as were most of the early playhouses, was often used for performances other than plays: such as fencing matches, "feats of activity," as gymnastic exhibitions were called; and there is reason to believe that The Theatre, as well as The Rose, Hope, Swan, and Newington Butts, could be hired temporarily by any one, much as a modern hall is let out upon occasion.

In the struggle against the theatres, one point constantly urged against them was that they bred

disorder. It is impossible to deny the charge; in
fact, the neighbourhood of The Theatre, and, later,
the Bankside, were two of the most unruly spots in
London. " By reason of no playes were the same
daye, all the city was quiet," writes one in 1584.
" Whereas, if you resorte to The Theatre, The Cur-
tayne, and other places of playes in the Citie, you
shall on the Lord's Day have these places, with
many others that I cannot reckon, so full as possible they can throng." (Stockwood's Sermon at
Paul's Cross, August 24, 1578.) " It happened
on Sundaie last that some great disorder was committed at The Theatre." (Lord Mayor to the
Privy Council, April 12, 1580.) In June, 1584,
Lord Burleigh wrote: " Uppon Weddensdaye one
Browne, a serving man in a blew coat, a shifting
fellowe, having a perrelous wit of his owne, entend-
ing a sport if he could have browght it to passe, did
at The Theatre doore querrell with certen poore
boyes, handicraft prentices, and strooke one of
them; and lastlie he, with his sword, wondied and
maymed one of the boyes upon the left hand, whereupon there assembled nere a thousand people;—this
Browne did very cuninglie convey himself awaye."
In Tarleton's *News out of Purgatory* one reads:
" Upon Whitson Monday last I must needs to The
Theatre to see a play, where, when I came, I found
such concourse of unrulye people that I thought it

better solitary to walk in the fields then to inter-meddle myselfe amongst such a great presse."

The elder Burbadge died in 1597. Legal complications and disagreements over a renewal of the lease for the ground on which The Theatre stood determined the heirs of Burbadge to take advantage of a stipulation in the original lease by which they were allowed to remove whatever buildings they had erected. In December, 1598, or January, 1599, The Theatre, or at least that part of it that was valuable as building material, was removed to Bankside and used in the construction of The Globe.*

Popular accounts sometimes lead careless readers to suppose that Cuthbert Burbadge came like a thief in the night and stole The Theatre away in violation of the law. Such was not the case. Below is an extract from the Bill of Complaint, Allen vs. Burbadge, 44 Eliz., (published by Halliwell, *Outlines*, page 375). Cuthbert Burbadge " unlawfullye combyning and confederating himselfe with the sayd Richard Burbadge and one Peter Street, William Smyth, and divers other persons to the number of twelve, to your subject unknown, did about the eight and twentyth daye of December in

---

* The two dates above are due to two conflicting contemporary accounts. It is possible that the removal did not all take place at once, and that both dates are correct.

the one and fortyth yere of your Highnes raygne, and sythence your highnes last and general pardon by the confederacye aforesayd, ryoutouslye assemble themselves together, and then and there armed themselves with dyvers and manye unlawfull and offensive weapons, as, namelye, swords, daggers, billes, axes, and such like, and soe armed, did then repayre to the sayd Theatre, and then and there, armed as aforesaid, in verye ryotous, outragious, and forcible manner, and contrarye to the lawes of your highness realme, attempted to pull downe the sayd Theatre; whereuppon divers of your subjects, servauntes, and farmers, then goinge aboute in peaceable manner to procure them to desist from their unlawful enterpryse, they the sayd ryotous persons aforesaid notwithstanding procured then therein with great violence, not only then and there forcyblye and ryotouslye resisting your subjects, servauntes, and farmers, but allso then and there pulling, breaking, and throwing down the sayd Theatre in verye outragious, violent and riotous sort, to the great disturbance and terrefyeing not onlye of your subjects sayd servauntes, and farmers, but of divers others of your Majesties loving subjectes there neere inhabitinge; and having so done, did then alsoe in most forcible and ryotous manner take and carrye awaye from thence all the wood and timber thereof unto the Bancksyde in the

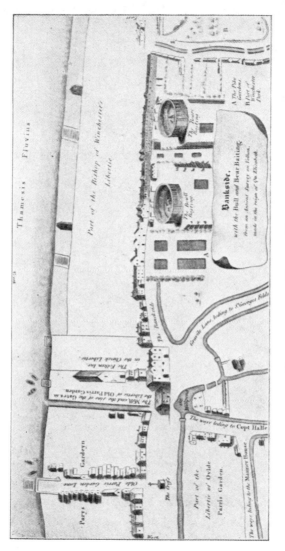

Thamesis Fluvius

Part of the Bishop of Winchester's Libertie

The Banke side

The Fishing house in the Clarke Libertie

The Mill and the site of the Gate in the libertie of Old Parris Garden

Parys Garden

Olde Parris Garden Lane

Garden

The logg

The way leding to Copt Halle

The way behind to the Manner House

Part of the Libertie or Oulde Parris Garden

Gunde Lane leding to S.Georges Felds

Bankside, with the Bull and Bear Baiting, from an Ancient Survey on Velum, made in the reign of Q.n Elizabeth.

The Bull Baytinge

The Beare Beating

A The Play Gardens.
B Part of Winchester Park.

BANKSIDE IN THE TIME OF ELIZABETH

parishe of St. Marye Overyes, and there erected a newe playehowse with the sayd timber and woode."

THE CURTAIN

This theatre was probably built in 1576, but a little later than The Theatre. It stood south of Holywell Lane, not far from the other playhouse. Much of what has been said about one applies to the other. One detail of its construction, that it was open to the sky, is proved by the following: "About this time new plays will be more in request then old, and if Company come current to The Bull and Curtaine, there will be more money gathered in one afternoon then will be given in Kingsland Spittle in a whole moneth; also, if, at this time, about the hours of four or five, it waxe cloudy, and then raine downright, they shall sit dryer in the galleries, then those who are the understanding men in the yard." (*Jack Dawes Prognostication*, 1623.) The Curtain derived its name from the plot of ground on which it was built, which name referred to a fortification in connection with London Wall.

BANKSIDE

Most maps of recent times, published to show the sites of ancient theatres, give an entirely erroneous impression of the populousness of this neighbourhood. It was chosen as the site of theatres because it was outside the city. The watermen frequently complained that the closing of the theatres stopped the traffic Southward Ho, from which we may infer that there was little else of moment on the Bankside. Stow tells us that in 1598 most of the houses were contained in a single row along the river bank between London Bridge and Paris Garden Stairs; and from Gerard's *Herbal* we know that this region abounded in wild flowers. Hence, one may consider the "network of blind alleys," so often alluded to, as a creation of the imagination. If they existed at all, they were merely mud paths to the few scattered houses that were not upon the principal thoroughfares of Bankside and Maiden Lane.

THE BEAR GARDEN

This theatre, originally a mere ring for baiting, stood between The Rose and The Globe, a short distance west of the line joining them. It was originally an open wooden fabric, which is figured with another like it in Aggas's map. It was a wooden structure and doubtless often needed repair. Some time before 1606 it was rebuilt in rectangular form. In 1606 it was again rebuilt for Henslowe and Allen by Peter Street, who had already built The Globe and The Fortune. The following inter-

esting description of its construction is taken from
the building contract preserved at Dulwich College
and quoted by Collier. (*Memoirs of Edward
Alleyn*, page 78.)

"That he, the said Peter Streete, his executors
administrators or assignes, before the thirde day of
September next comynge after the date hereof,
shall at his owne or their owne proper costes and
charges, not only take and pull downe for and to
the use of said Phillipp Henslowe and Edward
Alleyn their executors or assignes, so much of the
tymber or carpenters worke of the foreside of the
messuage or tenemente called the Beare Garden,
next the river of Thames in the parishe of St.
Saviors aforesaide, as conteyneth in lengthe from
outside to outside fiftye and sixe feete of assize,
and in breadth from outside to outside sixteene
feete of assize; but also in steade place thereof,
before the saide thirde day of September, att his
or their like costes and charges, shall well sufficiently, and workemanlike, make or erect sett up
and fully finishe one new frame for a howse, to
conteyne in length from outside to outside fyftie
and sixe feete of assize, and in breadth from outside to outside sixteene foot of assize, which frame
shalbe made of good, new sufficient and sounde
Tymber of oke, to be fynished in all thinges as
hereunder is mentioned; that is to say: that the

saide frame shall conteyne in height two storeyes
and a halfe, the two whole storeyes of the said
frame to be in height from flower to flower ten
foote of assize a peece, and the half story to be in
height fower foot of assize, and all the principall
rafters of the same frame to be framed with
crooked postes and bolted with iron boltes through
the rafters, which iron bolts are to be provided
at the costs and charges of the saide Peter
Streete his executors or assignes. And also shall
make in the same frame throughout two flowers with good and sufficient joystes, the same
flowers to be boarded throughout with good and
sounde deale boardes to be plained and closely
laid and shott. Al the principall longe upright
postes of the saide frame to be nyne ynches broade
and seaven ynches thicke: and shall be in the same
frame three maine summers, that is to say in the
uppermost story twoe summers, and in the lower
story one summer, every summer to be one foote
square; all the brest summers to be eight ynches
broade and seaven ynches thick. The same frame
to jetty over towards the Thames one foot of
assize. And also shall make on the south side of
the saide frame a sufficient staire case, with staires
convenient to lead up to the uppermost romes of
the saide frame, with convenient dores out of the
saide staire case into every of the romes adjoyn-

THE BEAR GARDEN

(Engraved by Wilkinson from the Antwerp View of London)

inge thereunto, in every rome of the same frame
one sufficient dore; and also by the same staire
case shall make and frame one studdy, with a
little rome over the same, which studdy is to jetty
out from the same frame fower foote of assize,
and to extend in lengthe from the saide staire
case unto the place where the chimneyes are
appoynted to be sett, with a sufficient dore into
either of the romes of the studdy. And the nether
story of the same frame shall seperate and devide
into fower romes: that is to say, the first towardes
the east to be for a tenemente, and to conteyne in
length from wall to wall thirteene foote of assize;
the next rome to be for a gate rome, and to conteyne in length ten foote of assize; the third rome
twenty foote of assize, and the fowerth westward
thirteene foot of assize. And the second story shall
seperate into three romes, the first, over the rome
appointed for a tenemente on the east end of the
said frame, to conteyne in length thirteene foote
of assize, the midle rome thirty foote of assize,
and the third rome westward thirteene foote likewise of assize. And the half story above to be
divided into two romes, namely over the said tenement thirteene foote, to be seperated from the
rest of the said frame, and the residue to be open
in one rome only. And cut of the said frame
towards the Thames shall make two dores, and one

fine paire of gates with twoe wickettes proportion-
able. And also at either end of the lower story
of the said frame shall make one clere story windowe [to] either of the same clere storyes, to be
in height three foote of assize, and six foote in
length, and the middle rome of the same frame,
conteyninge twenty foote, to have a clere story
windowe throughout the height of the saide former
clere storyes: and in the second story of the same
frame shall make three splay windowes, every windowe to be sixe foote between the postes; and in
the same second story shall make seaven clere
story windowes, every clere story to be three foote
wide a peece, with one mullion in the midst of every
clere story; and every of the same clere storyes
to be three foot and a halfe in depth. All over
the forsaid gate shall make one greete square windowe, to be in length ten foote of assize and to
jetty over the said frame three foote of assize,
standinge upon twoe carved Satyres, the same
windowe to be in wheight according to the depth
of the story, the same windowe to be framed with
twoe endes with mullions convenient; and over the
same windowe one piramen with three piramides,
the same frame to have fower gable ends towards
the Thames, and upon the top of every gable end
one piramide, and betweene every gable end to be
left three foote for the falling of water, and in

THE ROSE THEATRE

(From an engraving by Wilkinson, who, however, called it the Globe)

every gable end one clerestory, and backward over
the gate of the same frame towards the south one
gable end with a clere story therein, and under
the same gable end backward in the second story
one clere story windowe. And also in this parsell
of the saide frame as is appoynted for a tenement
shall make twoe paires of staires, one over another
by the place where the chimneyes are appoynted
to be sett."

This wooden structure, however, was in existence but a few years. "In 1613, August 29,
Gilbert Katerines of St. Saviours', Southwark,
covenanted with Henslowe and Meade that before
the 30th of November, he would pull down the
Bear Garden on the Bankside, and set up a new
house fit for players to play in, and for bulls and
bears to be baited in, in size and fashion like The
Swan, for £360." (Fleay, *London Stage*, page
202.) This structure was first called The Hope,
though it soon became known, as before, as The
Bear Garden. Its appearance is so familiar as not
to need description. It is represented alone by Wilkinson, and in the general views of London by
Vischer and Hollar. In the *Notes on London
Churches and Buildings*, 1631-1638, we read:
"The Hope on the Banks side in Southwark, commonly called The Bear Garden, a play-house for
Stage Playes on Mundayes, Wednesdayes, Fridays

and Saterdayes; and for the Baiting of the Beares on Tuesdays and Thursdayes, the stage being made to take up when they Please." It was probably not used for plays after the death of Henslowe in 1616.*

THE ROSE

This theatre was built by Henslowe for performances by Lord Strange's men and others. Fleay says that it was opened February 19, 1592. This date, however, is in all probability too early, a more likely date being towards the end of the year 1592. Henslowe's connection with this theatre ceased in 1603, and in later years the theatre was only used for non-dramatic presentations. It stood a little to the northwest of the site of The Globe, and at the end of Rose Alley. Wilkinson published several engravings of The Globe Theatre, one of which must be misnamed. It is

---

* West of Bankside stood the Manor of Paris Garden. Contemporary writers used the name loosely for all the adjacent territory, and so the Bear Garden in the Liberty of the Clink was sometimes referred to as Paris Garden. This fact has led many writers to jump at the conclusion that there was a baiting ring farther west within the actual limits of the manor park. An examination of the evidence, however, seems to warrant the assertion that no such ring ever existed. The contradictory statements of modern writers is the excuse for the insertion of such a detailed description of what was in reality one of the minor theatres.

THE GLOBE THEATRE
(Engraved by Wilkinson from a drawing in the collection of John
Charles Crowle, Esq.)

certainly a building of earlier construction than The Globe, and is near the river; it is not a picture of The Bear Garden, hence the inference that it is The Rose. It is circular, and much lower than the other theatres. The usual hut is lacking, and the thatch roof rises gradually upon one side as if to shield the stage from the weather and at the same time to provide room for the upper stage. The signal flag is attached to a staff that rises directly from the yard, instead of from the hut, as in the later theatres.

THE GLOBE

The materials of the demolished Theatre were transported to Bankside to be used in the construction of The Globe. It was originally built as a round theatre, early in 1599. This became the home of Shakespeare's company; here he acted minor parts in his own plays, and here were performed for the first time his great tragedies. The Globe served as the model for The Fortune, which will be described below, hence little need be said about the structure of The Globe. It stood in Bankside within 80 paces of the river, on a site now occupied by Barkley's brewery. The nearest river landings were Horseshoe Alley Stairs, distant about 450 feet, and Paris Garden Stairs, about 950 feet away. The Globe was burned to

the ground during a performance of *Henry VIII.*
in 1613.

"The King's Players had a new play called
All is True, representing some principal pieces of
the reign of Henry VIII., which was set forth with
many extraordinary circumstances of pomp and
majesty, even to the matter of the stage, the
knights of the order with their Georges and gar-
ters, the guards with their embroidered coats, and
the like. Now King Henry, meeting a masque at
the Cardinal Wolsey's house, and certain chambers
being shot off at his entry, some of the paper or
other stuff wherewith one of them was stopped, did
light on the thatch, there, being thought at first
but an idle smoke, and their eyes more attentive to
the show, it kindled inwardly and ran round like
a train, consuming in less than an hour the whole
house to the very ground; nothing did perish but
wood and straw, and a few forsaken cloaks, and
one man had his breeches set on fire." (Sir Henry
Wotton.)

The Globe was immediately rebuilt, octagonal
in shape, however, instead of round, and was
demolished in 1644 to make room for a pile of
tenements.

BLACKFRIAR'S THEATRE

This playhouse is often referred to in contemporary writings as a private house, *i. e.,* smaller, higher

priced, more select, and roofed. It consisted of a remodelled private house of large size that stood in the precinct of the Blackfriars upon a site now occupied by Playhouse yard near the Times Office. The renovation of this building for the purposes of making it usable as a theatre must have been very complete, for a document (quoted by Fleay, *Chron.*, p. 228) says: " And further say that if the sayd Hall were converted from a playhouse to any other ordinary use it would be of very little value, and nothing near worth the rent reserved by the sayd leas." The building, which stood next the Pipe Office, " consisted of all those seaven greate upper roomes as they are nowe divided, being all uppon one flower and sometime being one greate and entire rome, with the roof over the same covered with lead." (Deed to James Burbadge.) There are numerous other rooms mentioned, and it is not possible to tell whether the theatre was on the ground floor or above stairs. It is interesting to note that there were in this theatre three doors at the rear of the stage. (Cf. *Eastward Ho*, I, i., stage direction.)

THE FORTUNE THEATRE

In 1599 The Rose theatre was falling into decay, as is shown by a letter quoted by Collier (*Memoirs of Allen*, p. 55). A new theatre was planned, and a letter gives the following reasons why The Fortune should be built.

"First, because the place appoynted oute for that purpose standeth very tollerrable, nere unto the Fieldes, and soe farr distant and remote frome any person or place of accompt, as that none can be annoyed thearbie.

"Secondlie, because the erectours of the saied howse are contented to give a very liberall portion of money weekelie towards the relief of our poore, the nomber and necessity whereof is so greate, that the same will redonde to the contynuall comfort of the said poore.

"Thirdlie and lastlie, wee are the rather contented to accept this meanes of relief of our poore because our Parrishe is not able to releeve them. Neither hath the Justices of the Sheire taken any order for any supplie out of the Countye, as enjoyned by the late Acte of Parliamente."

As a result The Fortune was built by Peter Street for Henslowe and Alleyn. It stood on the east side of Golding (now Golden) Lane, between it and what is now called Upper Whitecross Street, in the parish of St. Giles's Cripplegate. The contract for building The Fortune was published by Halliwell-Phillipps (*Outlines*, page 462), and is dated January 8, 1599. The frame of the house was to be set square "fower score foote of lawful

THE FORTUNE THEATRE
(From an engraving by Wilkinson)

assize everye waie square without, and fiftie five
foote of like assize square everye waie within,"
with a strong foundation of piles, brick, sand, and
lime, "to be wrought one foote of assize at the
leiste above the ground." The theatre consisted
of three stories, of 12, 11, and 9 feet high respec-
tively. They were to be 12½ feet wide, "besides
a jutty forwards in eyther of the saide two upper
stories of tene ynches of lawful assize." There
were four "gentlemen's rooms," and sufficient and
convenient two-penny rooms; and all the rooms
were to be provided with seats. The theatre was
to have "suche like steares, conveyances, and divisions, without and within, as are made and con-
tryved in the late erected play-howse on the
Bancke, in the said Parish of St. Saviour's, called
the Globe." There was to be a tiring room, and
a "shadow, or covering," over the stage. The
length of the stage was 43 feet, and it extended
forward to the middle of the yard. Beneath the
stage and beneath the first gallery the space was
railed with oak boards. The roof of the shadow,
galleries, stairs, etc., were covered with tile, and
the rooms ceiled with "lathe, lyme, and haire."

The Fortune was opened in July, 1601. An in-
denture of May 20, 1622, (quoted by Wheatley,
vol. 2, p. 68) describes the spot as a "part or
parcel of ground upon part whereof lately stood

a playhouse or building called The Fortune, with
a Taphouse belonging to the same . . . con-
teyning in breadth from E. to W. 130 foote, and
in length 131 foote and 8 inches, or thereabout."
The theatre soon became popular, and from it
Alleyn derived most of the money with which he
endowed Dulwich College.

Little is known concerning the size and capacity
of the Elizabethan theatres. With the above exact
dimensions in mind it is interesting to note that
the Fortune is referred to in Middleton's *Roaring
Girl* (Prologue, l. 10) as "our vast theatre."
December 9, 1621, The Fortune was burned to the
ground. It was soon rebuilt, "a large round,
brick building" (Wright, *Sec. Gen. of Actors*,
1699), and became frequented by the meaner sort
of people. This theatre was adorned with a statue
that still ornamented the front of the building
when Wilkinson made his celebrated engraving.
It is thus referred to in Heywood's *English
Traveller:*

> "I'll rather stand here
> Like a statue, in the fore front of your house
> Forever, like the picture of Dame Fortune
> Before the Fortune playhouse."

Minor Theatres

Newington Butts in Southwark, nearly a mile
from the Bridge-foot, was probably built before

The Swan Theatre
(From an engraving by Wilkinson)

1571, doubtless either a tavern or a mere baiting ring. Its only real connection with the drama was in 1592, when plays were given there by Strange's men, and in 1594 by Strange's men and the Admiral's.

The Swan was where the present Holland Street is, not far from the Blackfriar's Road. Though one of the larger theatres, it was not long, and never exclusively used for plays. It, like The Hope, had a movable stage. "Lady Elizabeth's men had played here under Alexander Foster from 29th August, 1611, till March, 1613. Only during these two years had it any connection with the drama; before and after, it was used only for fencing." (Fleay.) The principal item of interest in connection with The Swan is that its interior is the subject of unique contemporary drawing of an Elizabethan stage.

The Red Bull stood on the upper end of St. John Street, and affords another interesting picture of a stage, of a later date, however. The Red Bull was not an important theatre, and may have been merely a tavern in Elizabethan times.

II

Just how much and how little is known concerning the construction of individual Elizabethan theatres may be inferred from the foregoing notes.

The following general description of a performance is compiled from various sources.

The river Thames was then the southern boundary of the city. Though there was but one bridge
across the river, the numerous ferryboats and private barges prevented it from being a serious
obstacle between the city and the Bankside, whence
the cathedral was in plain view. The neighbourhood of St. Paul's was not only the centre of the
religious and social activity of the city, but also
of the book trade. There appointments were made,
bargains struck, and duels arranged.   There,
among the bookstalls, quarto editions of the current plays were sold for sixpence, and we read
in Middleton's *Roaring Girl* that it was a common
habit to take "books of the play" to the theatre.
Playbills to advertise performances were often set
up in these shops; also posted about town, especially in the neighbourhood of the theatres. "Then
hence, lewd nags, away, Go read each post, view
what is played to-day." (Marston, *Scourge of Vil-
lainy.*)   It was also a common practice for the
players to parade about the streets of the city
with music on the day of a performance for the
purpose of drumming up a crowd. "In some
places they shame not in time of divine service, to
come and dance about the church."   (Stockwood's
Sermon at Paul's Cross.)   In July, 1582, the Lord

THE SWAN THEATRE—INTERIOR VIEW

Mayor writes to the Earl of Warwick that permission was given to John David, a fencer in the earl's service, to march in the city with drums, etc.

Open theatres and bad weather often prevented a performance. If a person in London wished to know whether a play was going to be enacted that afternoon, he had but to walk to the bank of the Thames and glance across the river. A signal for the performance was a flag suspended from a staff upon the theatre. These flags are represented in most of the old drawings of the theatres and are referred to in many of the contemporary plays and pamphlets. (Cf. Dekker's *Raven's Almanac;* Middleton's *Roaring Girl,* IV. ii.; *Mad World,* I. i.; etc.) If the theatre-goer had plenty of time he might ride around to Bankside by way of London Bridge; but if he were in haste, he would hail a ferryman with the cry of Southward Ho! and desire to be set down at Paris Garden Stairs. Dekker tells us that for this purpose it was more fashionable to hail a pair of oars than sculls. The Globe was near the Falcon Inn, where riders put up their horses during a play, and where all sorts and classes of people loafed and tippled before the play began.

From the outside the play-house looked like a huge squatty building, not like a high tower, as usually represented in the old maps. (Cf. dimensions of The Fortune above.) It was covered with a half-finished roof over the upper gallery, which was thatched in The Globe and tiled in The Fortune. All the theatres except the earliest probably possessed a little hut that rose above the main building. The Globe seems to have been the only one whose hut possessed a double gable. The purpose of this structure is not fully known. It carried the staff with the signal flag, and it afforded standing room for the trumpeter; it may have been connected with some of the stage machinery to be described. When the play was about to begin the trumpeter from the hut indicated the fact by three successive blasts at short intervals.

General admission to the theatre was collected at the outer door. (*Gull's Horn-Book.*) Extra money was paid for admission to the rooms, and for a stool upon the stage. A penny seems to have been the lowest price of admission. None who go "to Paris Garden, The Belle Savage, or Theatre, to behold bear-baiting, enterludes, or fence-play, can account of any pleasant spectacle unless they first pay one penny at the gate, another at the entry of the scaffolde, and the third for a quiet standing." (*Perambulation of Kent.* Ed. of 1596.)* Two pence, however, was a common admission fee. "If he be showed at Paul's it

---

* Money was then worth six or eight times its present value.

will cost you fourpence, if at The Theatre, two-pence." *(Lyly, Pap With a Hatchet.)* Two-penny rooms are referred to in connection with The Fortune, also in *A Mad World, My Masters; The Woman Hater; Satiromastix*, etc. The most popular seats were upon the stage it-self, where one paid for his stool. "Enter W. Sly, a tireman following him with a stool." (Marston, *Induc. Malcontent.*) Sixpence was the regular price for a stool, but a shilling was often paid. (Cf. *Induc. Malcontent, The Roaring Girl*, II. i., etc.)

The plays were performed by daylight, in the afternoon. Chettle, in the *Kind Heart's Dream*, alludes to the bowling alleys between the city wall and The Theatre, "that were wont in the afternoon to be left empty, by the recourse of good fellows unto that unprofitable recreation of stage play-ing." October 8, 1594, Lord Hunsdon wrote to the Lord Mayor, asking permission for his com-pany to play at the Cross-Keys. "They will play from 2 p. m. to 4, instead of beginning at 4 or 5, use no drums or trumpets, and be contributory to the parish poor." Performances at the private theatres were given by candlelight, though in the afternoon. Court presentations often took place at night.

Once within the doorway of the theatre the

spectator found himself within a large circular enclosure into which projected the stage. The early theatres were either square, hexagonal, or circular on the outside, but, with the exception of The Fortune and The Bear Garden during a part of their existence, they were circular within. The floor of the central area, the "yard" of public theatres, the "pit" of private, was bare clay or turf in the former, was provided with bench-like seats in the latter. About the yard were three or more galleries, one above the other, divided into sections called rooms. Entrance to a room, which in many cases contained seats, was extra, and paid within the theatre. The lower rooms could be reached by steps from the yard as well as from the door in the rear of each room. Reference has already been made to two-penny rooms and to gentlemen's rooms. Private rooms are mentioned in the *Induction to the Malcontent*. The music room, often referred to in contemporary plays, was a room next the stage, set apart for the use of the musicians. The people who occupied the yard were called groundlings. They were the commoner sort of tradesmen, apprentices, petty-venders, loose women, pick-pockets, and the like. The better sort of quietly disposed people sat in the rooms; the unruly gallants upon the stage. Respectable women sometimes accompanied their husbands

to the rooms, but on such occasions they went
masked.

The stage, which projected into the yard, was
rectangular and occupied about one-fourth of the
area.   The stage was merely an open platform
about three feet from the ground, and visible to the
audience from the front and both sides.   During
a performance the stage was strewn with rushes,
like the floor of a domestic hall.   At the rear were
two or three doors for the entrance and exit of
the actors.   The stage, however, was not wholly
given up to the actors.   It was here, upon either
side, that the gallants placed their stools or
"tripods," often arriving late for the mere
pleasure of creating a disturbance.

The space directly behind the stage was occupied by a three-story structure.   The stage doors
opened into the dressing room.   The second story
was a room open to the view of the audience,
called the "upper stage" or the "stage gallery."
In it were presented those parts of a play that
were distinctly separated from the scene that was
being enacted on the main stage.   In the balcony
scene of *Romeo and Juliet* Romeo stood on the
stage proper, Juliet on the upper stage.   The
play before the king in *Hamlet* was acted on the
upper stage.   In the Chronicle plays the defend-
ers of a city wall would appear upon the upper

stage. The third story of this rear structure was the hut that was visible from the outside of the playhouse. From a point above the upper stage a canopy projected far enough to cover about one-third of the stage. It was called the shadow, and served to shelter the actors in inclement weather.

When the third bugle had blown and the play was about to begin, the prologue entered, dressed in a black cloak and crowned with bay leaves. The superstitious Elizabethans believed that bay leaves constituted a perfect protection against thunder and lightning. Perhaps it was by design that the prologue wore this symbolic adornment, for the author of an unsatisfactory play was often the recipient of boisterous manifestations of contempt from the groundlings. When the prologue finished his speech, which usually contained an apology for the poverty of stage effects, or a forecast of all or part of the play, he withdrew and the performance commenced. The name of the play was indicated by a placard or "title" that was either hung up in some conspicuous place or carried by the prologue. The place of the scene was indicated in the same way. "How now, my honest rogue," says the prologue in *Wily Begiled*, "What play shall we have here to-night." " Sir," answers the player, " you may look upon the title." " Hang up the title: our scene is Rhodes," occurs in the *Spanish Tragedy*.

Several recent writers have gone slightly astray in their description of Elizabethan stage effects. The assertion that the Elizabethans possessed neither scenery nor curtain is not quite correct. In a sense, they possessed both. The numerous references to drawing the curtain to be found in the texts and stage directions of old plays proves the existence of a curtain of some sort. The position of this curtain, which was usually called the traverse, has given rise to considerable speculation. It is drawn in the death scene at the end of *Othello*, by which we know that it must have been in front of an area large enough to contain a bed. In the *White Devil* the traverse is drawn, discovering five persons and a corpse. It is not likely—at least there is no proof of the fact—that this space was a recess beneath the upper stage and between the stage doors.* A passage in Middleton's *Family of Love*, III. ii., makes it seem probable that curtains were sometimes used to close in the upper stage. It is hardly likely, however, that the scenes alluded to above were enacted on the upper stage. If this surmise is correct, the traverse must have been a part of the furniture of the lower stage.

* In the Blackfriar's Theatre this space was occupied by a third door.

All references to the curtain, however, do not necessarily refer to the traverse. An old engraving of the stage of the Red Bull Theatre (subsequent to Elizabethan times, however,) shows the back of the stage so draped as to conceal the doors. The frequent references to hiding behind the arras doubtless refer to the presence of such hangings as are represented in this old drawing.

It should be remembered that most of the old theatres contained a hut above the upper stage, whose purpose is not fully known, and that a roof covered about one-third of the lower stage. It is the present writer's opinion that overhead machinery operated the traverse, and that it could be dropped so as to divide the stage longitudinally or transversely. In the *Life and Death of Lord Thomas Cromwell*, III. ii., an attendant opens the curtains in order that the doings in another room may be visible to the audience. In Marston's *What You Will* a person who has been sitting upon the stage exclaims: "Come, we strain the spectators' patience in delaying their expected delights. Let's place ourselves within the curtains, for, good faith, the stage is so little, we shall wrong the general eye else very much."

The Elizabethan writers constantly allude to the poverty of their stage effects. Doubtless they spoke in comparison with the costly machinery of

the court masques. At all events they have sometimes been taken too seriously. They were certainly
rich in properties. The following are from the
numerous lists of properties quoted by Fleay and
others. The castle for Lady Peace or Lady Plenty,
and the prison in which Discord is watched by
Argus; frozen heads; Turk's Heads; a monster
in which Benbow played; women's maskers' hats;
fishers' maskers' nets; spears for play of *Cariclia;*
holly for Dutton's play; holly for forest; fisher-
men's trays; palmer's stuff; vizard for ape's face;
key and hailstones for Janus; altar for Theagines;
Andromeda's picture; black physician's beard;
palmer's hair; two squirts for Paul's children; the
monarch's gown; a basket to hang up diligence in
play of *Probia*, etc.

The following is a list of properties supplied for
some revels in 1575: "Monsters, mountains, forests, beasts, serpents; weapons for war, as guns,
dagges, bows, arrows, bills, halbards, boarspears,
fawchions, daggers, targets, pole-axes, clubs;
heads and head pieces; armour counterfeit; moss,
holly, ivy, bays, flowers; quarters; glue, paste,
paper, and such like; with nails, hooks, horsetails;
dishes for devil's eyes, heaven, hell, and the devil
and all."

In February, 1577, a play was prepared for
court presentation, in which " a counterfeit well "

was carried from The Bell in Gracious Street. Artificial horses often figure in the old plays; a box-
tree is used in *Twelfth Night;* Slitgut climbs up
into a tree in *Eastward Ho;* Isabella cuts down
the arbour in *The Spanish Tragedy;* ordnance was
constantly used in the Chronicle plays; in *Locrine*
there is a crocodile stung by a snake, and both of
them fall into the water; tents are pitched in
Richard III.; tables, chairs, beds, boxes, piles of
rock, etc., etc., are frequently mentioned.

Wright in *The Second Generation of Actors*
says that there were no scenes in Elizabethan times,
and it is impossible to disprove his assertion.
There is reason to believe, however, that there
was some scenery in the modern sense. There are
numerous passages in the old plays where people
point to and discuss certain things in a way that
would seem far more unreal if the actor was point-
ing to nothing in particular than if the passage
were altogether left out. The Elizabethans were
not shocked by certain situations that would seem
incongruous to our eyes, but this fact is hardly
warrant for supposing that they altogether lacked
the sense of congruity. While searching about
for a cheap substitute for the more elaborate scenery of the court masques that was perfectly familiar to the Elizabethans, one is struck by the
mention of painted cloths. These were popular

substitutes for tapestry and interior hangings of all kinds, decorated with pictures, often narrating whole stories by a series. Such properties the player possessed. Why should they not use them? why should not many of the passages that so readily apply to a visible scene have been uttered with the scene described actually present in the form of a painted cloth covering the back of the stage? The hut above the stage gallery seems to have been too pretentious a structure to serve no other purpose than a flag-staff support and a standing ground for the bugler. It may have contained rollers by which the painted cloths were let down. The idea of elaborate scenery was not unknown to the Elizabethans, though barred from the public stage by expense; nor can we understand the rapid development in construction of theatres built after the Restoration unless we imagine a beginning in earlier times. Such facts at least lend probability to the surmise that the Elizabethans had crude representations of scenes other than what was suggested by suitable properties.

The greatest money outlay noted in the expenses of Henslowe was for costumes. The clothes worn by the actors were often magnificent. They were, however, Elizabethan garments. Costuming in the modern sense was unknown. Cæsar wore a doublet, and Richard III. Elizabethan armour. One of the earliest allusions to the actual use of garments in correct historical setting is contained in Wotton's account of the performance of *Henry VIII.* (Cf. above, Globe Theatre.)

As the play progressed, the end of a scene was marked, with but few exceptions, by the complete clearing of the stage and change of title. The end of an act was indicated by an intermission, and the time occupied by music. This custom gave rise to such expressions as "Before the music sounds for the act" (*What You Will*), "Whilst the act is playing" (*Malcontent*), etc. At the end of a play was more music and a jig, a combination of song and dance by the clown. The verses at the end of *Twelfth Night* are such a jig. This diversion followed even a serious tragedy. A performance at court ended with a prayer by the players for the sovereign.

Such was the outward aspect of the performance. To complete the view, we must take into consideration the kind of people who composed the audience. That was a cruel, boisterous, half savage age. The people were superstitious; they believed ardently in witchcraft, ghosts, and fairies; many of the sports both of boys and men were cruel to a degree with which we have now no sympathy. Branding on the face, slitting the nose, clipping the ears, even hanging, were penalties inflicted for petty crimes. Men wore swords and were accustomed to take the law into their own hands. From such a people we must expect noisy behaviour in the play-house, though they were, in many respects, much more appreciative than the modern audience.

The people in the rooms were generally well enough inclined. The characteristic scenes happened in the yard and on the margins of the stage. The former, having no seats, tempted people to move about during the performance. Doubtless a person bent on crossing the pit used his arms and elbows freely, and trod on people's toes. If the audience were in a good humour this sort of behaviour would provoke a general laugh; but, likely as not, there would be angry words, blows, sometimes a general row.

During the play venders of apples, cakes, ale, tobacco, etc., hawked their goods about the yard and in the galleries. Sometimes a deeply tragic part was interrupted by a cry of " Pickpocket! Caught!" The play would be stopped while the luckless cut-purse was hustled out of the theatre.

The gentlemen on the stage were little better. It was thought a clever trick to come in late enough to interrupt the prologue with a lot of noise in placing one's stool. Once in their seats the gal-

lants did not scruple to bandy words with people
in the pit, flirt with women in the rooms, or interrupt the players during a speech. We are told
that sometimes these gallants crowded so close
upon the stage that the players came forward and
appealed to the audience to know whether more
room was not necessary in which to act. If the
play was not liked, the actors were pelted and
hooted off the stage.

Among the numerous pamphlets of Elizabethan
times, none is so racy, so amusing, or so useful as
a bit of social history as *The Gull's Hornbook.*
The following is taken from the direction to a
young gallant about to go to the theatre:

"Whether therefore the gatherers of the publique or private Play-house stand to receive the after-
noones rent, let our Gallant (having paid it)
presently advance himself up to the Throne of the
Stage. . . . on the very Rushes where the
Commedy is to daunce, yea, and under the state of
Cambises himselfe must our feathered *Estridge,*
like a piece of Ordnance, be planted, valiantly
(because impudently) beating downe the mewes
and hisses of the opposed rascality.

"By sitting on the stage, you may (with small
cost), purchase the deere acquaintance of the
boyes; have a good stoole for sixpence: at any time
know what particular part any of the infants

present: get your match lighted, examine the play-
suits, lace, and perhaps win wagers upon laying it
is copper, &c. And to conclude, whether you be
a foole or a Justice of the peace, a Cuckold or a
Capten, a Lord-Maiors sonne, or a dawcock, a
knave or an under-Sheriff; of what stamp soever
you be, current or counterfet, the Stage, like time,
will bring you to most perfect light and lay you
open: neither are you to be hunted from thence,
though the Scarcrows in the yard hoot at you,
hiss at you, spit at you, yea, throw dirt even in
your teeth; tis most gentleman like patience to endure all this, and to laugh at the silly Animals:
but if the *Rabble*, with a full throat, crie, away
with the foole, you were worse than a madman to
tarry by it: for the gentleman and the fool should
never sit on the stage together. . . . .

" Present not yourselfe on the Stage (especially
at a new play) untill the quaking prologue hath
(by rubbing) got culor into his cheekes, and is
ready to give the trumpets their Cue, that hees
upon point to enter: for then it is time, as though
you were one of the *properties*, or that you dropt
out of ye *Hangings*, to creep from behind the
Arras, with your *Tripos* or three footed stoole in
one hand, and a teston mounted betweene a fore-
finger and a thumb in the other: for if you should
bestow your person upon the vulgar when the belly

of the house is but half full, your apparell is quite
eaten up, the fashion lost, and the proportion of
your body in more danger to be devoured then if
it were served up in the Counter amongst the Powl-
try: avoid that as you would the Bastome. It
shall crown you with rich commendation to laugh
aloud in the middest of the most serious and saddest
scene of the terriblest Tragedy: and to let that
clapper (your tongue) be tost so high, that all
the house may ring of it. . . . As first, all the
eyes in the galleries will leave walking after the
Players, and onely follow you: the simplest dolt in
the house snatches up your name, and when he
meets you in the streets, or that you fall into his
hands in the middle of a Watch, his word shall be
taken for you: heele cry *Hees such a gallant*, and
you passe. . . . .

"Before the play begins, fall to cardes: you
may win or lose (as *Fencers* do in a prize) and
beate one another by confederacie, yet share the
money when you meet at supper: notwithstanding,
to gul the *Ragga-muffins* that stand aloofe gaping
at you, throw the cards (having first torn four or
five of them) round about the Stage, just upon
the third sound, as though you had lost: it skills
not if the four knaves ly on their backs, and out-
face the Audience; theres none such fools as dare
take exceptions at them, because, ere the play go

off, better knaves than they will fall into the
company.

"Now sir, if the writer be a fellow that hath
either epigrammd you, or hath had a flirt at your
mistris, or hath brought either your feather, or
your red beard, or your little legs, &c. on the stage,
you shall disgrace him worse than by tossing him
in a blancket, or giving him the bastinado in a
Tavern, if, in the middle of his play (bee it Pastoral or Comedy, Morall or Tragedie), you rise
with a screwd and discontented face from your
stoole to be gone: no matter whether the Scenes
be good or no; the better they are the worse do you
distaste them: and, being on your feet, sneake not
away like a coward, but salute all your gentle
acquaintance, that are spread either on the rushes,
or on stooles about you, and draw what troupe you
can from the stage after you: the *Mimicks* are
beholden to you, for allowing them elbow roome:
their Poet cries, perhaps, a pox go with you, but
care not for that, theres no music without frets.

"Mary, if either the company, or the indisposi-
tion of the weather binde you to sit it out, my
counsel is then that you turne plain Ape, take up a
rush, and tickle the earnest eares of your fellow
gallants, to make other fooles fall a laughing:
mewe at passionate speeches, blare at merrie, find
fault with the musicke, whew at the childrens Action,

whistle at the songs: and above all, curse the sharers. . . . ."

Though the *Gull's Hornbook* is a comical satire, Dekker truly represents the time. Yet the Elizabethan audience was not all bad. Their rudeness was, in the main, the good-natured rudeness of the age, not a rudeness due to malice. Furthermore, they knew a good play when they saw it. Many a poor comedy that satisfies the popular taste to-day would never have got safely through the first night three hundred years ago. This fact has much to do with the general excellence of the Elizabethan drama. After all, there was manifested in the audience of that day the genuine spirit of true sport, of every fellow for himself, and give the Devil his due, that has always characterised the English, whether of the time of the Armada or of Waterloo.

CHAPTER XV

THE TAVERNS AND TAVERN LIFE

THE poets' view of the Elizabethan tavern is
not altogether correct. To be sure, the ale-
house was the place of good fellowship and jovial-
ity *par excellence*, the place for combats of
" merry wit," where met the numerous clubs of the
Apollo type. Yet, on the other hand, the tavern
was something different. It was constantly
haunted by the most disreputable characters of
London, it was the scene of frequent brawls, and
the nursery of all sorts of deceit and cozenage.
Officers of the crown, in their search for a criminal,
usually began to gather information at the ale-
houses and ordinaries of London. It was a regular practice of mine host to entice unfledged
country youths into his tavern, to lend them a
guiding hand through the push of boisterous London, to obtain their confidence by a thousand acts
of trivial kindness, and then to persuade them to
excessive extravagance. To further the success
of this practice the host would advance money,
and, when the gull was deeply in debt, put on the
screws and collect with usury, often ruining the
would-be gallant altogether and lodging him in a

debtor's prison. "I tell you," says the First Officer in Middleton's *Phoenix*, IV. i., "our safest way will be to arrest him when he comes out a' th' tavern, for then he will be half drunk and will not stand upon his weapon."

The host of a tavern was responsible to his guests for the safety of their property while under his care—hence the long, narrow entrances, easily closed and defended, which gave upon the galleried courtyards. Not only were plays performed in many of these tavern courts, but they were also the scene of all sorts of business transactions. It was not uncommon for the inn-keeper to perform the office of a money lender and banker. In Middleton's *Michmaelmus Term*, II. iii., after a bond is taken, occurs the following line, "Come, let's all to the next tavern to see the money paid." As in later times, the Elizabethan tavern was a rendezvous for duellists, and also a place as popular as the streets with courtesans.

The most characteristic external indication of a tavern is referred to in the line, "I am not as well known by my wit as an ale-house by a red lattice." (Marston, *Ant. and Mel.*, I. iv. 1); and the bush the most frequent of tavern signs, is familiar to all readers of *As You Like It* (Epilogue). Though much ingenuity was exercised in choosing a variety of tavern signs, the same were duplicated

THE FALCON TAVERN
(From an engraving by Wilkinson)

quite as frequently as are street names to-day. Pennant records what was apparently an unique one.   Near Chancery Lane, between it and the turnstile, was a sign which bore a picture of St. John's head on a charger.   Below it was the motto, " Good eating within."   Booths and benches were other outside indications of a tavern, as well as a post on which were placed advertisements, announcements, and often bills of the play.

The scarcity of small coins in Elizabethan times gave rise to the habit of using tokens or counters of brass, tin, or leather, that were issued by the individual tavern keepers.   Of course these tokens were redeemable only at the tavern by which they were issued.   It was the custom to give each room of the tavern an individual name, as the Dolphin chamber, the Blue chamber, etc.   It was also the custom for guests to send presents of wine to each other from room to room, sometimes to a stranger, in which case a bottle of wine served the purpose of a card of introduction.   The score was usually written in chalk on a board by the drawer, or by the drinker himself ; and " score at the bar " was one of the common cries of tapsters.   It may be added that the host was generally a reputable member of one of the Livery Companies, and that he usually turned the management of the establishment over to his wife.

It would be impossible to give a complete list of the London taverns. A record dated 1574 asserts that there were 876 taverns in Middlesex, and 454 in Surrey. Most of these were in London. The following, from an old black-letter quarto whose title page has been lost, enumerates the principal taverns of the day:

> There hath been great sale and utterance of wine,
> Besides beer and ale and ipocras fine,
> In every country, region, and nation;
> Chiefly at Billingsgate at the Salutation,
> And Boar's Head ner London Stone.
> The Swan at Dowgate, a tavern well beknown,
> The Milk in Cheape and then the Bull Head,
> And many like places that make noses red:
> The Boar's Head in Old Fish Street, Three Cranes in the
>   Vintry,
> And now of late St. Martin's in the Sentree;
> The Windmill in Lothburry, the Ship at the Exchange,
> King's Head in New Fish Street, where roysters do
>   range;
> The Mermaid in Cornhill, Red Lion in the Strand,
> Three Tuns, Newgate Market, Old Fish Street at the
>   Swan.

(The above is quoted by Drake, vol. 2, page 133. The following is from the Harleian MS. 6850, fol 31.)

"On the way from Whitehall to Charing Cross we pass the White Heart, the Red Lion, the Mermaide, iij Tuns, Salutation, the Graihound, the

Bell, the Golden Lion. In sight of Charing Cross: The Garter, the Crown, the Bear and Ragged Staff, the Angel, the King Harry Head. There from Charing Cross towards ye cittie: another White Hart, the Eagle and child, the Helmet, the Swan, the Bell, King Harry Head, the Flower de Luce, Angel, Holy Lambe, the Bear and Harrow, the Plough, the Shippe, the Black Bell, another King Harry Head, the Bull Head, the Golden Bull, a sixpenny ordinary, another Flower-de-luce, the Red Lion, the Horns, the White Horse, the Princess' arms, Bell Savage's Inn, the St. John the Baptist, the Talbot, the Ship of War, the St. Dunstan, the Hercules, or the Owld Man Tavern, the Mitre, another King Harry Head, iij Tuns, and the iij Cranes."

The following quotations fully describe the condition of the Elizabethan inns. "Those towns which we call thoroughfares have great and sumptuous inns builded in them, for the receiving of such travellers and strangers as pass to and fro. The manner of harbouring wherein is not like to that of some other countries, in which the host, or goodman of the house, doth challenge a lordly authority over his guests, but clean otherwise, since every man may use his inn as his own house in England, and have for his money how great or little variety of victuals, and such other service

as himself shall think expedient to call for. Our
inns are also very well furnished with naperie,
bedding and tapestry, especially with naperie; for
besides the linen used at the tables, which is commonly washed daily, is such and so much as be-
longeth to the estate and calling of the guest.
Each comer is sure to lie in clean sheets, wherein
no man hath been lodged since they came from
the laundress, or out of the water wherein they
were last washed. If the traveller have an horse,
his bed doth cost him nothing, but if he go on foot
he is sure to pay a penny for the same; but whether
he be a horseman or a footman if his chamber be
once appointed he may carry the key with him,
as of his own house so long as he lodgeth there.
If he lose aught while he abideth in the inn, the
host is bound by a general custom to restore the
damage, so that there is no greater security anywhere for the traveller than in the greatest inns
of England. Their horses in like sort are walked,
dressed, and looked unto by certain hostlers or
hired servants, appointed at the charges of the
goodman of the house, who in hope of extraordinary
reward will deal very diligently after outward
appearance in their function and calling. Herein,
nevertheless, are many of them blameworthy, in
that they do not only deceive the beast oftentimes of
his allowance by sundry means, except their owners

look well unto them; but also make such packs
with slipper merchants which hunt after prey, that
many an honest man is spoiled of his goods as
he travelleth to and fro, in which feat also the
counsel of the tapsters or drawers of drink, and
chamberlains is not seldom behind or wanting.
Certes I believe not that chapman or traveller in
England is robbed by the way without the knowledge of some of them; for when he cometh into the
inn, and alighteth from his horse, the hostler is
forthwith very busy to take down his budget or
capcase in the yard from his saddle bow which he
peiseth slyly in his hand to feel the weight thereof;
or if he miss at this pitch, when the guest hath
taken up his chamber, the chamberlain which
looketh to the making of the beds, will be sure to
remove it from the place where the owner hath
set it, as if it were to set it more conveniently
somewhere else, whereby he getteth an inkling
whether it be money or other sort wares, and thereof
giveth warning to such odd guests as haunt the
house and are of his confidence, to the utter undoing of many an honest yeoman as he journeyeth
by the way. The tapster in like sort for his part
doth mark his behaviour and what plenty of money
he draweth when he payeth the shot [reckoning],
to the like end; so that it shall be an hard matter
to escape all their subtle practises. Some think

it a gay matter to commit their budgets at their
coming to the goodman of the house; but thereby
they oft bewray themselves. For albeit their
money be safe for the time that it is in his hands
(for you shall not hear that a man is robbed in
his inn) yet after their departure the host can
make no warranty of the same, since his protection extendeth no further than the gate of his
own house: and there cannot be a surer token to
such as pray and watch for these booties, than
to see any guest deliver his capcase in such a manner. In all our inns we have plenty of ale, beer,
and sundry kinds of wine, and such is the capacity of some of them that they are able to lodge
two hundred persons, and their horses at ease, and
there too with a very short warning make provision for their diet, as to him that is unacquainted
withal shall seem incredible. Howbeit, of all England there are no worse inns than in London, and
yet many are there far better than the best that
I have heard of in any foreign country, if all
circumstances be duly considered. But to leave
this and go in hand with my purpose. . . .
Finally there is not so much omitted among them
as the gorgeousness of their very signs at their
doors, wherein some do consume thirty or forty
pounds, a mere vanity in mine opinion, but so
vain will they needs be and that not only to give

some outward token of the innkeeper's wealth, but also to procure good guests to the frequenting of their houses in hope there to be well used." (Harrison, 1587.)

"The world affords no such inns as England hath, either for good and cheap entertainment after the Guests owne pleasure, or for humble attendance on passengers; yea, even in very poore villages. . . . For as soone as a passenger comes to an Inne, the servants run to him, and one takes his horse, and walks him till he be cold, then rubs him and gives him meate, yet I must say they are not much to be trusted in this last point, without the eye of the master or his servant to oversee them. Another servant gives the passenger his chamber, and kindles his fier; a third pulls off his bootes and makes them cleane. Then the Host or the Hostess visit him; and if he will eat with the Host or at a common table with others, his meal will cost him sixpence, or in some places but fourpence (yet this course is less honourable, and not used by Gentlemen); but if he will eat in his chamber, he commands what meat he will, according to his appetite, and as much as he thinks fit for him and his company, yea, the kitchen is open to him, to command the meat to be dressed as he best likes; and when he sits at Table the Host or Hostess will accompany him,

or, if they have many Guests, will at least visit
him, taking it for courtesie to be bid sit downe;
while he eats, if he have company especially, he
shall be offered musicke, which he may freely take
or refuse; and if he be solitary, the musicians will
give him the good day with music in the morning. It is the custom, and no way disgraceful,
to set up part of supper for his breakfast. In the
evening, or in the morning after breakfast (for
the common sort use not to dine, but ride from
breakfast to supper time, yet coming early to
the inn for better resting of their horses) he shall
have reckoning in writing, and if it seem unrea-
sonable, the Host shall satisfy him either for the
due price, or by abating a part, especially if the
servant deceive him any way, which one of experience shall soon find. . . . I will now only
add that a gentleman and his man shall spend as
much as if he was accompanied with another gentleman and his man; and if gentlemen will in such
sort joine together to eate at one table, the expenses will be much diminished. Lastly, a man
cannot more freely command at home in his owne
House, than he may do in the Inne; and at parting if he will give some few pence to the chamberlain and hostler, they will wish him a happy journey." (Fynes Moryson, *Itinerary*, 1617.)

The word ordinary properly referred to a meal

at which each paid a fixed sum and all sat down at the same table. Ordinaries were sometimes served exclusively at certain places, but also at many of the regular taverns; hence the name came into use for any kind of eating house. "The nurses of these (worse than heathenish) hellish exercises are places called *Ordinary Tables;* of which there are in London more in number to honour the devil than churches to serve the living God." (George Whetstone, 2d part of *The Enemy to Untruthfulness*, 1586.) We hear of ordinaries of all prices from three half pence to two shillings. Fletcher, in *The Wild Goose Chase*, I. i., mentions a ten crown ordinary, and Middleton, in *Father Hubbard's Tales*, tells of a person who spent five pounds at an ordinary.

Among the Darrell Papers, published by Mr. Hubert Hall, is an interesting account-book that gives information concerning the expense of meals in a reputable tavern frequented by gentlemen. On April 16, 1589, Wild Darrell paid for a dinner consisting of beef, mutton, chicken, bacon, pigeon, bread, and beer, 8s. 9d.; supper on the same day cost 4s. 10d. Dinner on the next day, however, was but 4s. 11d., and on the next Friday (a fish day) he spent for dinner 2s. 2d., and for supper "nil." This charge, however, did not include bread and beer, for we find 8s. 6d. set down as a

supper expense on the next Sunday "For Bread
and Beare since Thursday night." It is also interesting to note the separate articles charged in
the account for a single meal. On Friday at
dinner of May 2, Darrell spent for "A side of
habdyn, and another of green fishe, 14d.; Foure
playses, 12d.; 2 whitinges, 8d.; conger, 8d.; butter, 4d.; Lettise for sallett, 2d.; a pynt of white
wyne and another of clarett, 6d.; sugar, 2d.; a
pound of butter, 5d.; for dressing the fishe, 8d.;
Oyle and sugar for sallett, 2d; More for butter,
2d.; a pounde of candles, 4d."

On coming to London from the country the
traveller's first task, if he did not possess a town
house, was to go in search of a tavern, which he
chose in a neighbourhood that was convenient to
his affairs. Dekker tells us that the visitor's first
business was to become acquainted with the drawers.
These were the all-round officers of the tavern.
It was their duty not only to draw wine and ale,
but to meet the guest at the door, conduct him to
his room, run errands about the house, and afford
information in every possible way. We have
already seen the part they played in the numerous
robberies by the way, a characteristic of rural
taverns, however, rather than of London. The
visitor always called the drawer by his first name,
and the fellow replied by the characteristic " Anon,

sir." As soon as the gallant became well acquainted with the drawers he could begin to take liberties in the way of dominating the household and running up extravagant bills. He not only bought the commodities for sale in the tavern on trust, but also borrowed money and had it scored to his account. "Bring me money from the bar" is a cry not unusual in the old plays. In many of the taverns the ale was served by bar-maids. Their presence, however, unless a member of the landlord's family, was not so common as at present, and such a person was likely to be dissolute and characteristic of the meaner taverns. In Heywood's *Fair Maid of the West* people are always on the point of wonder that Bess Bridges, who has made the house so popular, should withal be chaste.

The host and hostess were great personages in those days. They knew everyone about the country, high and low, and in *Henry IV.* we find that they are fit companions for princes. The hostess particularly was the one to make her visitors welcome, a task she performed in a number of ways. "I am as common in the court as a hostess's lips in the country," occurs in the *Malcontent*. "My host drinking, my hostess dancing with the worshipful justice" (Peele, *Merry Jests*), illustrates the familiarity that existed between landlord and guest.

It was not an uncommon custom for a man to visit the kitchen of a tavern and examine it to see if its cleanliness suited his taste, or to superintend the cooking of his meals. Dekker, however, discountenances this habit in the following words: "The first question you are to make (after discharging of your pocket of Tobacco and pipes, and the household stuff thereto belonging) shall be for an inventorie of the Kitchen: for it were more then most Tailor-like, to be suspected you were in league with some Kitchen-wench, to descende yourselfe, to offend your stomach with the sight of the Larder, and happily to grease your Accoustrements. Having therefore received this bill, you shall (like a capten putting up deere paies) have many Sallads stand on your table, as it were for blankes to the other more servicable dishes: and according to the time of the year, vary your fare, etc."

Taverns were equally popular with people who happened in for a game of cards or dice, or merely to talk and while away the time with drink and tobacco. There was the large public room on the first floor where stood the bar. But this was not so popular as a lounging place as the numerous private rooms in the possession of every tavern. When one or more guests took possession of a room it was considered their personal property, so to

INTERIOR OF AN ELIZABETHAN TAVERN
(The Four Swans)

speak, until they left it. The entrance of another
person was considered an intrusion, and when ef-
fected was always done with profuse apologies
and protestations that the newcomer would leave
if there were the least objection to his presence.
Tavern fights were often the result of forcible
entrance into another room, and the habit was
often resorted to as a trumped-up excuse for a
duel. It is worth while to note in connection with
the use of rooms for gaming that the old plays
contain many references to calling upon the
drawer for a pair of false dice or a similar deck
of cards. One may exercise his fancy as to
whether this was one of the perquisites of familiar
acquaintance with the drawers.

Bragging and braggart should be the motto of
every Elizabethan tavern haunter. Note one of
the directions given by Dekker: " Enquire what
gallants sup in the next roome, and if there be
any of your acquaintance, do not you, (after the
City fashion) send them a pottle of wine, and your
name, sweetned in two pittiful papers of Suger,
with some filthy apology crammed into the mouth
of a drawer; but rather keep a boy in fee, who
underhand shall proclaime you in every roome,
what a gallant fellowe you are, how much you
spend yearly in Taverns, what a great gamester,
what custome you bring to the house, in what

witty discourse you maintain a table, what Gentlewomen or Citizens wives you can with a wet finger
have at any time to sup with you, and such like.
By which *Encomiasticks* of his, they that know
you shall admire you and thinke themselves to bee
brought into a paradice but to be meanely in your
acquaintance; and if any of your endeered friends
be in the house, and beate the same Ivybush that
yourselfe does, you may join companies and bee
drunke together most publickly."

Whether it was characteristic of Englishmen
three hundred years ago to elude paying honest
debts or not is a question, but certain it is that
this habit is made the subject of numerous jests in
the old plays; especially is this true in the case
of tavern bills. Dekker has this to say on the
subject. "But in such a deluge of drinke, take
heede that no man counterfeit him selfe druncke
to free his purse from the danger of the shot; tis
a usual thing now amongst gentlemen; it had wont
bee the quality of Cocknies: I should advise you
to leave so much brains in your head as to prevent
this."

The peculiar character of the ordinary has
already been alluded to. Though many taverns
were ordinaries, Dekker gives a separate chapter
to the behaviour in each of these places of entertainment. Half after eleven in the morning, he

says, is the proper time to repair to an ordinary;
that is, about half an hour before the meal is
served. One remembers the sports and customs
of an Elizabethan ordinary so graphically set
forth by Scott in the *Fortunes of Nigel*. The
picture is not overdrawn. Dekker goes into full
details. " Being arrived in the room," he directs,
" salute not any but those of your acquaintance:
walk up and downe by the rest as scornfully and
as carelessly as a Gentleman Usher: Select some
friend (having first thrown off your claoke) to
walke up and down the room with you, let him be
suited [dressed] if you can, worse by farre then
yourselfe, he will be a foyle to you: and this will
be a meanes to publish your clothes better than
Powles, a Tenniscourt, or a Playhouse; discourse
as lowd as you can, no matter to what purpose if
you but make a noise, and laugh in fashion, and
have a good sour face to promise quarrelling, you
shall be much observed."

Dekker, in his inimitable way, goes on to give
more detailed directions as to the manner of behaviour of different sorts of people, as the soldier,
courtier, and the poet. Against the latter class
of writers he seems to have an especial grudge.
" Observe no man," he says, " doff not cap to that
gentleman to day at dinner, to whom, not two
nights since, you were beholden for a supper; but,

after a turn or two in the roome, take occasion
(pulling out your gloves) to have some *Epigram*,
or *Satyre*, or *Sonnet* fastned in one of them, that
may (as it were vomittingly to you) offer itselfe
to the Gentlemen: they will presently desire it: but
without much conjuration from them, and a pretty
kind of counterfeit loathness in yourselfe, do not
read it; and though it be none of your owne,
sweare you made it. Mary, if you chance to get
into your hands any witty thing of another mans,
that is somewhat better, I would councell you then,
if demand be made who composed it, you may say:
faith, a learned Gentleman, a very worthy friend.
And this seeming to lay it on another man will be
counted either modestie in you, or a sign that you
are not ambitious of praise, or else that you dare
not take it upon you, for fear of the sharpness it
carries with it. Besides, it will add much to your
fame to let your tongue walke faster then your
teeth, though you be never so hungry, and, rather
then you should sit like a dumb Coxcombe, to
repeat by heart either some verses of your owne,
or of any other mans, stretching even very good
lines upon the rack of censure: though it be
against all law, honestie, or conscience, it may
chance save you the price of your Ordinary, and
beget you other *Suppliments*. Mary, I would further intreat our Poet to be in league with the

Mistress of the Ordinary, because from her (upon condition that he will but ryme knights and young gentlemen to her house, and maintain the table in good fooling) he may easily make up his mouth at her cost *Gratis*."

Dekker here loses grasp of the proprieties and gives a number of unquotable suggestions for all sorts and conditions of men, but resumes a more decorous tone when he reaches lastly. You must not fail " at your departure forth the house, to kiss mine Hostis over the barre, or to accept of the courtesie of the Cellar when tis offered you by the drawers, and you must know that kindness never creeps upon them, but when they see you almost cleft to the shoulders, or to bid any of the vintners good night, is as commendable as for a Barber after trimming to lave your face with sweet water."

THE END

INDEX